ML

D1394013

Books are to be returne
the last date

# Rating Management's Effectiveness

# Rating Management's Effectiveness

## With Case Studies in Telecommunications

Dimitris N. Chorafas

First published 2004 by
PALGRAVE MACMILLAN
Houndmills, Basingstoke, Hampshire RG21 6XS and
175 Fifth Avenue, New York, N.Y. 10010
Companies and representatives throughout the world

PALGRAVE MACMILLAN is the global academic imprint of the Palgrave Macmillan division of St. Martin's Press, LLC and of Palgrave Macmillan Ltd. Macmillan® is a registered trademark in the United States, United Kingdom and other countries. Palgrave is a registered trademark in the European Union and other countries.

ISBN 1–4039–3728–1

This book is printed on paper suitable for recycling and made from fully managed and sustained forest sources.

A catalogue record for this book is available from the British Library.

Library of Congress Cataloging-in-Publication Data
Chorafas, Dimitris N.
   Rating management's effectiveness : with case studies in
   telecommunications / Dimitris N. Chorafas.
      p.   cm.
   Includes bibliographical references and index.
   ISBN 1–4039–3728–1 (cloth)
   1. Organizational effectiveness—Evaluation.   2. Industrial efficiency—Evaluation.   3. Executives—Rating of.   4. Middle managers—Rating of.
   5. Telecommunication—Case studies.   I. Title.

   HD58.9.C496 2004
   384'.068'4—dc22

                                                           2004044687

10   9   8   7   6   5   4   3   2   1
13   12   11   10   09   08   07   06   05   04
Printed and bound in Great Britain by
Antony Rowe Ltd, Chippenham and Eastbourne

# Contents

# List of Figures

# List of Tables

# Preface

Some managers remain as keen as ever to understand what makes business decisions and actions *effective*. Others pay only lip service or no attention at all to effectiveness, and their companies go under. Effectiveness is not just a matter of calm reflection. It is the skill of doing things in the most successful way. *Efficiency* is achieving one's mission at least cost. What this text tells the reader through case studies is:

- how to be effective, and
- what happens in the case of ineffectiveness.

Documented through extensive research, the text also demonstrates that ethical values and transparency are at the source of effectiveness. Today this is more true than ever, because market discipline starts to work.

Independent rating agencies are market discipline's agent. To grade a company's creditworthiness they are looking not only at its balance sheet, but also, if not primarily, they examine the quality of its management and its ability to deliver results. What is now called *external rating risk* weighs heavily on an enterprise. For the company as a whole to be effective, the standards of corporate behaviour must be high.

This book is designed both for professionals and for the academic market, particularly senior level and graduate studies in Business Administration and Management, in colleges, universities and in-house postgraduate training centres. The text is based on an extensive research project done by the author in 2003 and 2004 in the United States, England, Germany, France, Italy and Switzerland.

Most of the case studies in this book come from telecommunications, both from the telephone companies and from their suppliers. Although these case studies focus on each firm individually, the message they bring to the reader is that of a *pattern*: how, why and when ineffective managements brought the organizations they were entrusted with to the wall – and what they could have done to avoid such an ending.

The text outlines the reasons why **management effectiveness** must be examined within the perspective of each company's business challenges. The effort of reaching management objectives should capitalize on the synergy which exists between shareholder value and business ethics.

Honesty is the best policy at the level of the board, the CEO and senior management.

Effectively run companies appreciate the risks associated with near-sightedness, skills obsolescence, overcentralization and dubious deals. As several case studies will demonstrate, cooking the books through leveraging, derivative instruments and construction of a maze of offshore companies is no proof of management effectiveness – but of extreme management weakness. Growth is dictated by the customer, not by superleveraging one's company and giving hostages to fortune. Neither is fiddling with financial figures a proof of improvement in revenues, earnings, or shareholder value.

Lies have short legs, and no matter how well covered different misdeeds may be, eventually they will come unstuck. Italy's Parmalat – the hedge fund with dairy products on the side – has been the latest case to demonstrate that management ineffectiveness and outright malfeasance correlate.

Europe's largest bankruptcy adds itself to the long list of painful American bankruptcies, from Enron to WorldCom and other scandals. In all likelihood, these will continue in 2004, 2005 and beyond, not least because legal proceedings in ongoing scams are far from over.

The book divides into two parts. In five chapters, Part One explains *why* and *how* management's effectiveness makes the difference between success and failure, in any organization and in any mission. This is particularly true in a business and industrial enterprise; it is less so in a bureaucratic state organization where the criterion of 'effectiveness' is that of not making mistakes – which means doing absolutely nothing.

Chapter 1 addresses the concepts underpinning management effectiveness, starting with an outline of the functions of management. It defines effectiveness and efficiency, associates effectiveness with leadership and the ability to make focused decisions, and underlines the role of personal accountability – which is indivisible from management functions.

The theme of Chapter 2 is rating management effectiveness, and the company's creditworthiness, by independent rating agencies. To a fairly significant extent, such agencies work as a proxy for market discipline. Every company's activity, as well as inaction, engenders external rating risk. Independent agencies can be expected to play a key role in the coming years in judging management effectiveness.

Through case studies, Chapter 3 demonstrates that mismanagement is by no means an exception. The case studies in this chapter include the Ahold scandal, Parmalat's scams, the failure of Cable & Wireless, Bridgestone's and Ford's fiasco, and Mitsubishi Motors cover-ups.

Chapter 4 advises that to survive, a company must reinvent itself time and again, over the years. This means reinventing the functions of management, and the company's product line, but also abstaining from actions which are a show of ineffectiveness. The case studies in this chapter centre on: Standard Life, Equitable Life, Mannheimer Life, Imperial Chemical Industries, Canary Wharf, the European air transport industry, and the ten countries joining the European Union in 2004.

Chapter 5 concentrates on management and mismanagement in the telecommunications industry, starting with irrational exuberance regarding the equity of telecoms, and continuing with evolution in telecommunications services. Essentially this chapter provides background for the case studies in Part Two. Hence, it includes sections on:

- voice over internet protocol (VOIP)
- digital subscriber line and its challenges
- Wi-Fi wireless technology and its limits
- Liquidity, indebtedness and external rating risk

All six chapters in Part Two are dedicated to case studies on management effectiveness in the telecommunications industry. Chapter 6 provides the general perspective, taking as an example European telecoms which brought themselves to the edge of the abyss through unprecedented mismanagement: France Télécom, Deutsche Telekom, British Telecom and NTL.

The theme of Chapter 7 is the rise and fall of Vivendi Universal. This is a curious outfit which, having slid all the way to illiquidity, could not quite make up its mind whether it was a telecoms joint, Hollywood outfit, or water and sewage company. In the late 1990s, Vivendi looked like a company that had lost control of its future.

Chapter 8 concentrates on WorldCom, the fallen telecommunications giant which combined management ineffectiveness with falsified financial accounts and a myriad of scams – supposedly done to enhance shareholder value, but really leading to the delusion of all its stakeholders. WorldCom's problem was not just one of taking high risk, but of ineptitude in thinking that financial malfeasance could be hidden for ever.

Chapter 9 presents a *bouquet* of case studies on management ineffectiveness, as well as on abuse of protection from creditors by hiding behind 'Chapter 11'. These case studies include Global Crossing, its capacity swaps and its bankruptcy; McLeod USA, Williams Communications, Marconi, Viatel, Qwest, Adelphia Communications, Exodus, Metromedia and Mobilcom.

The theme of Chapter 10 is the money gone down the drain with third-generation (3G) mobile, because of ineptness and blunders associated with huge unwarranted investments – to the tune of $130 billion to buy fresh air. 3G is an example of business blunder and plans built on quicksilver; killer applications that were imaginary; the ego of EU bureaucrats, and government greed which capitalized on have-brained telecoms.

Chapter 11 closes this book with case studies on Alsthom, Ericsson, Alcatel, Lucent Technologies and Nortel. These four are the vendors of telecommunications equipment who overleveraged their clients, the telcos.

Through vendor financing, they pushed them into overbuilding capacity, which ended in self-inflicted wounds for all concerned. The concluding remark, in this chapter, is the 2004 modest pick-up in telecoms vendors' activities, which is good news. The bad news is that these are only early signs of a recovery. They are not definite.

The Stone Age did not end for lack of stone. Through analogical thinking, one should not expect the age of ineffectiveness and malfeasance to end because of lack of opportunities for doing silly things. There is no point in trying to change human nature. But there is plenty of scope in demonstrating that honesty and effectiveness are policies much more rewarding than their alternatives.

My debts to a long list of knowledgeable people and organizations who contributed to this research are enormous. Without their contributions this book would not have been feasible. I am also indebted to several senior executives and experts for constructive criticism during the preparation of the manuscript.

Let me take this opportunity to thank Jacky Kippenberger for suggesting this project and seeing it all the way to publication, and Linda Auld for the editing work. To Eva-Maria Binder goes the credit for compiling the research results, typing the text, and making the camera-ready artwork and index.

Dimitris N. Chorafas
Valmer and Vitznau
June 2004

# Part One

# Management Makes the Difference between Success and Failure

# 1
# The Concept of Management Effectiveness

## 1. Introduction

Goldman Sachs, the investment bank, puts senior executives to the test. This is an excellent idea. Every company should be testing and grading the people entrusted with corporate governance, and therefore with the entity's survival and its profits. When in the 1960s IBM was the high-growth, well-run enterprise, every one of its senior managers – including the chief executive officer (CEO) – was rated by two of his colleagues, and sometimes there were surprises in terms of rating results.

The management of an enterprise is a complex operation which necessitates personnel well trained for this role. Members of the board, the CEO and his or her immediate assistants must have the ability to anticipate change and identify new opportunities. If they can figure out what changes are in store for the marketplace, they gain extraordinary leverage against their competition. They must also be able to take – and manage – a reasonable amount of risk. To be one of the first into a new territory, they cannot wait for large amounts of evidence.

While the future cannot be precisely planned, many events can often be foreseen at least in terms of direction and trend. This requires strategies enabling managers not only to prognosticate but also to take advantage of new realities and convert market turbulence into opportunity. This rests on two pillars:

- anticipating where the greatest changes are likely to occur, and
- what they are likely to be, as well as their aftermath.

As this book will document through case studies, particularly in the telecommunications industry, good management is by no means a widespread practice. As a fund manager, Goldman Sachs estimates that nearly one-quarter of Britain's top 100 companies are run by managers who are either

3

incompetent or poor in execution of their functions. The investment bank has also rated one in six of the best-known cross-border European companies as poorly managed.[1]

Low-grade management skills, failure to appreciate that management has not only one but six major functions and that these are interrelated (more on this in section 2); lack of attention to detail; decisions which are undocumented or whose aftermath has been poorly examined, are among the reasons for low-grade management performance. Such failures have most significant consequences for the life of the enterprise, because corporate governance becomes so much more complex with globalization and rapid product innovation, as Figure 1.1 suggests.

Another basic reason for poor corporate governance is the decay in ethics and disappearance of personal accountability, which has characterized the 1990s and first years of the new century. Corporate scandals and bankruptcies engineered to avoid facing obligations have led to growing unease about the worth of board members, the skills of chief executives and role of their immediate assistants, prompting greater scrutiny by investors. Ranking management quality, as Goldman Sachs is doing, helps to rate a company's leadership on:

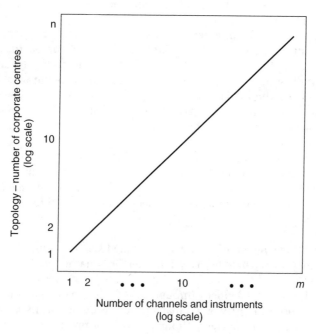

*Figure 1.1*   Corporate governance becomes so much more complex with globalization

- competence,
- integrity,
- board structure, and
- commitment to shareholders.

Is the company's growth an illusion based on cooked books, as has been the case with telecommunication companies in the late 1990s, or is it truly dictated by its customers? Goldman's rating system uses two scales of measurement. One is a managerial quality score (MQS); the other is a business quality score (BQS). Both MQS and BQS help the investment bank's analysts to:

- reach an overall judgement of a company's leadership, and
- evaluate the entity's business prospects, its ability to make judgements, and its courage to act on them.

The American investment bank awards points on a scale of one to five, with 1 high and 5 low. The lowest grade means that a rated company's management may be placing their own interests above those of their shareholders, and have a record of making bad deals. Such deals could have been driven by factors other than those that preserve the shareholders' interest, including misbehaviours which cast a shadow on a company's future.

The results of the scoring of corporate governance by Goldman Sachs make sad reading. About a quarter of companies in the FTSE 100 scored either 4 or 5 – at the bottom of the scale – while in continental Europe 36 known companies also received a score of 4 or 5. Such low ratings raised questions about job performance of top executives, and put under the magnifying glass their spiralling pay cheque and fringe benefits.

At FTSE 100 companies, for example, executives enjoyed an average salary rise of 9.7 per cent during 2001 compared to the previous year, while the shareholders lost plenty of money with stock market blues. Other cash elements of senior managers' earnings have been rising by an average of nearly 11 per cent – all this while management skill and performance were nearly dismal. A similar pattern prevailed in France, where in year 2000 shareholders experienced a loss in value of 35 per cent on average, because of the market's downturn, while executive pay in these same companies *rose* by more than 30 per cent on average.

Somehow both ineffectiveness and greed have taken hold of the executive suite, with a growing number of directors, CEOs, chief financial officers (CFOs) and others forgetting that their first and foremost duty is to the company's stakeholders – not to themselves. In fact, even from the much narrower viewpoint of self-interest, the practice of underperformance and overpay is counterproductive, because capitalism is an evolutionary process and the market will find its way to reward and punish according to deliverables.

## 2.   The functions of management

No discussion on management performance and effectiveness can be factual and documented without first defining the *functions of management*, as well as examining what is that we really measure. In a nutshell, management must perform, in the most able manner, six functions: (1) forecasting, (2) planning, (3) organizing, (4) staffing, (5) directing, and (6) controlling. Their positioning in Figure 1.2 corresponds to the relative structure of the information environment within which they must be executed.

An unstructured environment has many degrees of freedom and plenty of uncertainty. Therefore, it involves a significant element of risk. By contrast, a structured information environment is procedural, defined step by step. The act of directing day-to-day operations – which, to a large extent, is an administrative duty – is an example.

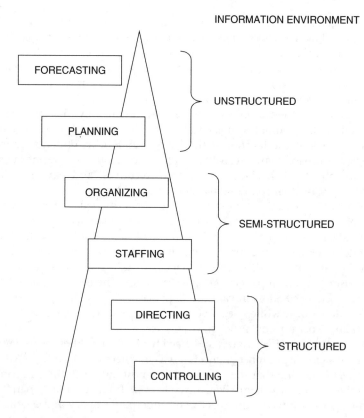

*Figure 1.2*  Pyramid of managerial functions and the information environment to which they belong

Whether structured or unstructured, each one of these six management functions is vital to corporate governance. To plan, we have to prognosticate future events, particularly their likely evolution, as well as evaluate the aftermath of our current decisions and actions. At the same time, we must be able to foresee the impact of our plans. These activities are a 'must', and constitute the main targets of forecasting.

One of the mistakes made with forecasting in daily practice is to try to come up with a precise number. An unstructured information environment involves many uncertainties, which means stochastic variables. Therefore, it is better to obtain a distribution of values at different levels of probability, rather than just one expected value.

In an article in *BusinessWeek*, Dr Robert J. Barro provides an excellent example of this issue in relation to employment numbers:

> A forecasting equation I use shows that monthly changes cannot be predicted accurately. This equation considers the history of employment and gross domestic product and recent claims for unemployment insurance. The current prediction is for a January (2004) gain of 65,000 payroll jobs. But the range could be –90,000 to +225,000.[2]

The expected value is 65,000, while the other values in the range have a lower probability of showing up.

Precisely because it is unstructured, the art of prognostication helps in distinguishing a great manager from an average one. It is also a basic ingredient in strategic planning. Strategy is a master plan against our corporate opponents. Strategies are established in boardrooms, and they are driven by underlying changes in the market – as well as by our own company's strengths.

Insensitivity to market switches leads to downfall. For instance, as we shall see in Chapter 11, in the late 1990s telecommunications equipment suppliers had become used to a market where customers increased their spending on new equipment by overleverging themselves. They did so because newer-and-newer technology was thought to deliver, giving them increased efficiency. Post mortem, after the downturn, it has been found that:

- only some of the expected efficiency has been delivered; the majority will never be realized;
- the new message from customers has been that they, not the telecoms, dictate how much channel capacity is needed – and they want much better value for their money.

The wild expansion of channel capacity through fibre optics, projected mobile communications broadband via UMTS (universal mobile telecommunications systems; see Chapter 10), and rapid corporate expansion by means of mergers and acquisitions (M&A) are examples of strategic plans based on wrong assumptions. The hypotheses nearly all telephone companies have made that the market can absorb all bandwidth they make available, and that revenue per user will keep on increasing at a rapid pace, proved utterly wrong.

Other bad news for telephone operators has been that commitments in capital expenditures, made through leveraging, grew much faster than the revenue to serve them. Contrary to their expectations, average revenue per user fell. In the developed countries, where fixed and mobile penetration is already high, it is very hard to increase or even hold steady overall revenue in a highly competitive market.

The argument by many telecoms that 'they could not know better' is no excuse. Since the end of World War II efficient companies have become serious about the need for detailed and well-documented plans. The best example of a plan is the budget, which is essentially a financial plan. Few companies today would do without a budget, and those whose budgets are unrealistic are not well managed. Apart from the *financial plan*, it is necessary to have a:

- product plan,
- market plan,
- human resources plan, and
- technology plan.

All these integrate into the strategic plan, which should be established by the board and top executives. One of the most important planning decisions is that of choosing the area in which to compete. This is a difficult decision, because it requires not only careful choice of new products and processes, but also the courage to exit from various areas of the market, and consolidate in the company's chosen area of operations.

One of the most important domain-strategic choices is that of dealing with the disruptive effects of change. For instance, what does a telecommunications company have to do to position itself against the disruptive change that Dell drove in computing and easyJet in travel? Can it deliver the sort of service that helps in value differentiation, and makes it possible to move to a different level of service and cost?

Planning decisions have constraints. Competing is hard for the big telcos that have an aged infrastructure and outdated information technology (IT) systems. It takes much more effort and focus to develop a truly new business model while still trying to operate the existing network than most of the old telcos are capable of.

As Figure 1.2 indicates, the next two managerial functions lie within a semi-structured information environment. A great deal of the task of organizing is centred around providing a description of authority and responsibility channels, as well as setting the ground for personal accountability. Organizational solutions constitute the structural linkages which sustain a two-way information flow within the enterprise:

- top–down, better known as line of command, and
- bottom–up, whose mission is to feed management with information, provide market/product/client feedback, and report on performance.

Because organizations are made up of people, a vital managerial function is that of staffing. In terms of salient problems in the performance of managerial duties, staffing follows organizing, and it includes personnel selection, hiring, training, screening, evaluating, promoting, and again evaluation. All this is part of managing human resources. The principle is that *if* able-brained people don't come at the bottom of the pyramid, *then* the day will come when they will not be found at the top.

Human resources must be administered in an able manner; they must be led, motivated and steadily trained. Knowledge and skills become obsolete. The company's human resources should be provided with lifelong learning, and this evidently costs money – but as Derek Bok, a former president of Harvard University, once said, 'If you think education is expensive, try ignorance.'

Only the best-managed companies appreciate this dictum. The others try to manage their human resources through a hit-and-run approach, which costs the firm dearly. In its heyday, Enron had a performance review committee that met every six months. Known as 'rank and yank', it consisted of a group of senior managers getting together in a hotel for a week or so to:

- rank employees, according to a list of criteria, and
- sack the bottom 10 per cent to 20 per cent of current employment.

This summary-type decimation of a company's human resources is not a good idea. In fact, post-mortem evidence shows that in Enron's case the results were trivial: the 'system' simply did not work.[3] Good management does not take such shortcuts, but sees to it that there is steady development and screening of human resources to make sure that:

- know-how and hard work are rewarded through merits, and
- demerits for poor performance carry penalties.

Contrary to the foregoing four functions of management, which address both the present and the future, directing is a day-to-day business. It takes place in a structured information environment, with few degrees of freedom, and its objective is to ensure that everything goes according to plan. Directing is performed within a structured environment, because the framework of operations has been set by planning; and it is supported by organization, while staffing looks after human resources.

The framework of antecedent functions is precisely what makes the company tick – and it also makes management control feasible. Control is the sixth basic function of management, which must be exercised at different levels and by different organizational units, each fulfilling specific goals. Auditing, for instance, is quantitative financial control.

Traditionally, auditing has focused on the accounting books, but it has recently begun to expand into evaluation of management performance, compliance and the internal control structure. As this example demonstrates, management control is both quantitative and qualitative, because many elements which come into control activities are based on judgement.

In an organization-wide sense, risk management is also a control activity, but incorporated into it are other managerial characteristics. The careful reader will notice that 'management' is one of the two words in 'risk management'. Therefore all the outlined six functions find themselves represented in risk management. A similar statement is valid in regard to economic capital allocation, which is basically a planning activity – and, at the same time, a management process which fully integrates with risk control.

In banking, an example of risk management responsibilities is the control of limits set by the board. These may be simple quantitative guidelines, or (preferably) more complex, involving rating, maturities and market conditions. Limits are never one-dimensional, as many people believe. They are two-dimensional and three-dimensional. An example involving a three-dimensional framework is given in Figure 1.3.

In telecommunications, management control activities include both product offerings, such as bandwidth management, and financials, for instance assets and liabilities management. Tactical control objectives for a telco are to plug revenue linkages and swamp fraud. Examples of strategic control objectives are to reduce problems through better customer service, improve 'wallet share' through focused service targeting, and drive more new services with reduced time to revenue (TTR).

Whether we talk of telecommunications, banking or any other industrial sector, management control cannot be effectively exercised without a plan. For instance, no limits can be controlled if such limits are not explicitly established in the first place by the board and senior management. The functions of management planning and control correlate – and, for both, the members of the board and CEO are the organization's highest-ranking authorities, with all this means in terms of effectiveness and personal accountability.

## 3.  Effectiveness and efficiency defined

In literature, and in day-to-day practice, effectiveness and efficiency are two terms very often used interchangeably. This is incorrect. A managerial action is *effective* if it meets its established goals, which have been defined and elaborated by the plan. Such goals must be specific and measurable. It is

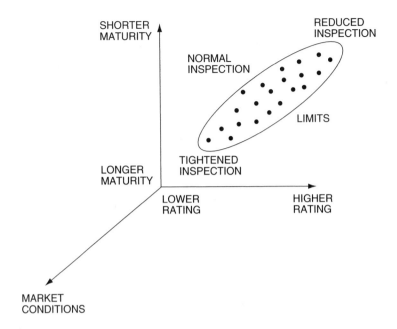

*Figure 1.3* Limits are usually set in a three-dimensional space

impossible to be effective on generalities and/or imprecise guidelines, which mean different things to different people.

*Efficiency* relates to the use of the minimal resources necessary to do the assigned job. Costs matter. Resources should not be spoiled, but used in the most cost-conscious manner in accomplishing a given mission. In that sense, effectiveness and efficiency complement one another: they are the two sides of a job well done. Both are evaluators which should always be kept in mind when decisions are made about the quality of corporate governance.

Let's look first at some practical examples connected to effectiveness. A more or less precise formulation of what has to be done is provided by the manager's and the professional's job description, which is part of the staffing job. The job description should cover the concrete objectives which have been assigned to a given manager. In a telecommunications company, for example, one division – and its general manager – will be responsible for network infrastructure, another for the system platforms, still another for customer relationships, and so on.

The effectiveness of forecasts and of plans, as well as of their execution, must be steadily judged. To be accurate, such a rating should start from the hypotheses leading to the elaboration of business plans. After the 2000–2001 downfall of the telecommunications industry, many telcos established their plans for recovery on the hypothesis that value-added services would help them redress their finances. But in December 2003, in an exclusive interview with Total Telecom, Masanobu Suzuki, chief executive of NTT Communications, said that value-added services still only represented a very small part of the data services business. The original hypothesis proved wrong.

Strategic plans based on wrong hypotheses are absolutely ineffective. When Fred Smith started Federal Express, he *sensed* the public's willingness to pay a premium fee for guaranteed overnight delivery – and he has been successful in putting his vision into practice. Smith's intuition, combined with his knowledge of the hub-and-spoke system of dispersing a fleet of airliners, made him a successful pioneer. By contrast, chief executives of companies who spent billions of euros to buy UMTS licences ruined their firms, and made a bad name for themselves in the telecoms market.

The hypothesis made in the 1999 to 2001 timeframe by the majority of these ineffective CEOs and planners was that there is a great deal of money to be made through mobile office applications, mobile commerce, mobile banking and financial services, and mobile automotive services. Some telecoms even developed overblown quantitative guestimates. All of these estimates have been sharply reviewed downwards over the years.

Management planning is not done by throwing the dice, or by following the flock. Going along with the flock may be good for sheep, but it is bad for companies. Yet this is what was done by the telecoms (and many other firms) in the late 1990s. While the latest revisions of mobile telephony's market potential vary from country to country, 2003 statistics and 2005 forecasts for the South Korean market, shown in Table 1.1, are fairly representative of this industry in most European countries and in the US.

Effectiveness in corporate management rests a great deal on the accuracy of the prognostication of market potential, and this has become quite difficult as companies increasingly operate in many countries and different product markets. Joint ventures, alliances and outsourcing agreements add

*Table 1.1*  Mobile telephony applications market. Per cent of revenues by product channel in South Korea*

|  | Mobile office applications (%) | Mobile commerce market (%) | Mobile banking & financial services (%) | Automotive application market (%) | Mobile messaging (%) | Mobile information & entertainment** (%) |
|---|---|---|---|---|---|---|
| 2003 statistics | 0.3 | 0.7 | 2.8 | 0.2 | 51.0 | 45.1 |
| 2005 estimates | 0.6 | 3.0 | 2.7 | 0.5 | 45.3 | 47.9 |

* *Total Telecom Magazine*, November 2003.
** Whatever 'mobile entertainment' may mean. A 29–30 January 2004 London conference on mobile content included in it adult pornography, violent crime, gambling and gay dating services – hardly a market to crow about.

further to complexity. At the same time, with downsizing, layers of middle management have gone and more divisions report directly to a senior manager's span of control. This is positive in terms of efficiency (more on this later), but, at the same time, it increases the challenges associated with forecasting and planning (see section 2).

Another key factor which imposes its own prerequisites on management effectiveness is that the pace of innovation accelerates as new technologies are applied faster and product life-cycles become shorter. This means that corporate leaders are struggling to keep up the momentum in their business, and prevent their market from passing to competitors who are lean and mean.

A further challenge to corporate leadership is presented by the fact that financial markets harbour great expectations. 'The pressure people are feeling at the top of organizations is unbelievable,' suggests John Kotter, of Harvard Business School. If earnings growth drops 3 per cent, Kotter says, the share price may fall by 30 per cent. Yet earnings are unlikely to grow faster than GDP for more than short periods.[4] Indeed, the gap between expectations and reality has grown since the stock markets declined in 2000.

To ensure that there is a basis against which to measure the effectiveness of his or her decisions and actions, it is in a manager's interest to map authority and responsibility for him/herself and his/her subordinates into *job descriptions* which are dynamically updated and regularly re-evaluated. Experience teaches that the best job description includes not only an outline of *responsibilities*, but also:

- *indicators* which help to qualify the assigned responsibilities, and
- specific *quantitative objectives*, which should be renewed at least annually.

The functions a manager or professional is expected to perform in an efficient way should be part of his/her job description. Figure 1.4 presents in a nutshell this threefold approach to the definition of a given job. Responsibilities, indicators and objectives summarize what each senior member in the organization needs to do. Effectiveness of execution will be judged against these.

Notice that each of these three parts of the job description needs upkeep, but at different paces. Responsibilities change rather slowly because they relate to the company's structure. In the rapid transition of modern business stability is provided by the underlying organization and structure, outlined through assigned responsibilities.

By contrast, maintaining a fast pace in innovation is possible by means of keeping dynamic the indicators of functional performance. Moreover, job indicators change with reorganization and re-engineering. Updating of job indicators is not a goal but a means of measuring a manager's effectiveness. The quantification and qualification of managerial responsibilities and objectives are crucial both to the person and to the company.

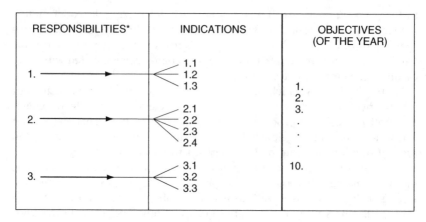

*Figure 1.4* A valid job description is threefold, and should always be subject to management control

* Responsibilities must be few and clearly phrased; 3 or 4 indicators for each responsibility will do.

Let's now examine what management can do to make job performance more efficient. Keeping overhead low is a prime example. Overhead is no direct labour invested in a product or service; it is a functional performance, which should be highly effective. *Low overhead* for the same unit of work produced and delivered means less organizational fat.

A different way of making this statement is to say that too many supervisors for the same number of productive workers is a sign of inefficiency. Another reason for inefficiency is inexperience. Most people who lead companies today are sitting in the boss's chair for the first time. Even CEOs recruited from outside are less likely than in the past to have done the top job elsewhere. Yet the CEO's job is polyvalent, and therefore complex, and lack of experience often leads to missed opportunity, high costs or both.

It is most likely that the most skilful and experienced managers, who have a policy of challenging the 'obvious', are those best able to bring about transformations which improve overall performance. Along with large overheads and low productivity, high taxes are a characteristic of inefficiency – this time around, at government level. Figure 1.5 compares business taxes in the US, Germany, the UK and France.

Factors affecting efficiency tend to correlate among themselves. Take management culture as an example. One of the metrics is 'Baumol's disease', named after William J. Baumol of New York University. Baumol's hypothesis is that jobs in which productivity does not increase substantially over time

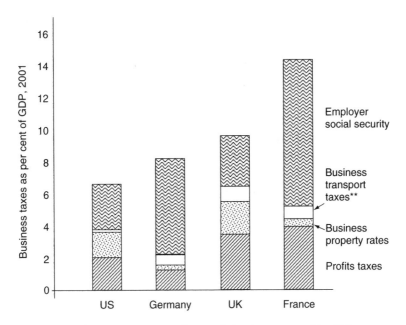

*Figure 1.5*   High business taxes are a characteristic of government inefficiency
* Based on statistics by *The Economist,* 15 November 2003.
** Half road-fuel duty and non-household vehicle duty.

tend to wind up as part of government – and share in its inefficiency. Examples are:

- the postal service,
- the railway system (in some countries),
- sanitation services, and
- the performing arts.

All of these were once private, but at some time they came to depend on government funding because they had not been able to become more productive. At the root of Baumol's disease lies the fact that as socially useful enterprises become unable to sustain themselves they lose out in the marketplace. When this happens, the government steps in with funding and eventually takes them on to keep them going, turning them into bureaucratic monopolies. This increases the government's obligations, which must be funded through taxation, and further demotes the 'taken-over' products and services by overbloating their overhead and confirming their non-productive status.

It needs no explaining that Baumol's disease has had, and will continue to have, severe consequences for government deficits. The more entitlements there are, the more non-productive spending there will be – and the more non-productive spending there is, the more government deficits will grow, leaving it to future generations to pay to clear up the mess.

Yet efficiency and effectiveness are a company's, and a nation's, competitive advantage. Other competitive advantages are gained through research and development (R&D), ingenious marketing, rigorous financial controls and high technology. Competitive advantages, however, can be fast consumed by the action of competitors, as well as the inaction on the part of *our* company's managers and professionals. Therefore, successful entities appreciate that to survive they have to reinvent themselves not only by rapidly renewing their products, but also by:

- cutting their products and processes to pieces,
- taking these pieces of products and processes apart, and
- putting them together again in a different, more *efficient* way.

Companies able to reinvent themselves benefit from the law of *survival of the fittest*. Value is created by reaching specific goals. Therefore, as already stated, goals should be regularly re-evaluated and sized so that they can be met. Setting the same goal in two consecutive years is a sign of ineffectiveness, because it means the outlined objective has not materialized in the first place.

In conclusion, a manager is *effective* if he or she fulfils the outlined responsibilities and achieves assigned annual goals. But he or she may or may not be *efficient*. Efficiency requires that assigned aims are achieved by engaging and using available resources (human, financial, or other) while attaining objectives.

## 4.  Management effectiveness and leadership

Two types of leadership characterize business and industry. One is so-called charismatic leadership, which is full of promise and glamour. This is based on the personal strategy of avoiding the problem and making gambles, but in the majority of cases delivery is substandard or downright non-existent. After the manager has failed, he lies about it – as Napoleon did after his disastrous expedition in Egypt.

A critical question which is as old as humanity but has never been answered definitively is: 'Are corporate leaders born or made?' The answer seems to vary with the people one asks. Some experts say, without much proof to back it up, that between 35 per cent and 50 per cent of the qualities associated with leadership are due to genetic factors. Others suggest that the difference between a good and a bad CEO is made through intensive training: formal and on the job. Still others think that the difference is made through hard work, opportunities and incentives to make use of training and/or genetic leadership characteristic.

A leader may find the opportunity to show his or her skills and effectiveness, or may create it. Without the opportunity to develop abilities and character, people will not be able to train themselves in good judgement, 'the ambition for the cause', strong values, the ability to take tough decisions, and the skills to see them through. Ambition is a human trait which should never be underestimated in the search for the right person to lead a company.

- Training and ambition are two reasons why companies should think about succession early enough.
- Every firm must have in place a succession-planning process which works in collaboration with, but is independent of, the CEO.

Succession planning is an integral and critical part of the management of human resources. Indeed, in the early years of the twenty-first century it has become an important topic discussed by boards. Not surprisingly, CEOs are less likely to retire of their own will than other senior managers. When Chris Gent, Vodafone's CEO, said he would leave in a year's time, the company discovered that it had no succession strategy.

With few exceptions, such as Citibank's Walter Wriston, who put three senior executives in competition before choosing John Reed as his successor, chief executive officers don't dominate the search for their own replacement, because they think they will be in place for ever: 'Their company needs them.' CEOs, however, should look after renewal in the line of command, rather than leaving it to the head hunters.

Experts participating in the research which led to this book suggested some guidelines. One of them is that whether leadership rests on genetic or acquired characteristics, leaders should have a clear sense of direction for their business, as well as the ability to communicate with and motivate people. Communicating about goals and values, as well as progress towards fulfilment of goals, is crucial in making everyone throughout the organization feel that they know the CEO, and appreciate what he or she expects of them.

In many cases, successfully communicated goals and direction make the difference between mediocrity and success in business. Getting the human relationships right determines whether the best people in the organization stay with it or leave. There is little that can be gained in terms of performance and effectiveness from people who feel undervalued, misunderstood, frustrated, and that they have no future.

This last reference brings the spotlight back on the evaluation process mentioned in the Introduction, with the examples from Goldman Sachs and IBM. While all evaluation depends on judgement, and judgement is to a very large extent subjective, it is wise to provide an infrastructure which permits a reasonable amount of objectivity. This is significantly helped through clear signals regarding what the personal evaluation is all about.

It is appropriate to remember in this connection that, in management evaluation, efficiency and effectiveness are often confused. This makes rating very much more difficult. Understanding the difference between effectiveness and efficiency is key to better appreciation of performance. Do we wish to have a leader who is effective but inefficient? Efficient but ineffective?

In what proportion should these two factors coexist? What is the mix we wish to accept, since we are unlikely to find both of them at a high rate? The most eloquent judgement frequently comes post mortem. After Cardinal Richelieu, Louis XIV's prime minister, died, an unknown poet wrote on his grave: 'Here lies a famous cardinal who did more bad deeds than good. The good deeds he did poorly; the bad deeds he did very well.'

Take as an example of deeds a bank's economic capital allocation in conjunction with its target rating by an independent rating agency. High rating, for instance AAA or AA+, is a judgement based on a number of factors with own capital at the top of the list. But while capital reserves are crucial, they are not everything in rating. 'We look at capital but also beyond capital,' said Walter Pompliano of Standard & Poor's in a meeting in London. For instance, the factors scrutinized by S&P include:

- Management decisions
- Management actions
- Corporate outlook
- Risk appetite
- Risk control, to keep exposure in check
- Access to funding
- Franchise and diversification
- Changes taking place in risk profile.

Deficiencies identified in any one of these criteria may disallow AA or better credit rating, even if the bank has complied with regulatory capital requirements. Rating has also a great deal to do with the dynamics of the company and of the market – as well as with the characteristics of the management, which are reflected through the effectiveness and efficiency of each manager and professional in performing his or her job.

This is stated on the understanding that both effectiveness and efficiency are crucial criteria for human capital, and for the well-being of an organization as a whole. A longer list of criteria concerning human capital would include knowledge, experience, wisdom, trust, loyalty, precision, continuing personal development, inspiration, creativity, relationship handling, productivity

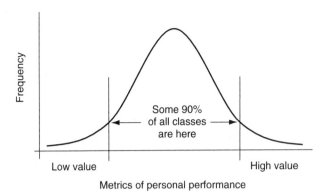

*Figure 1.6*  The values of personal characteristics tend to cluster around the mean; exceptional people are at the right-hand tail

and leadership. In a university environment, in connection with accreditation of the institution by an independent evaluation committee (as practised in the US), the number of books and articles published by the faculty will also be part of such a list.

The characteristics of any list made for evaluation purposes should be described so that it is easy to understand what is necessary for good standing. A factual and documented evaluation of management effectiveness is needed more today than at any time in the past. To a significant extent, the fulfilment of effectiveness prerequisites characterizes exceptional people (or entities) to the right tail of the distribution curve shown in Figure 1.6. On the contrary, negative evaluations position a person (or entity) to the left tail, which is synonymous with underqualification.

The search for proven leadership and performance is commendable, but it is wrong to believe that good managers with a pedigree will be excellent leaders no matter what job they do and what challenges they face. While several leadership qualities are more or less general, others – such as the deeper know-how of a given line of business, and the ability to thrive in a given culture – are specific to a given situation.

In the 1960s, when IBM was flying high, other companies believed that the foremost computer maker of that epoch was so crammed with good leaders that it was enough just to pick one to make the right choice. This did not work with Univac, and plenty of other firms that followed this mistaken hypothesis. Although IBM and Univac were in the same industry sector, that of mainframe computers, Univac did not have IBM's support environment, which its managers knew so well that for them it was second nature. Without the multilayered support for managerial decisions and actions, and having to live outside IBM's culture to which they were accustomed, these transplants to the CEO's chair of other companies failed.

In the first years of the twenty-first century the same story repeated itself with General Electric. As an article in *The Economist* had it,[5] the parachuting by 19 of GE's star managers immediately added an astonishing $24.5 billion to the share prices of the companies that hired them. But there was a caveat. GE executives tended to join severely underperforming companies whose shareholder returns over the previous year(s) had been worse than marker performance. Right after these transplanted CEOs joined their new company, the shares in the firms that hired them jumped. However, there have been cases where the stock market performance of the company that hired a GE senior executive as its new CEO got worse, and in some cases much worse. Table 1.2 provides a startling example with two negatives and a neutral out of a sample of seven. Such statistics put paid to the idea that an industrial leader parachuted to the summit of another firm can turn any situation around and work a miracle.

*Table 1.2*   Percentage by which share price beat the market after the transplant of a GE executive*

| Company hiring | GE manager | Hire date | Cumulative abnormal return in % | | Result |
|---|---|---|---|---|---|
| | | | 1 year before hire date to 2 days before hire | 2 days after hire date to 1 year after hire | |
| **Intuit** | Steve Bennett | 25 Jan. | 147.6 | −37.4 | Negative |
| *Competitors* | | 2000 | 24.3 | −17.0 | |
| **Conseco** | Gary | 28 Jun. | −92.8 | 75.5 | Mildly |
| *Competitors* | Wendt | 2000 | −24.6 | 70.2 | positive |
| **Honeywell** | Larry | 3 Jul. | 21.3 | 15.7 | Positive |
| *Competitors* | Bossidy | 2001 | 12.7 | −25.1 | |
| **3M** | James | 4 Dec. | 11.8 | 16.4 | Positive |
| *Competitors* | McNerney | 2000 | 17.2 | 0.9 | |
| **Home Depot** | Robert | 5 Dec. | −21.7 | 20.7 | No |
| *Competitors* | Nardelli | 2000 | −11.4 | 20.1 | difference |
| **Comdisco** | Norman | 28 Feb. | −54.5 | −93.0 | Very |
| *Competitors* | Blake | 2001 | −13.2 | −1.2 | negative |
| **Albertsons** | Larry | 24 April | 7.6 | 18.8 | Positive |
| *Competitors* | Johnston | 2001 | 11.7 | 9.5 | |

* Statistics by *The Economist*, 25 October 2003 and Harvard Business School.

## 5.   The sense of effective and focused decisions

Every decision is a judgement, and it is usually part of a process of selection among alternatives. Decisions are rarely a matter of choosing between 'right' and 'wrong', nor are they often based on facts – because 'facts' are so frequently unknown or uncertain. For the most part, decisions are based on opinions, and these tend to reflect untested hypotheses about events which are probable or expected.

What tends to turn the aftermath of decisions sour, and post mortems make these decisions look ineffective, is that unexpected events happen, and there has been little or no attention paid to them because of oversight or plain misjudgement. Such unexpected events may be internal or external.

- *Internal unexpected events* reflect in a very negative way on management's effectiveness.
- *External unexpected events* are those outside the entity's control, but their likelihood should have been understood at decision time. This is the role of prognostication (see section 2).

Examples of internal unexpected events are inefficiencies such as a shortfall in marketing and sales efforts, and misjudgements concerning cash flows, or a shortfall in human resources and skills. Other examples are price changes which constitute a business risk; changes in the cost basis, sometimes due to outsourcing; and an unexpected shortfall in connection with critical projects, such as R&D. The last results in delays in product innovation which may damage a company's market share, and even its reputation.

External unexpected events often relate to economic developments, in the local national or global market; higher competitive pressure than projected, affecting market share and/or pricing; strategic changes by competitors, including new entrants and their products; unexpected impacts of regulation and supervision; and unexpected change in independent agencies, known as external rating risk (see Chapter 2).

Quite often, the possible existence or subsequent appearance of unexpected events can be revealed through contrarian opinion. This is why effectively managed companies encourage contrarian opinion, and most particularly dissent. It is always prudent to assume that:

- hypotheses may have little to do with reality,
- 'facts' might be wrongly selected or even biased, and
- traditional measurements are not the right ones for the decision at hand, because they reflect yesterday's conditions.

In all these cases, disagreement is salutary because it provides an understanding of what the decision is all about. One of the characteristics of a leader is his or her appreciation of the need to listen to, and test, different opinions, making it absolutely clear that subordinates do not start out with the conclusion and then look for facts that will support it. Another important characteristic of effective management is the appreciation that decisions should not be made by acclamation:

- one does not make a decision unless there is disagreement about it,
- good decisions are typically based on a clash of conflicting views.

Both Alfred Sloan, the legendary CEO of General Motors, and Carlo Pesenti, the CEO of Italcementi and of five Italian banks,[6] appreciated that there is a great deal to be gained in terms of insight and foresight by means of *adversary proceedings*. The essence of this is a dialogue between different viewpoints. This leads not only to a factual and documented choice among alternatives, but also to a choice between different judgements.

Franklin Delano Roosevelt was a master in following a policy of adversary proceedings. He surrounded himself with brilliant people with controversial ideas, and gave them free rein in debating them in front of him, because this helped him to make up his mind. At the end Roosevelt chose the one or the other of these opinions – and sometimes, says one of his biographers, both of them, even if they were adverse to one another.

Dr Carlo Pesenti had a similar strategy. He wanted his immediate assistants to come to executive meetings with their ideas, so to speak, virgin. He did not want their judgement compromised in preparatory meetings among themselves. Executive committee meetings were characterized by concentration on different viewpoints. 'Concentration', says Peter Drucker, 'is the executive's only hope of becoming master of time and events instead of their whipping boy.'

Neither did Dr Pesenti care that much whether the decision was 'right' or 'wrong'. What he was particularly after was that it should be based on thorough analysis, which considers the strengths and weaknesses of all alternatives. There is always a probability that the decision will prove wrong because of external uncertainties. It might have been wrong to begin with, but most probably whereas it was right when it was made, changing circumstances made it wrong.

The sense of these real-life examples is that making a 'correct decision' means exercising judgement which is *in focus*. 'I always stop when things are out of focus', the Italian businessman and financier used to say. And he wanted his immediate assistants to focus only on important issues. 'The magistrate does not consider trifles' (*De minimis non curat praetor*) said Roman law, more than two thousand years ago.

In order to focus on what is important, decision-making must benefit from a problem list which states the unresolved issues and identifies the one that is salient. A *salient* problem is the one on which management must first focus its full attention. Alternative solutions should be noted in as much detail as the problem dictates, with emphasis placed on *management objectives*. That's what Sam Walton called the process of 'putting our hands around the problem'. Effective management ensures that there is an action list associated with the problem under study. The aim is to identify personal responsibilities not just for thinking about the problem but also for presenting a solution answering Cicero's prerequisites: what, why, where, when, and how. This process should also identify knowledge gaps in one or more issues connected to the problem, as well as answer questions such as:

- What is the effect of the agreed-upon solution?
- Is this decision consistent with the overall objectives of the firm?
- How will the decision influence later requirements in terms of commitments?

It is most likely that the best solutions will be multidimensional. Product decisions, for example, usually have a great deal to do with R&D priorities, manufacturing technology, financial resources, human capital, marketing policies, salespeople training, client support, maintenance costs and so on. Furthermore, every new product decision must recognize that its success depends on the successful outcome of the preceding product decisions – and, to a certain degree, on those that follow. Efficiency is most crucial; an advanced technological product must be designed to:

- fit different markets,
- develop into a coherent product line,
- use standard component parts, and
- minimize maintenance requirements.

As Figure 1.7 suggests, a good example is the Boeing 707 series. Aérospatiale, Boeing's No. 1 competitor, emulated this strategy, but before this, in the 1960s, it had designed, with British Aerospace, Concorde – a high-technology product which had boxed itself into a one-and-only version. Because development costs are so high, monolithic products don't succeed; they don't recover their costs. Product continuity requires:

- spreading the R&D investments,
- protecting one's flanks against competition,
- making possible specific market focus, and
- capitalizing on both mass effect and customization.

Moreover, changes in specifications while the product is in development and, even worse, in manufacturing are indications of failure in management decisions. Such changes can greatly upset timetables of deliverables, impede effective marketing, and eventually turn a projected profit margin into a massive debt.

A good example is the flexibility provided by the Boeing 737

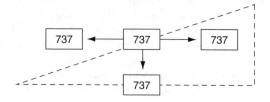

A bad example is the monolithic Concorde

*Figure 1.7*   Flexibility in design does not ensure market success, but it's most likely

## 6.   The role of personal accountability

To paraphrase an old real-estate property maxim, the three most important things in picking the right company for investment are management, management and management. Other than knowing something of the company's track record, the clearest indication for a prospective investor is the quality of the board of directors and of the CEO (see also Chapter 2 on rating by independent agencies).

In the light of many corporate collapses and alleged senior management fraud, it is rewarding to establish that a company has independent-minded, non-executive directors who seem both qualified and respected in their field. Protection of shareholder value also makes it wise to know which members have reputations for integrity, honesty and business acumen and which don't.

A basic investment rule is: beware of boards that are overly large – more than a dozen – or too small – fewer than six. Too few means that the board, as a strategy-making body, is probably missing some crucial skills; or is a rubber stamp. By contrast, boards with too many directors become little parliaments with interminable arguments, rather than focused debated and documented decisions.

Big boards are also cumbersome and costly, and may lead some investors to suspect that businessmen are offered directorships as prizes rather than for particular skills they are able to contribute to the company's management. Moreover, *personal accountability* – a critical factor in effective management – tends to diminish with large boards, as it becomes quite difficult to trace:

- *failed strategic decisions* which led to downgrading the company's competitiveness,
- losses due to events which damaged the franchise of the business, and
- adverse conditions in revenue because of miscalculation of macroeconomic and other factors, such as competitive pressure.

CEO malfeasance unveiled through a wave of prosecutions by the attorney-general of New York State and the Securities and Exchange Commission (SEC) is a case in point in personal accountability.[7] CEO malfeasance is a display of management ineffectiveness. Other examples are poor risk management, which has turned several companies belly up; and defective internal control as well as failure in compliance with rules and regulations.

White-collar crime flourishes when top management is ineffective, or is even an accomplice to it. At the beginning of October 2003, an advisory group in the US urged the US Sentencing Commission to hold directors and executives in leadership posts, at companies and government agencies, fully responsible for overseeing programmes to prevent white-collar crimes.

According to the advisory group, the sentencing guidelines should directly address violations of compliance programmes that companies and government agencies set up to prevent white-collar crime. Programmes aiming at preventive measures have been established by many big companies and have associated with them penalties and sentences if a crime is committed within a company. What the advisory panel said beyond this is that:

- people responsible for overseeing such programmes shouldn't be treated leniently, and
- senior management must be responsible for enforcing the company's own rules and supervisory guidelines.

In defining merits and demerits in the foregoing frame of reference, boards of directors can profit by following sentencing guidelines used by judges, prosecutors and attorneys to assign punishment and fines for particular crimes. Establishing rules for compliance with in-house anti-white-collar-crime programmes gives the whole effort more prominence, a necessary step after the recent run of corporate scandals. The US Sentencing Commission also recommended that the governing authority of an entity should be held responsible for lack of appropriate anti-crime initiatives – which should address not only rank and file but also the highest echelon in company management.

Lack of such rules is an excuse for wrongdoing. When Robert Fomon, the former head of E. F. Hutton Securities, was asked in the 1980s whether he should take some responsibility for an illegal cheque overdrafting scheme, he replied, 'No chief executive can be held accountable for any single thing that happens in a corporation.'[8] But some experts on ethical issues, as well as prosecutors and several corporate officers, now say that upper management must accept a great deal of responsibility.

New regulations, recently put in place by the authorities, ensure that even if top management does not know explicitly about the actions of subordinates, executives might be found culpable if they have created a climate in which wrongdoing is condoned or encouraged. A wave of scandals at top management level, some of which are becoming *déjà vu*, has been instrumental in changing the attitude of supervisors and governments towards personal accountability.

'Senior management should be held accountable for unethical actions if they have put severe pressure on their employees and have not emphasized that these goals should not be achieved by cutting ethical corners,' said Kirk O. Hanson, a professor at the Stanford Business School and president of the Business Enterprise Trust, a non-profit institute at Stanford that examines issues of business ethics. He and other experts suggest that the pressures on companies today to improve performance pose a special risk of questionable behaviour. In some instances:

- top officers put forth performance goals with the message: 'I don't care how you do it, just do it,' or
- the upper echelon deliberately turns a blind eye to wrongdoing, or even implicitly agrees to it while remaining shielded from blame.

'I think that top management has the responsibility to create a climate where that kind of behaviour never arises,' says Richard M. Rosenberg, former chairman and chief executive of BankAmerica Corp. 'That's maybe a naive statement, but I really believe it.'

Even laws enacted to help companies re-establish themselves having gone through tough times are exploited with the aim to gain major financial benefits. This is, for instance, the case of using protection from creditors under 'Chapter 11', to reduce one's cost base, get rid of pension and health care liabilities, shed infrastructure, fire staff, sell off or shut down unprofitable businesses units.[9] Sprinkle the magic dust and companies emerge from 'Chapter 11':

- with little or no debt,
- with a restructured balance sheet,
- with a focus on bottom line,
- with a skinny workforce, and
- with plenty of money ripped off from banks, whose loans have been cancelled, and investors whose shares and bonds become worthless.

In the end, this is a denial of personal accountability and also works against the sense of being competitive by sustaining our people, our organization, our products and our financial conditions. Personal accountability, and sound principles of management effectiveness, require that we act against market forces in terms of costs, innovation, flexibility, value differentiation, and delivery channels. A basic principle of personal responsibility is a steady watch over profitability, cash flow and documented accountability for results. This is what rating management effectiveness is all about, as we shall see in Chapter 2.

## Notes

1. *Financial Times*, 18 November 2002.
2. *BusinessWeek*, 26 January 2004.
3. *The Economist*, 11 January 2003.
4. Ibid., 25 October 2003.
5. Ibid.
6. To whom I was consultant for sixteen years.
7. D. N. Chorafas, *Management Risk. The Bottleneck Is at the Top of the Bottle*, Basingstoke: Palgrave Macmillan, 2004.
8. *International Herald Tribune*, 2 August 1990.
9. D. N. Chorafas, *Corporate Accountability, with Case Studies in Finance*, Basingstoke: Palgrave Macmillan, 2004.

# 2
# Rating Agencies, Management Effectiveness and Creditworthiness

## 1. Introduction

In a market economy, financial and industrial companies must have the possibility to go bankrupt. If the supervisory authorities or the prevailing laws and regulations have an eleventh-hour salvage policy, or too much tight rein to avoid bankruptcies, then in the first case it will lead to huge risk-taking, and in the second it will kill entrepreneurial activity. Both policies are, therefore, counterproductive.

On the other hand, people and companies dealing with a counterparty want to feel comfortable with the relationship. The gap is filled through the activity of independent rating agencies. Regulated by the Securities and Exchange Commission (SEC) as 'nationally recognized statistical rating organizations', independent rating outfits are essentially information agencies which provide an expert opinion on creditworthiness, based on both objective and subjective criteria.

- Objective rating criteria are quantitative and reflect the results of the study of financial documents such as balance sheets, profit and loss statements and reports to supervisors.
- Subjective criteria are mainly qualitative – the result of interviews with senior management of the company being rated, as well as an analysis of management's decisions and actions.

Both objective and subjective criteria help in defining, or at least in projecting, a company's ability and willingness to perform according to its contractual obligations. Subjective criteria are always present in management decisions, and as this chapter suggests, management's ethics and effectiveness play a key role in evaluating creditworthiness.

In the longer term, management effectiveness and willingness to perform are more important than capital adequacy, because management action and reaction are continuous, while capital adequacy is a snapshot. In the banking industry, for instance, regulators only set a minimum capital standard. They cannot, and they should not, target 100 per cent financial security because this is the responsibility of the bank's management; the regulator's mission is to:

- provide conditions for orderly market behaviour,
- create market transparency,
- avoid systemic risk, and
- ensure protection of investors, up to a point.

The regulators don't aim at stockholder protection beyond that of guaranteeing an orderly market. Stockholder and bondholder protection is not part of their charter. Again up to a point, bondholder protection is the mission of independent rating agencies, which address the default probability of bonds and companies.

Stockholder protection is basically provided by the effectiveness of the management of the company in which the investor takes a stake. Other things equal, shareholders who can judge management effectiveness and who know the probability of default assigned by rating agencies have better protection than those who don't.

What the investor needs to know is not only how effective and efficient management is (see Chapter 1), but also the company's financial staying power and risk tolerance, which affects the economic activity it undertakes. In this connection the rating agency can give a perception from the outside, while exact knowledge of the entity's internal limits goes deeper than the external view. However, this external view is very important, and every major company today is subject to *external rating risk*.

External rating risk is associated with market discipline. Every sector of the economy has its own criteria which affect the default probability of companies operating in it, though some of these criteria are industry-specific. For instance, in the insurance industry the credit risk of the insurer is judged by the company's ability to pay the claims arising from the policies it has underwritten. In a way, this rating corresponds to bond rating, but in reality it accounts for criteria proper to the insurance company.

These introductory paragraphs set the context for this chapter. It should be remembered that independent agencies are not the only ones to rate creditworthiness. Many banks have their own credit rating system, and they depend on it for approving loans. This raises a number of queries: What are the advantages of a global, external credit rating system versus an internal one? Why, in a globalized economy, should the probability of default also be universally defined? Will universal credit rating improve or exacerbate the pattern of default likelihood? How far can external rating risk go?

## 2.  External rating risk

Section 1 made reference to the notion of *counterparty*. This term denotes an entity or person to whom the bank has an on-balance-sheet and/or off-balance-sheet credit or market exposure, or potential exposure of another type. Counterparty obligations may, for example, take the form of loans, derivatives transactions, guarantee, warrants, or other commitments.

When a bank rates its clients in terms of their creditworthiness, it does so in the context of a certain deal, such as a loan. By contrast, the independent rating agency is not a counterparty to a transaction; essentially it is an information provider on somebody else's creditworthiness. This helps to explain the use of the term 'independent': the rating agency is independent of the transaction(s).

This independence of opinion forms the background of external rating risk, which has after-effects on the rated company's business. It might be possible to influence an external evaluator, but not to determine what he says. Independent rating agencies do their work with diligence, and their rating is subject to a well-organized and knowledgeable – in short, effective – rating review process.[1]

The act of rating can be polyvalent and espouse other objectives than creditworthiness. Indeed, its concept is expanding. On 12 July 1999, John Kiskinen, then Chairman of the White House Year 2000 Conversion Council, announced that the United States would begin publicly rating foreign countries on their degree of year 2000 (Y2K) preparedness.

Rating agencies have a franchise which takes years to develop, and plenty of effort to keep active. Not only is it difficult to get an SEC designation to operate a rating agency in the US, but also it is not that easy to acquire the necessary skills, particularly so as to create a global presence. Rating agencies vary significantly in their size, from the big four: Standard & Poor's (S&P), Moody's Investors Service, Fitch Ratings and A. M. Best, To a score of small entities, which have acquired an independent rating agency franchise, and are asked by their clients to rate a bond, some other instrument, or the creditworthiness of a whole firm.

Some of the independent rating agencies are specialized: A. M. Best originally rated only the claims-paying ability of insurance companies. But specialized agencies increasingly look towards the more general rating market. Since 1999, A. M. Best has also been rating insurance companies' corporate debt.

Whether the independent rating entity is big or small, specialized or more general, local or global, the objective of its rating is to provide an unbiased opinion. This opinion is *not* an advice or a recommendation.

- Independent rating agencies aim to inform.
- It is not part of their mission to protect anybody.

As stated in section 1, up to a point the protection of investors is the job of bank supervisors (more on this later). The parties responsible for uncovering and punishing corporate malfeasance are the attorney-general, police and judiciary.[2] Independent rating agencies have nothing to do with this. As an example, what the independent rating agencies provide, for information purposes, is shown in Table 2.1.

For their part, regulators establish minimum standards. They don't have the latitude to rate a credit institution's risk profile according to the 22 thresholds shown in Table 2.1, or any other scale. Rating agencies do it because granular credit rating is a sort of fundamental analysis, permitting evaluation of an entity's credit risk at different levels of reference. Indeed, with Basle II, this evaluation will increasingly involve:

- stratification of creditworthiness, and
- support through credit risk rating models.

*Table 2.1*  Long-term senior debt rating by Moody's, S&P and Fitch Ratings

| S&P and other agencies | Moody's | Credit message |
|---|---|---|
| **Investment grade** | | |
| AAA | Aaa | Very high quality |
| AA+ | Aa1 | |
| AA | Aa2 | High quality |
| AA− | Aa3 | |
| A+ | A1 | |
| A | A2 | Good payment ability |
| A− | A3 | |
| BBB+ | Baa1 | |
| BBB | Baa2 | Adequate payment ability |
| BBB− | Baa3 | |
| **Speculative grade** | | |
| BB+ | Ba1 | |
| BB | Ba2 | Uncertainty in payment ability |
| BB− | Ba3 | |
| B+ | B1 | |
| B | B2 | Higher risk investing |
| B− | B3 | |
| CCC+ | Caa1 | |
| CCC | Caa2 | Vulnerability to default |
| CCC− | Caa3 | |
| CC | | |
| C | Ca-C | Bankruptcy likelihood or |
| D* | | other major shortcoming |

* Fitch Ratings further distinguishes between DDD, DD and D.

Moreover, rating agencies are not an arm of the regulators. 'Regulators have a different role than the rating agencies,' said David Beers, of S&P. 'We try to define those banks that are likely to keep their license.' 'The rating agencies themselves don't want to be an arm of the regulators,' said Alastair Graham, of Moody's. 'Our role is independent, and our focus is that of assuring the soundness of debt.'

Granularity in credit rating can be helped by analysis which, as mentioned, involves both qualitative and quantitative issues – not only the study of balance sheets and income statements. As this activity expands, it may bring independent credit rating agencies into equity analysis, which has so far been the domain of investment banks. In my research, I asked: 'Does the following order of priority make sense?':

- Regulators
- Rating agencies
- Public.

'I don't think this is unfair,' answered David Beers, of S&P. 'Regulators look after the depositors and the rating agencies care for the bondholders.' Readers will notice that in terms of the creditworthiness of an institution, bondholders

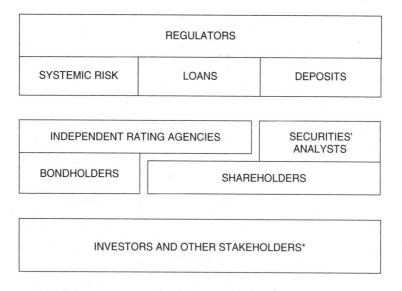

* For instance, in insurance, the policy-holders.

*Figure 2.1*  The role of regulators, rating agencies and analysts vs the investors

are more at risk than depositors because depositors are protected through state-run deposit insurance.

Figure 2.1 positions regulators, rating agencies and equity analysis outfits as perceived by the majority of participants in the research which led to this book. Though their goals may be different, analysts working for rating agencies and investment banks share common characteristics in terms of background and deliverables. They:

- study the past to detect strengths, weaknesses and trends,
- project into the future based on management effectiveness,
- analyse cost structures as a proxy for profit margin(s), and
- evaluate assumed risks, their distribution and their future impact.

When the processes identified by these four points are not executed in an effective manner, external rating risk rises. Downgrading is bad news (see section 5). However, if accurate, bad news can be as important as good news, because it obliges management to take immediate corrective action. The principle of institutional survival is to bring up the bad news yourself. This can be done through internal rating (see section 4).

## 3. Evaluating management effectiveness

A rating system is not just grades and thresholds. As the Basle Committee on Banking Supervision aptly suggests, it comprises all methods, processes and controls – including data collection, datamining and other information technology (IT) supports vital to the assessment of credit risk, and the dynamic upkeep of grades pertaining to every rated entity or issue. Therefore, the Basle Committee says that, to qualify, a rating solution must have two distinct dimensions:

- risk of borrower default, and
- transaction-specific factors influencing creditworthiness.

While the reference made by the Basle Committee addresses specifically the banks' internal rating based (IRB) methodology, the foregoing concept can be generalized to all rating procedures with the addition of one more point to the two already mentioned:

- management-specific factors influencing the entity's survivability.

All three points are key to estimating credit risk. By using the information they provide, we come to a conclusion regarding a counterparty's credit-worthiness. What these points imply is that we can never have an exact idea of the counterparty without having seen the:

- financial figures,
- management controls,
- top people at the steering wheel,
- evidence of effectiveness, and
- policies of compliance to regulatory rules.

The challenge associated with the observation of each of these milestones in analysis is that it is not actually possible to track each one of them for each loan or other type of transaction. This enhances the role of independent rating agencies, and promotes the need for an international regulatory body to establish a level playing field.

The party responsible for both day-to-day operations and longer-term survival of the firm is its top management, not the rating agencies or the regulators. But both the independent rating outfits and supervisors observe whether or not senior management runs the business in an effective manner, keeps exposure under lock and key, and appreciates the longer-term consequences of what is now happening, as well as why it is happening in the way it is.

Rating agencies take note of whether top management has made the correct decisions, sometimes by going back to these decisions and evaluating their effects. Such post mortems are not particularly common, but both their need and their popularity are rising. Financial and industrial companies are themselves becoming increasingly keen to do post mortems because of the benefits they derive from them, in terms of:

- an evaluation of the effectiveness of past decisions, and
- the opportunity to improve the focus of future top management decisions.

The issue of effectiveness of senior management decisions and actions is so important because criters of the performance of an enterprise – from investors, to rating agencies and regulators – now appreciate that while sound capitalization is necessary, it is not a sufficient condition for survival – and nor, therefore, for credit rating. 'We look at capital but also beyond capital,' said Walter Pompliano of Standard & Poor's. Pompliano mentioned ten crucial management-related factors which come into rating:

- Management decisions
- Management actions
- Corporate outlook
- Risk appetite
- Risk control
- Access to funding
- Franchise
- Buybacks
- Diversification
- Change in risk profile.

Note that even if the quantitative financial evaluation gives positive results, any one of these largely qualitative factors may not confer 'AA' credit rating. Capital is needed to take care not only of expected risks, but also of unexpected risks which are usually tail events in a risk distribution. As Figure 2.2 shows, a confidence interval, $\alpha$, is connected to the single-, double- and triple-A rating. Beyond this financial factor, management-related issues ensure that rating has a great deal to do with the dynamics of the company and of the market.

Years ago I was consultant to the chairman of a large financial group who was more concerned that the presidents of his banks made fact-based decision than that they were always 'right' in their choices. The rationale for this policy was that the market changes and while at the time it was made a decision seemed 'right', over time it might prove to be wrong. But if the background factors of a decision have been researched in a rigorous manner, considering all the alternatives, then this decision has the best chance of withstanding the test of time and of overcoming the market's whims. Basically, that its what management effectiveness is all about. Management quality can also be judged in connection with compliance to the new rules drawn up at the Basle Committee on Banking Supervision, to ensure that banks cannot stretch their capital so thinly that they risk collapsing when their lending and/or trading transactions go bad. This underpins the new capital adequacy framework, which forces banks to pay more attention to creditworthiness of the countries and companies they lend to.

Through the use of a risk-based evaluation of capital needs, Basle II tunes reserves to assumed exposure, and makes the issue of creditworthiness more transparent. Under the original 1988 Capital Accord, known as Basle I, banks did not have to provide capital against the loans they make to governments that are members of the Organization for Economic Co-operation

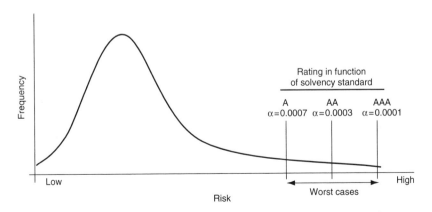

*Figure 2.2* Economic capital, solvency standard and level of confidence, according to A. M. Best

and Development (OECD). As a result, Hungary, rated BBB, was treated the same as Germany, rated AAA; and Mexico went bankrupt right after it gained OECD status.

The OECD loophole was significant because banks had to set aside an 8 per cent reserve for loans to other countries which may have a higher rating than some OECD members. As this example demonstrates, there are merits in a credit evaluation framework which charges capital reserves not through club membership, but according to a country's credit rating.

Much better focus must be the objective of every evaluation. But as explained in section 1, a well-rounded evaluation system needs both an objective and a subjective part. The latter is based on interviews and the discovery of facts which are based largely on qualitative assessments but help explain why the figures look the way they do – and what might be the most likely development.

## 4.   Internal ratings and external ratings

There are two different, indeed contradictory, approaches to credit rating by independent agencies. One is positive, and the other somewhat negative. The positive approach sees the work done by independent rating agencies as complementing internal credit rating efforts. The negative approach, which I have seen in use at some credit institutions, sees external rating as a not very reliable outsourcing of credit risk analysis – which is the wrong approach.

The principle is that a common, well-understood and believable indicator of exposure adds transparency to any financial institution's credit risk measurement profile. Whether internal or external, credit rating procedures can only be effective if each banker and investor understands their meaning in the context of his own portfolio of exposures, and from the perspective of his own risk tolerance.

According to the transparency principle, even if there were no other reason than that of providing a nearly universal, fairly standardized, credit risk measurement profile, external ratings would be worth their salt. To appreciate this statement it should be remembered that until very recently, practically until Basle II came along, internal rating systems featured by financial institutions had very few thresholds, about six or seven, plus one for default. By contrast, rating systems by independent agencies have a much finer granularity, with up to 20 credit rating thresholds, which allows greater accuracy in evaluation of creditworthiness.

When, in 1999, with the first draft of Basle II as a consultative paper, the Basle Committee on Banking Supervision promoted external ratings, many commercial banks did not like the idea. 'Compared to what we do in terms of rating in our bank, what the independent rating agencies do is retrograde, a step backwards,' said a senior commercial banker in London. 'Besides this, they cover less than the 8 per cent of the population we deal with.'

This assertion contains two statements, one of which is true and the other false. In my experience, the methodology used by independent rating agencies is way ahead of that of the average commercial bank, and even of many of those consider who themselves advanced in credit rating. On the other hand, there is no argument that independent rating agencies address only part of the population of counterparties a commercial bank deals with.

Another commercial banker critical of the new role of independent rating agencies stated: '[Their system] is behind the state of the art and it has deficiencies. For instance, its coverage of the population of borrowers is uneven.' The main reason behind this criticism is ego. The statement has nothing to do with the rating methodology of external rating agencies, whose deliverables cannot possibly be expected to be symmetrical for all entities with which a given bank deals.

In fact, as the discussion with this particular credit institution progressed, it became evident that a main worry of this executive was that, compared to his bank's internal rating system, the one by independent agencies afforded no credence to portfolio diversification. This, however, is not the objective of credit rating, whether internal or external. The confusion stems from the fact that we talk of a two-step process:

- Credit rating should be based on qualitative and quantitative factors connected to counterparties.[3]
- After counterparties have been rated comes the task of evaluating portfolio concentration and diversification along rating thresholds.

To make this discussion more meaningful, it should be added that other commercial bankers were more positive about ratings by independent agencies. Several of the executives of credit institutions I met in my research consider external ratings as positive, though some are worried that they might lead to herd behaviour. To avoid this, the bankers suggested that it would be wise to have a solution incorporating external rating *and* credit modelling, which is internal to the bank. The result should permit documented credit opinions on creditworthiness. This is practically what is now happening with Basle II.[4]

Another contrarian opinion which surfaced during the research done for this book was that independent credit rating agencies are very professional in assessing country risk, but not obligor risk. This is by no means a valid argument, thought it might apply to rating by export insurance agencies – a different set of entities – whose judgement has been integrated into the new Basle capital adequacy framework.

A British banker, who was more critical of Basle I than of Basle II, added the thought that, in the general case, expert classification by governments and government-sponsored entities is not a reliable index. It is very difficult to be objective when political arguments have the upper ground, and premiums most often become political ploys. 'For instance,' he said, 'the criterion of membership to the OECD is worth practically nothing.' I agree with this statement, but membership of clubs of nations and rating by independent agencies are not correlated.

Continental European bankers, with whom I met in Paris and Frankfurt, had different reservations. To them, the most negative issue is that S&P, Moody's and Fitch have by and large concentrated their rating effort on American companies. This gives American banks a lead, since on their home base much of the rating work has already been done.

As these quotations from research meetings reveal, there is no consensus about internal ratings and external ratings in the banking industry. Opinions and reasons behind different criticisms of ratings by independent agencies vary widely from one institution to another, but altogether they are not necessarily negative. A growing number of bankers, investors and regulators appreciate that they can benefit from an independent agency's credit grading efforts.

Also, on the positive side, it is appropriate to include the widening range of ratings on bonds, companies and sovereignties which is producing a fundamental change in the world's financial system – with consequences yet to be fully appreciated. Some analysts believe that in the longer term the effects may be comparable to those of derivatives, where goods and commodities were replaced, as the principal components of international trade, by derivative financial instruments based on:

- stocks,
- bonds,
- currencies, and
- other commodities.

By analogy, through futures, forwards, swaps and options, the global financial market has been instrumental in reshaping the world's economy. Research done at end of the twentieth century demonstrated that, in notional principal amount, the total worth of financial derivatives trades in 1998 was nearly 14 times the worth of the entire world economy. With the global economy growing on average by 2 per cent per year, while derivatives grow by 25 per cent to 30 per cent per year, today this has become a much higher multiple – to about 50 times at the end of 2004.

One more observation should be added before closing this section. The immensity of the market for derivative financial instruments has created a major reason why, on its own, each financial institution cannot provide for integration of credit exposure across all of its counterparties in trading loans, investments and the other channels of commercial banking. Neither can the regulators grade the myriad of entities and instruments all by themselves. These facts help in documenting the importance of external ratings, and their role in improving internal credit ratings made by financial institutions.

## 5. The high cost of downgrading

The new rules of competition in a globalized economy and its fast pace of innovation in derivative instruments require senior managers to start by asking what's important to their companies and to their customers, as well as where their bank can make good money – and what's the associated risk. With this information in hand, senior managers need to reinvent their businesses to create the next profit zones, always keeping an eye on overall market discipline, and the way independent rating agencies evaluate their company, themselves, and the results they obtain.

Rating the counterparty with which bankers, insurers, investors and other entities deal is important both in the short term and in the longer run. From time to time, financial ruptures have characterized virtually every downturn in the economy, leading to an increased frequency of defaults, and from there to a credit crunch.

Stresses in the financial system cause credit to be tightened on a national or even international basis. That happened most recently within the Japanese economy, as a whole, as well as in 2000 when the telecommunications industry's bubble burst, and in 1988 with the LTCM débâcle, which led the capital markets to freeze briefly, until the Federal Reserve eased aggressively. Other stresses are more local and, therefore, more limited. Such is the case of the inability of 'this' or 'that' counterparty to face up to its obligations.

Individual big-company stresses are events limited in duration, but they are still painful. Investment-grade companies nearly always have easy access to the bond market, and there may be no disruption to the flow of consumer credit, but companies suffering from a downgrade in credit rating have a difficult time. Counterparties turn away from them because their possible bankruptcy, or insolvency, is unsettling to the bankers and investors who extended them credit.

Economic history shows that when cases of insolvency multiply, bank lending standards become stringent, and loans to business and consumers may not grow at all. The result is a slow-down in money supply, swamping demand and leading to a rapid involuntary build-up of inventories, at both the retail and factory level. This too acts to depress economic growth, through a vicious cycle.

It is only reasonable that companies suffering a credit downgrade should have to pay more, sometimes much more, for their credit. In late July 2002, the credit rating of Ericsson, the Swedish telecommunications equipment maker, was cut to junk status, in a move that threatened the Swedish company's plans for a heavily discounted SKR 30 billion ($3.2 billion) rights issue.

In the aftermath of the downgrade, Ericsson said the financial impact would lead to an increase in the company's financing costs by about SKR 101 million ($10.2 million) per year. While since then Ericsson has been able to turn its fortunes around, this remains a good example of the cost of a one-notch downgrade from BBB– to BB+. Note that the company's share price reflected the event, as can be seen in Figure 2.3.

The lesson to retain from this, and many other similar examples, is that rating by independent agencies influences the cost of funds in a significant way. It is appropriate to appreciate, however, that the credit rating issue has two sides. Other things equal, a higher grade requires more equity and this tends to lower the company's return on equity (ROE).

The reason for stating 'other things equal' is that, as we have already seen, there are many other factors – including senior management effectiveness – involved in rating than capital alone. Therefore, independent rating agencies think that, of themselves, small changes in capital adequacy are not necessarily a reason for credit downgrading. As Samuel Theodore, managing director and global banking coordinator, Moody's Investors Services, said, 'There is no strong correlation between rating and level of regulatory capital. Economic capital is essentially a management tool.'[5]

Samuel made the point that so far Moody's has not downgraded any bank's rating solely because of a decline in its regulatory capital ratio – for instance, following share buybacks. By contrast, an institution's material

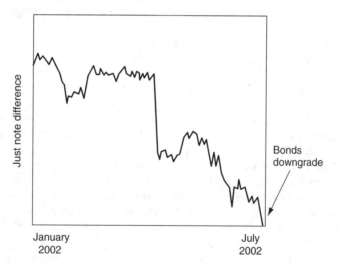

*Figure 2.3*  Ericsson's B share price relative to European telecom equipment equities

decapitalization often signals the presence of structural issues, problems with earnings, challenges with franchise, an ineffective or obsolete business model – all aspects of management performance that leaves much to be desired. These are key rating drivers. Other crucial rating factors include:

- Liquidity shortage
- Asset quality crisis
- Troubles with brand name
- Acts of mismanagement
- Major fraud, and
- Systemic issues which are negative.

Therefore, while there seems to be no apparent statistical relation between a certain level of volatility in capital adequacy ratio and credit rating, the aforementioned background factors may influence both the bank's rating and its Tier-1 capital. This statement is valid both ways: in upgrading and in downgrading the entity's creditworthiness.

For instance, following a couple of years of bleak financial results, in the second quarter of 2003, Crédit Suisse Group continued to strengthen its capital base, due primarily to earnings generation and the sale of non-core businesses. The Group's consolidated Tier-1 capital was 11.1 per cent as of 30 June 2003, an increase from 10.0 per cent as of 31 March 2003. This change has been positive for Crédit Suisse stakeholders, but most probably rating agencies did not consider it to be sufficient, because the rating of Crédit Swiss Group was not upgraded from A+.

Correctly, independent rating agencies have a long memory and, as already explained, they integrate a good deal of critical factors into their rating procedure. A credit institution may have 8 per cent Tier-1 capital and still get a B rating if the effectiveness of its management is wanting. By contrast, an AA bank would not have less than 4 per cent Tier-1 capital out of an overall 8 per cent capital adequacy ratio (the balance being Tier-2).

The fact that capital adequacy is not everything in credit rating in no way diminishes the role liquidity plays. The liquidity of a bank is indicative of its reserve ratio and vice versa. There are, however, two ways of looking at liquidity. One is *orthodox* (or conservative), and the other represents a more *liberal* view:

- The *orthodox* view is that the resources of a bank which ensure liquidity are cash and other assets quickly convertible into cash.
- The *liberal* view identifies liquidity with *shiftability* of assets; therefore it includes in the liquidity of the bank any investments that can be readily sold in the market.

Notice that over-the-counter derivatives are not part of that sort of easily liquifiable assets. Aptly, a paper issued on 2 July 2003 by the European

Central Bank (ECB) outlines four categories of Tier-1 capital; these stand a good chance of becoming standard criteria in the judgement of capital adequacy.

*Category I* (highest liquidity) includes central government securities, and debt securities issued by central banks. Part of *Category II* are local and regional government securities, supranational securities and securities of government agencies. *Category III* includes credit institution securities and corporate securities, while in *Category IV* are asset-backed securities traded in the capital market. A fairly similar classification exists for Tier-2 capital.

Moreover, any credit rating system worth its salt should be aware that illiquidity and insolvency are correlated. Theoretically, liquidity and solvency are two different concepts, but in practice this is not always the case.

In the stock market crash of October 1987 a key question for the Federal Reserve was the likelihood of systemic risk: was some big bank in trouble, and maybe insolvent? 'In the short run, [Gerald] Corrigan [the president of the New York Fed] argued. There was no way to tell the difference between just short term liquidity problems and outright insolvency.'[6]

Risk events which are at the high end of the risk distribution's tail may damage the bank's liquidity or solvency, or both. Therefore a financial institution must watch liquidity most carefully – both its own and the market's as a whole. It should also target and stress-test its own solvency, including the possibility of fast realization of assets under conditions other than fire sale.

## 6.   Rating agencies, capital requirements and management effectiveness

So far in this chapter fulfilling capital requirements and evaluating management effectiveness have been considered as two separate factors contributing to company rating, the first being more objective and the second more subjective. It is clear, however, that the two correlate both between themselves and with other factors, as we will see in this section.

Let's start with capital adequacy, which is a good basis on which to judge management's effectiveness in terms of compliance with regulations. 'Since 1999, we don't believe banks to be overcapitalized,' said Barbara Ridpath of S&P. 'It is rather the opposite.'[7] Ridpath made the point that while regulatory capital keeps an institution's banking licence, 'more capital' means the bank is safer, from the viewpoint of:

- shareholders
- bondholders
- lenders
- depositors, and
- the capital market.

It is only reasonable to add to this statement that, apart from capital adequacy, management effectiveness plays a key role in satisfying the (often conflicting) requirement advanced by the above parties. A company's senior management can never feel (let alone be) immune to the market's reaction. For any practical purpose, the members of the board, CEO, CFO and other senior executives are personally accountable for whatever the company does, and does not do while it should have been doing it.[8]

Because, however, different types of mishaps do take place – both in connection with fulfilling regulatory capital requirements and in regard to a long list of other issues – to make sure no entity uses funny money, in its rating S&P excludes all hybrids from core capital (Tier-1 and Tier-2 hybrids are not covered in this book). For evaluation purposes, S&P has introduced its own measures:

- adjusted total equity (ATE), and
- adjusted common equity (ACE).

Some but not all hybrid capital instruments are included in ATE. Each is evaluated from the viewpoint of three conditions: permanency, loss absorption, and cushion to debt-holders in liquidation. Standard & Poor's adjusted, risk-weighted assets incorporate several criteria which deal directly with the effectiveness of a company's management. Examples are:

- sound qualitative assessment of portfolio quality,
- evidence of effective market risk management,
- able use of securitization and risk mitigation techniques,
- detection of concentration and effective diversification of risk,
- much better than average asset and liability management, and
- operational risk control which keeps the most prominent exposures under lock and key.

As adjusted capital measures, ATE and ACE exclude hybrid capital instruments from core capital, incorporate specific assessment of hybrid capital characteristics, and make deductions for investments in unconsolidated subsidiaries. What the independent rating agency is after is the ability to identify both management effectiveness and capital sufficiently to absorb all risks through an economic cycle, particularly at its low level when the market does not support capital replenishment. Run through a recession scenario, the S&P capital model assumes:

- three years without access to capital markets,
- forced rollover of maturing loans,
- no market liquidity for the bank's loans, and
- enough capital at the end to remain in business and make new loans.

This means in practice sufficient capital to absorb all risk, without going 'cap in hand' to the credit market. Key to such evaluation is the quality and make-up of the risk portfolio, as well as the way risk is managed. Both are telling examples of the credit institution's management effectiveness.

Effective handling of counterparty risk and of position risk embedded in the bank's portfolio is a demanding management task. Take as an example Citigroup, with its more than 36 counterparties, doing 100 transactions every day. Only first-class management skill and high-technology, real-time solutions can keep counterparty risk under control. Doing business in these conditions is a balancing act. One desk may be short with a given party, while another desk may be long with this same party. Overall, corporate-wide internal control requires a system which works:

- 24 hours per day
- 7 days in the week
- anywhere in the world.[9]

Dr David Lawrence, of Citigroup, provided an example of how precisely this system must function. On a given Sunday, a company in Australia asked Citigroup for a $100 million loan. This entity was not a customer of the bank but Citi had rated it because of its corporate policy of keeping ratings up to date, including probability of default (PD) and loss given default (LGD). On the basis of this information, which was interactively available to the loan office, the $100 million loan was approved.

Banks should appreciate that there are clear competitive advantages in steadily improving the effectiveness of their risk management. Apart from the stated reasons, disclosure requirements for the most advanced internal ratings-based method under Basle II help in detailing to the fullest extent possible existing risks. Most evidently, another important consideration is the quality of the institution's internal evaluation processes, which are themselves a reflection of management's effectiveness.

Queries associated with operational risk provide an example of what is necessary: is the institution able to collect and report the granularity of operational loss data, as well as management's ability to understand the implications of its decisions in regard to credit risk? market risk? the many facets of operational risk? Has senior management real-time access to:

- length of commitments,
- concentrations of risks, and
- detail regarding instruments and counterparties?

The new regulations ensure that large institutions, with global or multiple holdings, pay particular attention to operational risk, and to issues related to consolidation of assets and liabilities. Both are critical issues in the calculation of minimum capital requirements, as well as in the allocation of economic capital which goes beyond the regulatory level and signals to the market that the bank has financial staying power.

Last but not least, management effectiveness can also be judged by the way the CEO and his immediate assistants look at the critical role played by internal control. The confidence that management places on organizational systems and procedures is key to the effective execution of the board's decisions. The new regulatory regime, under Basle II, exposes failings more harshly than has been the case so far, and this biases the market's perception of *our* firm and the likelihood of its survival.

## 7.   The strategy of deception in gaining higher rating

To attract an AAA client base, banks must have a strong balance sheet, top credit rating, and a top management of demonstrated ability and cunning. Because transactions made by important clients can be large and of a much longer duration than typical cash market operations, relationship banking has taken on new aspects, such as:

- ample documentation of counterparty risk,
- ability to access market liquidity, and
- a rigorous ongoing risk management process, which permits both detection and correction of anomalies.

In a highly competitive market like that of the early twenty-first century in the Group of Ten countries, the skill set for effective relationship management includes not only knowledge of derivative financial products, proficiency in rocket science, and effective risk control, but also familiarity with laws and regulations in every country of operation. Legal risk is very important to specific segments of the client base. Its control helps in answering the question whether or not *our* bank is an appealing counterparty to AAA clients.

This question goes well beyond the domain of correspondent banks. Today, the only non-government-supported credit institution with an AAA rating is Holland's Rabobank. For one reason or another, all other credit institutions have lost their triple A but, as section 3 pointed out, the better managed try to hold on or regain an AA. Most do so through honest effort. There are, however, some banks that have chosen to use tricks.

Frank Partnoy, a former investment banker, describes how Morgan Stanley tried, and finally succeeded, in convincing an independent rating agency that its new securitized bonds were entitled to an AA rating.[10] These structured instruments were issued in dollars and the problem was that a similar Mexican bond, also in US dollars, carried much lower rating. The not-so-clean deal was made for Benamex, the Mexican credit institution for which Morgan Stanley acted as investment banker.

The US investment bank argued that because the underlying Ajustabonos were denominated in higher-rated Mexican pesos, the bonds really were Mexican peso bonds, not Mexican dollar bonds. This made a difference because, in most cases, a sovereign's internal debt is rated higher than its foreign currency debt. But from an investor's perspective, the bonds looked as if they were dollar-denominated. Morgan Stanley seems to have offered two concessions that persuaded S&P to assign an AA rating.

1. It issued two classes of bonds, and S&P would rate only the safer of the two.

Benamex, the Mexican bank, would keep the riskier bonds, which remained unrated. It would also purchase some US Treasuries as back-up for the AA bonds, named PLUS Notes. This virtual integration of largely useless bonds with the more select class which made up PLUS Notes exploited a clause in the US Generally Accepted Accounting Principles (GAAP) which says that a firm which owns another includes all assets and liabilities of that firm as part of its own assets and liabilities (A&L).

Generally, this is a sound rule, but at times it can become a loophole which makes possible creative accounting practices in the twilight zone between what is legal and what is illegal. In essence, this is a deceptive practice which nevertheless permitted the Benamex bond to get an AA rating. The second concession offered by Morgan Stanley was that:

2. It would commit itself to executing foreign currency transactions in which it would convert peso payments on the Ajustabonos into US dollars.

To give investment grade rating, according to Partnoy, S&P also required Morgan Stanley to advertise the PLUS Notes with a clause which said that the AA– rating does not reflect risk associated with fluctuations in currency exchange rate between pesos and dollars. Such a fluctuation in parities involves forex risk.

To better understand the deception associated with this particular case, it is necessary to keep in perspective that few investors truly understand the message conveyed by rating. As it has been explained, in their work independent rating agencies target counterparty risk. The problem is, however, that many investors tend to confuse credit risk and market risk, wrongly thinking that an AA, or similar rating, covers all types of risks – which is not true.

This can evidently be exploited in marketing a certain instrument. The strategy in this particular case was that, with good rating, PLUS Notes became a sexy financial product: Rated AA–, PLUS Notes paid a relatively high interest in dollars, and were protected by a cushion of unrated bonds and some US Treasuries. Theoretically, but only theoretically, these bonds diversified risk in an investor's portfolio, because of their Mexican base, but at the same time, misinformation meant that they were telling the investors very little about their risky nature. By playing the system, Benamex bonds have been instrumental in positioning Morgan Stanley and the Mexican bank ahead of the curve in the perceived analysis of risk and return by a score of investors. A slow-witted investment manager might well have bought the rather hollow diversification argument, and he could have missed some of the risks associated with the offer.

Frank Partnoy also reveals other gimmicks which can blur the vision of independent rating agencies. He says: '[the rating agency] called to notify me that they would be changing the rating of several Morgan Stanley derivatives sales, including FT Trust [a derivatives contract]. The deals would retain their AAA rating, but S&P would add an R subscript to the AAA. R stood for Restricted... This was awful news [in terms of sales].'

In the end the news was not that awful because as this and many other cases demonstrate, investors rarely pay attention to subscripts and footnotes. Even if they read the subscript, the chances are that they would not understand what R means. While rating as triple and double A has become legend, and many investors run for it, the intricate aspects of a rating system are not so well known – let alone understood.

Few investors bother to inform themselves about their impact, yet they are putting their money on the block. Investors are wrong to turn away from the resource-intensive analysis which can provide them with evidence on how solid their investment is. Instead, they should focus attention on management issues associated with rating. Failing to do so has materially adverse effects on their business, and leads to a deterioration of their financial condition.

At the same time, institutions that have been able to deceive investors should not think that this is evidence of management effectiveness. If anything, precisely the contrary is true. As the case studies in Chapters 3 to 11 will demonstrate, tricky business is the characteristic of weak and ineffective management, which sacrifices the company's reputation and its survival in the longer term for quick gains.

## Notes

1. D. N. Chorafas, *Managing Credit Risk, Volume 1, Analyzing, Rating and Pricing the Probability of Default*, London: Euromoney, 2000.
2. Chorafas, *Management Risk*.
3. D. N. Chorafas, *Managing Credit Risk*.
4. D. N. Chorafas, *Economic Capital Allocation with Basle II. Cost and Benefit Analysis*, London and Boston: Butterworths-Heinemann, 2004.
5. International Capital Allocation Conference, Zurich, 16/17 September 2003, organized by IIR.
6. Bob Woodward, *Maestro. Greenspan's Fed and the American Boom*, New York: Simon & Schuster, 2000.

7. 'Basle II Masterclass', organized by IIR, London, 27/28 March 2003.
8. D. N. Chorafas, *Corporate Accountability, with Case Studies in Finance*, Basingstoke: Palgrave Macmillan, 2004.
9. D. N. Chorafas, *Implementing and Auditing the Internal Control System*, Basingstoke: Palgrave Macmillan, 2001.
10. Frank Partnoy, *F.I.A.S.C.O. The Truth About High Finance*, London: Profile Books, 1997.

# 3

# Is Mismanagement an Exception?

## 1. Introduction

The case studies which start in this chapter and continue to the end of the book will demonstrate that there is plenty of poor management in financial and industrial organizations. They have been purposely selected on the principle that bad examples are thought-provoking, because they show what can go wrong and in how many ways this may happen.

We should always learn from other people's errors, and the misfortunes which followed them. One thing fifty years of professional experience have taught me is that not only is mismanagement not an exception, but also management weaknesses are more easily imitated than management strengths. Moreover, because they are characterized by drift, weaknesses are provocative in two ways:

- they encourage clones, which repeat more or less the same silly things done by the parties they imitate, and
- they adopt creative accounting practices in a fruitless effort to pull themselves up by their shoestrings.

Take Daewoo and Kim Woo-chong, its chairman and founder, as an example. The bankruptcy of Daewoo with $80 billion in debt (!) has been South Korea's most dramatic event since the collapse of the country's economy at the end of 1997. One cannot but be surprised that banks and other creditors advanced all that money to an untrustworthy counterparty – as if credit risk counted for nothing (see Chapter 2).

Daewoo's oblivion was accompanied by the disappearance of Kim Woo-choong. For South Koreans, speculating about his fate became a national pastime. Newspapers reported sightings of him in France and in the United States, but little had been heard from the conglomerate's chairman and animator until the week of 20 January 2002, when Kim ended years of silence by granting an interview to *Fortune* magazine. In this, he described his fugitive lifestyle and answered allegations that he was guilty of the world's biggest accounting fraud. In the meantime, in his absence:

- Twenty Daewoo executives were jailed for accounting fraud that inflated Daewoo's assets by $30 billion, and
- South Korean prosecutors made it clear that they considered Kim the chief villain of this whole business,[1] as if he alone could have created and sustained the huge scandals characterizing his company.

In his interview to *Fortune*, Kim described how he built Daewoo from a tiny trading company, founded in 1967 with $10,000 of assets, into a global manufacturing giant generating $50 billion of annual sales. Its products ranged from cars and ships to pianos and televisions, and the company had negotiated lavish financial support from many countries in exchange for setting up plants.

Kim said in the interview that in its heyday, together with other family-owned conglomerates (*chaebol*), Daewoo turned South Korea into a leading exporting nation. In the last analysis, however, it was the South Korean taxpayer who footed a good part of Daewoo's bill, as government-directed domestic banks eagerly granted billions of dollars in loans to fund the *chaebol*'s breakneck expansion into ever more diverse, and uncontrollable, industries and markets. At its height, Daewoo was active in 110 countries, ranging from construction operations to electronics, but this reckless expansion turned out to be its downfall: sales grew while profits shrank, as the empire and its management became overstretched.

In a way quite similar to that of so many other mismanaged companies, which think they have found the elixir for perpetual growth, successful parts of the Daewoo empire were used to subsidize failing units. To cover up different scams, transparency was at rock bottom, while an ever-growing amount of cash was borrowed from banks to keep the group afloat.

In this *Fortune* interview, Kim Woo-chong admitted 'window dressing' of Daewoo's financial accounts to make the balance sheet look healthier than it was. Then, like other failed entrepreneurs who overleveraged themselves and their companies, he said creative accounting was 'not a big thing'. It just reflected the fact that the practice was widespread in South Korea's corporate sector – probably one of the few true things said in the interview.

In other words, it is OK to cheat as long as you are not caught. This is evidently wrong, and not only ethically. Abraham Lincoln once said that you can fool some of the people all of the time or all of the people some of the time. But not all of the people all of the time. Lincoln's dictum sums up eloquently both the reach and the limits of creative accounting and of mismanagement.

Making false financial statements is a practice which characterizes the large majority of failing corporate empires and nations on their way to bankruptcy. Among the latter, Argentina provides a recent example. Towards its end, Daewoo was borrowing money in one place simply to pay debts elsewhere, incurred until lenders eventually turned off the tap. 'All the world's financial institutions were asking us to pay,' said Kim. 'But there was no way.' Years of mismanagement had exhausted the company's resources, and this precipitated its end.

## 2. The Ahold accounting scandal

Headlines about scandals brought the message home to every investor that things were looking down in the board room of more and more companies quoted on the exchanges. Starting with Enron in early December 2001, the following years have seen new revelations of mismanagement, associated to 'this' and 'that' bankruptcy characterized as 'the largest ever'.

Three cases have been labelled 'Europe's Enron': Vivendi Universal (see Chapter 7); Parmalat (see section 3 in this chapter) and Ahold. Curiously enough, France Télécom (see Chapter 6) and Deutsche Telekom (also in Chapter 6) escaped this label, yet without doubt they deserved it even if they did not go bankrupt thanks to the deep pockets of taxpayers. All of the aforementioned cases, and many others, have raised questions about the effectiveness of European corporate governance.

On Monday, 24 February 2003, Dutch retailer Ahold disclosed 'significant accounting irregularities' at US Foodservice, one of its American subsidiaries.[2] This is a food distribution company where income had been overstated by more than $500 million. The revelation of this accounting scandal earned Ahold the label 'Europe's Enron', and deepened a dispute between the US and the European Union (EU) over the reach of the new accounting regulation by the Securities and Exchange Commission (SEC).

The controversy surrounding Ahold further heated up after the Dutch Ministry of Justice said it would consider whether to investigate allegations of insider dealing. At the same time, European stock market regulators stated that they would launch an inquiry aimed to establish if Ahold had complied with disclosure rules about market-sensitive information.

What the preceding paragraphs have described were just the opening shots. A few months down the line, by mid-May 2003, it was revealed that the fraud was worse than originally announced, as Ahold said that over three years, millions of dollars had been falsely declared as pre-tax profits. This case followed a classic pattern: beginning relatively modestly with $110 million in 2000, then escalating to $510 million in 2002, when Ahold's US unit reported $850 million of pre-tax profits to its parent.

As this accounting fraud hit the news, pressure on Ahold intensified. Its credit rating was cut on 8 May 2003, while angry shareholders attending its annual meeting five days later, on 13 May, blamed the company's management for everything that went wrong. Neither was the fraud at US Foodservice an isolated incident in food distribution. In 2002, Fleming, an American grocery chain, got into trouble after it first inflated the amounts it received from suppliers, and then misled its auditors through creative accounting practices.

Another case was that of Nash Finch, a wholesaler based in Minneapolis, also under investigation for its use of promotional allowances. Notice, however, that some of these practices are quite widespread in America and in Europe, and it is likely that more fraud will come to light, as investigations continue.[3]

Ahold's scandal and other, similar investigations also had an interesting twist. Correctly, American regulators believe that the Ahold accounting scandal undermines European arguments against non-US firms being forced to register with the new accounting oversight board. Many European accountants admit that the Ahold scandal has harmed their case, which sought to soften the SEC rules, even if EU officials were privately threatening retaliation if non-US companies were not granted exemptions.

Behind the verbal exchanges lies the fact that – at least on paper – accountancy regulation in most of Europe is weaker than in the US. 'May be', answer the Europeans, 'but the big accounting scandals happened in the US.' Time, and that's one of the reasons why American regulators are determined to force many non-US accountants to register with the new Public Company Accounting Oversight Board, opening them up to rigorous inspections and disciplinary action.

A thorough inspection not only of the companies' accounting, but also of certified public accountants' (CPAs') practices, is a 'must', since Ahold's auditors, the Amsterdam-based office of Deloitte & Touche, failed to pick up the problems in 2001 – even though worries about the company's accounts were widely expressed in the markets. Neither is there evidence that Ahold's board did any close questioning of the company's financial statements. Instead, it extended the CEO's term for up to seven years. Even the Dutch market regulator admitted that it had no powers of discipline over faulty auditing.[4]

In its way, the Ahold case poses another major challenge for auditors. Enron and WorldCom (see Chapter 8) were followed by the bankruptcy and criminal conviction of Andersen, which had audited both companies. Thereafter, the remaining Big Four hinted that Andersen was an exceptional case. Yet most of the other auditors have also been tarnished by scandal in the past year or so:

- KPMG over Xerox (see section 6),
- PricewaterhouseCoopers over Tyco,
- Deloitte over Adelphia Communications, and now Ahold.

With these references in the background, one thing which particularly worries market experts is that what happened to Ahold can happen to *any other* company where internal controls are lax and the auditors are careless or too complacent – or where top management is in a race to show higher and higher profits.

Even if this race to declare false profits, to beef up equity value and justify more and more executive options[5] does not reflect outright conflicts of interest, it poses deep ethical questions. 'Higher profits at any cost' are not an admissible policy, because it makes an entity's financial reporting more and more unreliable. No wonder Ahold's shares slumped after the revelations, wiping out billions in shareholder equity (more on this later).

Board members, CEOs and senior executives of companies manipulating their accounts should realize that they are not off the hook of justice, even if their names don't come up in the weeks or months following their wrong-doings. It may take a couple of years, but the scandals will come to light. In February 2003, in the US, lawsuits were filed against two former vice-presidents of Kmart, a grocery chain which went bust years ago, on charges of conspiracy and making false statements to the Securities and Exchange Commission.

Neither is the resignation of some of the top brass a way of claiming indulgence. The fact that on 24 February 2003 Ahold announced the resignation of its chief executive officer and finance director did not stop the company's capitalization from plunging by 63 per cent that day, to €3.3 billion. This is just 10 per cent of the high-water mark, in late 2001, when Ahold's capitalization exceeded $33 billion.

Expressed in the most practical way possible, from corporate mismanagement to outright malfeasance, freak events show up in many ways, and end by decomposing a former 'industry leader's image'. Like Kenneth Lay at Enron, and Dennis Kozlowski at Tyco, Cees van der Hoeven, Ahold's departed boss, had won a reputation from turning a dull company into a growth engine – but at what cost?

- Investors who did not know about the malpractices applauded the 'transformation' long after they should have started asking hard questions.
- When they eventually came round to ask them, Cees can der Hoeven scorned them for daring to doubt him, after all his 'successes'.[6]

Nobody so far has accused van der Hoeven of personally profiting from his mismanagement and falsified accounts. What analysts suggest is that Ahold's former boss had become addicted to his reputation as supermanager, and the public applause that went with it. Since 1993, over the years of his reign he bought some fifty firms for a total of $20 billion, and lured investors with up to 23 quarters of double-digit profit growth in a row. Then, when the company's growth slowed, as it inevitably does, Cees van der Hoeven seems to have been unable to admit to shareholders and the market Ahold's true condition. That's when, most probably, Ahold started to bend the accounting rules, claiming profits of acquired firms as organic growth, booking capital gains from sale-and-leaseback deals as profit, and keeping billions in debt off its balance sheet. Eventually credibility went out of the window, and with it management ethics.

On 2 October 2003 it was revealed that the troubled Dutch food retailer had lost $1.4 billion in 2002, citing in a long-delayed report big charges for the reduced value of its holdings in the US, Argentina and Spain. But other figures indicated that its core operations were still reasonably healthy, with sales in 2002 rising 16 per cent and operating profit up 4 per cent.[7]

When the first semester's financial figures were released, a few weeks later, they reported that Ahold had crept back into profit in the first half of 2003, making €60 million ($60 million). The company also indicated that it hoped to retain its place as the world's third-largest retailer, while a rights issue was expected to raise around €2.5 billion.[8]

Divestments are expected to bring a similar amount into Ahold's treasury, helping to repair its balance sheet and maybe pay for top management's frills and generosities. But on 4 September 2003, while Ahold shareholders approved the appointment of Anders Moberg as new chief executive, many of them complained that he would be paid too much money to help rescue the company. Moberg would receive more than €6 million, or about $6.5 million, for his first two years on the job. 'This is absurd,' said Peter Paul de Vries, director of the Dutch shareholders' association VEB. 'You cannot pay someone this much.'[9]

### 3.  Parmalat: Europe's biggest bankruptcy

On Christmas Eve, 2003, Parmalat, the Italian food multinational, filed for bankruptcy protection under an emergency government decree. Up to €14.8 billion ($18.5 billion)[10] had disappeared from the company's accounts through a maze of affiliates at home and abroad, as well as a worldwide series of false billings and fake statements made over many years, investigating magistrates believe.[11]

Calisto Tanzi, founder, chairman and CEO of Parmalat, whose family controlled 51 per cent of the Italian dairy-products company, resigned. He was arrested on 27 December 2003 – three days after his company's bankruptcy – on suspicion of fraud, embezzlement, false accounting and misleading investors. Prosecutors also allege Tanzi ordered the destruction of company documents.

Prosecutors say they suspect Tanzi diverted €1 billion ($1.27 billion) in company funds to his own use. Tanzi's lawyer claimed that no money disappeared. It was just a case of 'nonexistent assets . . .'. But Tanzi confessed to misappropriating €500 million. Prosecutors believe that the real sum is much higher.

Nobody knows for sure whether missing funds were used to cover operating losses, or illegally line certain people's pockets. On 30 December 2003, Tanzi admitted to prosecutors that he knew the company's accounts were being falsified to hide losses of as much as $10 billion, mainly in Parmalat's Latin American subsidiaries. Allegedly the fake balance-sheet figures allowed Parmalat to continue borrowing. Tanzi's departure opened the way for Enrico Bondi to become the new CEO. Bondi, a turnaround specialist, had been drafted into Parmalat's senior management team a couple of weeks before the company's bankruptcy by the banks who saw their loans and investments go down the drain. A decade earlier, Bondi had rescued the Montedison food and chemicals group from bankruptcy.

Parmalat's fate, its misdemeanours and the embarrassment which resulted was particularly acute for those Europeans who have been claiming that corporate governance has significantly improved. On all evidence, gambles with derivative financial instruments were part of the company's 'fast-growth' tricks.

Like Enron, another master of deception, Parmalat was over-fond of elaborate bond and derivatives deals, often using complex instruments and offshore structures that involved some of its many subsidiaries. By all evidence, investigators will be struggling to understand Parmalat's balance sheet and gauge the true extent of its liabilities.

Indeed, Parmalat had used derivatives and other complex financial trans-actions for many years, both to gamble and to shore up its balance sheet. An article in *BusinessWeek* suggested that the now defunct company did its derivatives deals through investment banks such as Citigroup and Merrill Lynch. In one 1999 transaction with Citigroup, done through a subsidiary of the bank called Buconero LLC, Italian for 'black hole', the bank made a €117 million ($146 million) 'investment' in return for a chunk of the company's net profit.[12]

By setting up the transaction as an investment and not a loan, which is, ironically, a legal manoeuvre, Parmalat made its borrowing costs appear smaller than they actually were. Derivative financial instruments helped all the way from tax evasion to bloating up the balance sheet and investor deception. In fact, Parmalat was a hedge fund with dairy products on the side (more on this in section 4).

To make matters worse, Parmalat had acquired a reputation for lack of transparency. In mid-2002 analysts at Merrill Lynch advised investors to sell their shares, because they could not understand the need for such opaque finances.[13] But other brokers, and several commercial bankers with them, were impressed by Parmalat's performance and advised their clients positively about the company's equity.

At least one auditor had also given a warning. As reported on 29 March 2004, by the Wall Street Journal, a Deloitte Touche Tohmatsu auditor in Brazil raised concerns in 2001 and 2002 about a Cayman Islands unit of Parmalat, later found to be at the core of the dairy giant's accounting scandal.

Citing Deloitte emails and memos, WSJ said that in March 2001 Wanderley Olivetti sent a message from Brazil to Adolfo Mamoli, a partner at Deloitte Italy, with concerns about Bonlat Financing Corp's ability to repay debts about $225 million owed to Parmalat in Brazil.

What some bankers and investors seem to have appreciated was how Parmalat, a dairy-products family-owned firm, had expanded from its origins in the region around Parma, Italy, to become one of the world's best-known producers of milk and other food products. And of creative accounting, too.

Some bankers and lots of investors looked at the company as 'the new Nestlé'. Parmalat had a $3.3 billion business in North America, where it sold its trademark milk-in-a-box, and also owned Black Diamond Cheese, Archway Cookies and Sunnydale Farms dairy products. It also operated in 30 countries around the globe.

Floated on the Italian stock market, but still controlled by the founding Tanzi family, on the surface Parmalat has thrived for several years, and to many investors looked like an unqualified success story. Its shares traded in New York and it had sold more than $1.5 billion in bonds to US investors. In 2002, its turnover was €7.6 billion ($9.65 billion), reporting good profits, and by the time it crashed it was employing more than 35,000 people, operating in over 30 countries around the globe.

Then, suddenly, the 'success story' turned sour and Parmalat needed urgent help. Enrico Bondi was appointed to the rescue mission because he was well trusted by the banks who would like to get over Parmalat's credit risk, but he had a tough assignment in:

- determining how everything went so horribly wrong, and
- staving off the threat of a short-term liquidity crisis which, in a matter of ten days, ended in bankruptcy.

The Bondi mission came too late. As a group, Parmalat had many bonds coming due, but the real emergency was to find $400 million by 17 December 2003 to pay off minority investors representing 18.18 per cent of its controlled subsidiary Empreendimentos e Administracao in Brazil. Optimists had said in this connection that Bank of America, which represented the minority holding of Dairy Holdings and Food Holdings, was willing to wait – but this was not the only big debt Parmalat had to run after.

As far as credit risk is concerned, appearances have been deceptive. While to bankers and investors unaware of what was going on, Parmalat was a successful operating company with good brands and strong market position, its financial entanglements were legion. Behind the prevailing opacity was hiding a rotten balance sheet, and lack of transparency had led some investment analysts to query some of the company's strange deals:

- Parmalat supposedly held large cash balances but also had big debts;
- its gross debt stood at €6 billion ($7.66 billion) at the end of November 2003;
- but the company also claimed to have more than $4.9 billion of cash or equivalents.

Supposedly 38 per cent of Parmalat's assets were held in a $4.9 billion account at Bank of America, in the name of a Parmalat subsidiary in the Cayman Islands. On 19 December, however, Bank of America said that no such account existed. This, too, proved to be one more deception. Not only were there no billions in the custody of a big bank, but what then surfaced was that several billions had disappeared in one of Parmalat's foreign subsidiaries.

Bank of America revealed the huge gaping hole in Parmalat's accounts, when in early December 2003 it told Grant Thornton, auditor of Bonlat, a Cayman Islands subsidiary of Parmalat, that there was no account with $4.9 billion at the bank, despite documents to the contrary. For their part, Italian investigators expressed the belief that up to €6 billion, some of it invented, was used to finance acquisitions, many of which produced losses that needed covering.

Italian prosecutors also seem to have discovered that managers simply invented assets to offset up to $16.2 billion in liabilities and falsified accounts which accumulated over a 15-year period. All of these accounts were characterized by total lack of transparency throughout Parmalat's network of companies operating in 30 countries.

According to ongoing investigation, auditors first enquired about the Cayman Islands account in December 2002, and received a letter on Bank of America stationery in March 2003 confirming the existence of the account. That letter is now said to have been a forgery, concocted by someone in Parmalat's Collecchio headquarters.[14] The surprise is that when such a 'forgery' was produced, nobody bothered to investigate, yet the size of the alleged account should have raised queries. Even a $1 million bank account is cross-verified by the auditors.

As rumours in the market spread, it gradually emerged that Fausto Tonna, the company's finance director until he resigned in March 2003, had helped the Tanzi family to construct a complex web of financial obligations, many of them in off-balance-sheet vehicles.[15] One of the problems was that nobody seemed to know precisely how this web worked.

Moreover, Parmalat's financial accounts for 2002 had failed to disclose that €496 million ($622 million) of its cash had been invested in Epicurum, a mutual fund based in the Cayman Islands. Besides that 'investment', reminiscent of how bankers play derivatives and loans games with other bankers, Parmalat had also entered into a huge currency swap with Epicurum.

The *Parmalat–Epicurum connection* is a classic example of the sacrifices that can be demanded with overleveraging and derivative financial instruments – yet, by its banks, Parmalat seems to have been considered a well-managed company with relatively low credit risk. The company's curious relationship with Epicurum was disclosed in November 2003, after Consob, Italy's stock market regulator, asked for information about it.

With the market getting wind that things were not as pristine as they were thought to be, Parmalat tried to quell market fears by saying, on 12 November, that it would withdraw its money from Epicurum within 15 days. This, of course, did not take place because, as happens so often with leveraged and uncertain deals, when rumours (let alone news) of financial instability break out, everyone tries to exit from the same door.

## 4.   Exploits of a hedge fund with dairy products on the side

Parmalat's case is one more proof that credit risk and market risk reinforce one another, and together they see to it that events move way beyond management control. Mindful of the impending withdrawal of €496 million, other 'investors' in Epicurum feared for their own funds and triggered a rush of withdrawals. The result was, unsurprisingly, that Parmalat was unable to get its money out, and when it asked its banks for short-term help, it was rebuffed.

On 8 December 2003, when this rebuff emerged, trading in Parmalat shares was suspended and the company's board reluctantly convened the next day. Enrico Bondi's appointment, initially as a consultant since Tanzi would not relinquish his CEO job, was the price of the banks' support. This meant that the executive powers of the turnaround specialists were rather limited – until a week or so later when all hell broke loose.

In retrospect, Parmalat was a mismanaged, opaque and tricky enterprise – a sort of *hedge fund with a dairy products and milk distribution business on the side*. But this does not justify a collective lapse of judgement – by bankers, investors and regulators. Large banks and big investors failed utterly to use their leverage to alter the behaviour of Calisto Tanzi and Fausto Tonna. In fact, it is not clear whether the company's counterparties ever made any real effort to demand:

- better financial disclosure,
- an end to spurions business practices, and
- withdrawal from derivatives gambling.

Critics say that bankers and investors did not care until the bad news broke lose. As a result big financial entities are now caught in competing claims for priority in getting repaid. In the end, with the Italian government moving in to save Parmalat, it is taxpayers' money that will be lost. Reputational risk, however, will hit bankers, investors and supervisors head on.

- Why did major institutional investors continue to buy Parmalat's shares and bonds?
- Why did the banks continue lending, and arranging questionable derivatives deals?
- Why the auditors and regulators failed in their duty to uncover the mare's nest?

Post-mortem investigators have found 'a whole set-up for falsifying documents'. This went on for years. How did it happen that certified public accountants got no wind of it? Investigators now believe executives of the Italian food multinational invented numerous transactions at headquarters and at subsidiaries in countries including Singapore and the Cayman Islands. 'It appears they would invent contracts, commercial and financial, which they would then show to banks to raise fresh cash,' said a flash by the *Financial Times* on the internet.

The Parmalat scandal also involved two major auditing firms. From 1990 to 1999, Parmalat's auditor was the Italian branch of Grant Thornton, one of the larger American accounting firms. In 1999, under Italian law, Parmalat was forced to change its auditor, replacing Grant Thornton with Deloitte Touche Tohmatsu – but Grant Thornton continued to audit Parmalat's offshore entities, originally based in financial companies that were in the Dutch Antilles then closed down and re-established in the Cayman Islands.

The puzzle is how, over the years, two major international auditors did not uncover a blatant accounting fraud – let alone the fact that allegedly Grant Thornton had advised Parmalat on how to hide losses (more on this later). After all, *investigative auditing* is a major part of a CPA's mission. That's why they are paid by their clients, and trusted by the regulators, the markets and the general public.

Deloitte says that it first raised questions about Parmalat's accounts in October 2003 – that's shortly before the company's crash. That's too little, too late and too thin as an excuse. Grant Thornton issued a statement calling itself a victim of the deceit. This, too, is a thinly veiled excuse, as well as a covert admission that auditing responsibilities had been disregarded.

With the auditors failing to do their job and inform the authorities and the markets, steady cash-raising through different gimmicks enabled Parmalat to cover up operating losses. Some of the revelations about the company's debts followed lengthy interrogations of Calisto Tanzi and Fausto Tonna.

Police searched Tanzi's house in Colléchio, a town near the northern city of Parma, where Parmalat has its headquarters. One of Parmalat's plants in Colléchio was also searched. For his part, Silvio Berlusconi, Italy's prime minister, issued a decree that will speed up the nomination by the Ministry of Industry of three commissioners to oversee the bankrupt company, one of them being Enrico Bondi.

Berlusconi also said that, as the French government did with Crédit Lyonnais ten years earlier, the Italian government will use taxpayers' money to save Parmalat from falling in the abyss. Before its fall, Parmalat was Italy's eighth-biggest industrial group, with a market capitalization of €1.8 billion and a workforce of 35,000 people, and plenty of subcontractors providing raw material such as fresh milk.

In fact, many of these business partners have found themselves in financial straits because they are family businesses depending for 70 per cent to 90 per cent of their produce on one and only client: Parmalat. Relief from creditors granted by the Italian government can lead several of these small entities, as well as cooperatives of milk producers, to outright bankruptcy.

At a totally different level of reference, the financial vortex of the fallen Italian hedge fund with dairy products and milk distribution on the side is drawing many of the world's largest banks and at least two big auditing firms to the attention of Italian and US regulators and investigators. On 23 December 2003, Bank of America met Italian prosecutors, and filed a criminal complaint in accordance with Italian law in connection with the Parmalat investigation. But other global banks now find themselves much deeper in the Parmalat scandal.

- Enron's scandal destroyed the reputation of Arthur Andersen.
- The Parmalat scandal means that Deloitte, and Grant Thornton, its accountants, must now explain themselves.

One of the criticisms directed at Parmalat's banks is that they were too close to their customer and allowed the company's financial managers to run amok. Critics say this is precisely what French banks have done with Vivendi, Alstom and Cirio, a food producer that defaulted on its bonds. Yet there is a saying in French banking: 'Le banquier bon, est un banquier con.'[16]

Italian banks were not the only to benefit from, and eventually pay for, this cosy and highly ineffective relationship with Parmalat and its top brass. Global banks, including Citigroup, JP Morgan and Deutsche Bank, were too willing to earn lucrative fees by constructing derivatives deals by which Parmalat: transferred funds offshore and speculated with them.[17]

In a way quite similar to that of Ahold, Vivendi Universal (see Chapter 7), Enron, WorldCom (see Chapter 8), and some other firms, Parmalat's financial problems have been ignored for too long by its bankers, auditors and supervisors, maybe because of inordinate laxity, maybe because these entities were taken in by the wrongdoers' constant self-promotion – and they did not have the brains to challenge the 'obvious'.

Credit-rating agencies, too, have some explaining to do, though they may find refuge behind the statement that it is difficult for outsiders to monitor what has been going on behind closed doors. Like Vivendi, Parmalat failed to disclose a great deal of information to Standard & Poor's, but the agency should not have issued investment-grade ratings on its bonds (see Chapter 2). Instead, it should have brought this lack of disclosure to public attention.

While, at the time of writing, much remains unknown, substantial assets have disappeared from Parmalat much as hundreds of millions of dollars were siphoned off from Enron, WorldCom and the other ex-high-flying bankrupts. In fact, in Parmalat's case Calisto Tanzi has admitted that he diverted, read misappropriated, funds from the group. The former CEO admitted this to the tune of hundreds of millions of euros over seven or eight years.

In connection to Parmalat Finanziaria, SpA, Calisto Tanzi told magistrates that he moved €500 million from the company to tourism businesses owned by his family. The money was shifted into 'a series of companies that now we'll have to analyse one by one to verify the cash flows,' Fabio Belloni – one of Tanzi's lawyers – told reporters outside Milan's San Vittore jail, where Parmalat's former boss is being held after his arrest on 27 December 2003.[18]

For its part, on 29 December 2003, the US Securities and Exchange Commission sued Parmalat with fraud for filing misleading financial statements during 2002 and 2003. The suit in a New York court alleges that Parmalat 'engaged in one of the largest and most brazen corporate financial frauds in history'. An Italian judge said Grant Thornton, one of Parmalat's auditors, had advised the group to set up a Cayman Islands subsidiary to 'modify the system used up until then to hide losses'. If this is true, Arthur Andersen could not have done better.

Guido Piffer, the Milan judge, accused Tanzi of having 'perfect knowledge of the fraudulent mechanisms' that were used to inflate Parmalat's assets and conceal billions of euros in liabilities. This accusation, which does not amount to a formal criminal charge, was contained in a seven-page ruling drafted by Judge Piffer to justify the decision on 28 December 2003 to continue holding under lock and key Parmalat's former chief executive.

In his ruling, Judge Piffer alleged that Tanzi had 'instigated and endorsed' the financial schemes that led to the discovery of a big black hole in Parmalat's accounts. 'It could not have been otherwise, taking into consideration the enormity of the financial breakdown that had to be concealed, and considering that Tanzi himself, and people in his family, were the beneficiaries,' the ruling stated.[19]

At the end of March 2004, three months after the largest scandal in European business broker out, Enrico Bondi presented Parmalat's financial results. Of its liabilities accounting to €14.8 billion, more than 28 per cent (€4.2 billion) were bank loans. Bondi's proposal to the creditors has been an accord through which, after a hefty writedown, creditors would convert their loans into equity in the wounded company.

In the background has been the hypothesis that after heavy cuts in operations; shrinking its debt by nearly 90 per cent to €500 million; reducing geographic coverage from 30 countries to 20, with commensurate personnel reductions; and cutting the number of its labels from 120 to 30, would leave a functional, profitable company. The downsizing was projected to reduce Parmalat's annual revenue from €5.8 billion to €3.8 billion, but double its operational margin from 3 per cent to 6 per cent, with 10 per cent further out goal. All these were hypotheses advanced to lenders to sugar-coat the bitter pill of debt-forgiveness.

No matter how you look at them, scams like Enron, WorldCom, Parmalat and several others, have been engineered by people who put 19th century robber barons to shame. And even as crooks they have not been effective, since at the end they were caught.

## 5.  Cable & Wireless, and the CEO's head

On 21 January 2003, it was announced that Graham Wallace, the CEO of Cable & Wireless (C&W), and architect of its failed attempt to turn itself into a global carrier of Internet traffic, will step down as soon as a replacement is found. This announcement followed intense shareholder pressure for his departure, and came just weeks after Richard Lapthorne, former finance director at British Aerospace (BAE Systems), was appointed as C&W's new chairman.

As part of other changes at top management level, C&W announced the appointment of two non-executive directors. Investors welcomed the news, sending shares in the troubled telecommunications company up 12 per cent in early trading. Later on the same day, however, profit-taking saw those gains pared, leaving C&W shares up only 3.6 per cent.

The CEO who was asked by the board to vacate his seat opened his golden parachute. Wallace has been on a two-year rolling contract with a base annual salary of £775,000 ($1.13 million), which means his pay-off could be as much as £1.55 million ($2.64 million). Shareholders were not happy about such huge pay for ineffectiveness, which resulted in £6.5 billion ($11 billion) lost by Cable & Wireless in just one year: 2002.

The Association of British Insurers, whose members control some 20 per cent of the British equity market, said: 'We will be looking at the company to bear the strongly held views of shareholders in mind, in terms of a severance pay package of the chief executive.' One top-ten investor commented that he would be 'horrified' if Wallace received a payment of two years' salary. Another leading shareholder said C&W should ensure the failed CEO received the 'minimum' severance package.[20]

How much was Graham Wallace responsible for C&W's debts? Some experts say the company's whole strategy was blurred, characterized mainly by a 'me too' approach. Others, however, suggest that what particularly failed was C&W international expansion. This led some experts to the hypothesis that if Cable & Wireless really wished to survive, then it should retrench to:

- the UK, where it is number two player,
- the Caribbean, where it enjoys a profitable incumbency position, and
- the Middle East, where it has been able to hold its own.

'It may be logical and rational [to retrench], but would the management have the incentive to do that?' asked one of market observers. Cable & Wireless is a £4.5 billion ($7.65 billion) business by revenue. If it were to reduce its activities to a tripartite operation, it would still have revenues of nearly £3 billion ($5.1 billion) according to estimates from Citigroup Smith Barney – but it would also have to close down or put on fire sale units producing $2.5 billion annual revenue.

For this reason, some analysts doubted whether such drastic downsizing could solve C&Ws survival problems. As evidence they advanced the company's June 2003 decision to retreat from the US market, which did little to address enterprise concerns about entrusting networks to operators. 'Companies have to see carrier stability before they trust their networks to them,' said Meta Group's Willis. 'What C&W has done in pulling out of the US will have a negative impact on other companies looking to offer managed services.'[21]

Regardless of this particular case on the impact of retrenchment of operators on outsourcing[22], it is appropriate to note that Cable & Wireless has not been the only operator falling back on its home market. British Telecom (BT) has done much the same, and Sprint closed its $60 million web hosting business at a cost of nearly $500 million. Retrenchment and downsizing often hide significant costs.

Are there lessons to be learned after downsizing about the soundness of relentless expansion? Perhaps the most interesting disclosure by Francesco Caio, C&W's new chief executive, is that global business provided only 7 per cent of the company's revenues. Apparently £9 billion ($15.3 billion), spent over two years, only managed to support this tiny share of the company's business.

On the other hand, Cable & Wireless cannot operate as a national telco because it is not one, and it may have to continue to be a global services provider, whether it likes it or not, because over the years its strategy has been not to care about regional or national markets. C&W concentrated its marketing on multinational enterprises, and with mobile operations enterprise revenue grew faster than any other business for C&W in 2002.

The thesis and antithesis in the preceding paragraphs demonstrate how confused downsizing can be. Some analysts questioned what C&W would get from the sale of its US operations, which it had acquired for $2.5 billion – which, according to some estimates, had risen to a cool $5 billion (more on this later). A parallel was drawn with the painful withdrawal of Sony. In 1989, Sony paid $3.4 billion for Columbia Pictures, about 340 times the studio's earnings, to buy the company largely for prestige reasons. To this were added other costs, such as:

- poaching a production team from Time Warner,
- rebooting the studio's production schedule, and
- redecorating every office in sight, to serve the ego of executives.

These additional unwise expenditures pushed up the total initial amount invested to Columbia Pictures beyond $5 billion. Sony justified this high spending by arguing that there is some kind of synergy business. But by November 1994 a string of embarrassing failures added themselves to the overspending, to produce for the mother company a $3 billion loss.

Eventually, as 2003 came to a close, so did the C&W American adventure. In November 2003 the UK-based carrier sold Cable & Wireless America (CWA) for $125 million to Gores Technology Group. According to some analysts, the company had really spent some $5 billion amassing network, hosting and data facilities, but eventually the profitless CWA filed for Chapter 11 bankruptcy protection.

With these $5 billion invested in CWA and lost, C&W, the former owner, has been reduced to leasing facilities to provide services in the US for its European-based customers. In terms of shareholder value, some experts said, C&W would have done much better to remain a sleepy UK telecoms company. But management effectiveness had departed, and shareholder value was put on the back burner.

Overpaying and overspending have pushed many firms over the cliff, starting with a sharp drop in their equity which for obvious reasons has unsettled investors. In the case of Cable & Wireless major shareholders did not take the loss of capitalization lightly. The Ontario Teachers' Pension Plan, which manages the retirement funds of 334,000 past and present Canadian teachers, filed a class action suit claiming that C&W misled investors by:

- engaging in sham capacity swap transactions (see Part Two),
- inflating its revenues through fraudulent exchanges of network capacity,
- failing to disclose $1.3 billion of lease commitments, and
- misrepresenting the amount of cash available to it by not revealing a £1.5 billion tax-related obligation.[23]

The claim, filed in May 2003 in Virginia, rolled up a string of US class action suits filed after the company's near collapse at the end of 2002. The Canadian Teachers' Fund has been seeking damages for all aggrieved investors who bought C&W shares from August 1999 and December 2002, with the heart of the claim being that between 1999 to 2001 Cable & Wireless was a counterparty to improper exchanges of network capacity, with US network operators Qwest and Global Crossing (see Chapter 9).

Since it takes two to tango, it should be kept in perspective that Qwest restated its accounts by $2.2 billion once the nature of these fraudulent transactions came to light. A Securities and Exchange Commission investigation of capacity swaps tried to get to the heart of the matter, and put Global Crossing under investigation, eventually ordering it to restate $19 million to swap-related 'sales'. Swaps dynamics is a derivatives trick which deserves the most careful scrutiny for all sorts of mismanagement and malfeasance.

## 6. Downfall of Xerox and public accountants' responsibilities

The 1999–2001 downfall of Xerox, the photocopier company, is a tale of management failure and the board's irresponsibility going well beyond the impact of technological change. It is also a case study on what certified public accountants should *not* have done. An estimated $38 billion in shareholder wealth was destroyed in less than two years; therefore Xerox's fall presents an important lesson for every company.

The huge loss in capitalization suffered by a company which was a leader in copier technology makes an interesting example of irresponsibility and ineffectiveness of management. It should also be remembered that in the 1960s and 1970s, its years of glory, Xerox had challenged the established computer firms; this too has been a case of where the firm lost a great deal, but was able to recover. All this makes Xerox a classical lesson in the rise and fall of industrial firms.

Figure 3.1 shows the pattern of Xerox's stock price over 11 years, more than a decade after the computer fiasco. Like IBM, Hewlett-Packard, Compaq, AT&T, Lucent Technologies, Nortel, Ericsson, Siemens, and dozens of other entities around the world, Xerox has been struggling to make the

*Figure 3.1*   Eleven years of rise and fall in the capitalization of Xerox

transition from a monoliner, selling copiers, to a broader product range setting. In the 1990s, its new goal, which it failed to reach, was that of selling high-tech solutions and services. The change was inevitable because with its mainstay of copiers Xerox had found itself losing market share to Japanese rivals, but lack of clear vision and a silly game of musical chairs meant that Xerox was unable to carve out a profitable place in the digital world.

Mismanagement was compounded by infighting in the executive suite. G. Richard Thoman left IBM in 1997 to become president and chief operating officer of Xerox. Brought in by then-CEO Paul A. Allaire to succeed him, Thoman was expected to do at Xerox what Louis V. Gerstner did at IBM. The plan was to change from a seller of copiers to a consultant on how to use digital documents more effectively. Agency cost (read: internal quarrels) destroyed that plan.

It seems that Paul Allaire decided not to leave the steering wheel of Xerox. He stayed around as the centre of authority, breaking one of the cardinal rules of succession. When Thoman became CEO, Allaire moved on to chairman, and he continued to control the board of directors. He also sat in on key management meetings with Thoman, leaving managers wondering who was really in charge.

The answer to this query has been: nobody. In 1999, Xerox lost $1 billion, or 13 per cent of its net worth, because of foreign currency blunders. Much of debt was incurred in Brazil. A short time thereafter, accounting manipulations were found at the company's Mexican unit. It seems that nobody was in control of the company's international operations.

In the two years (2000–2002) since a company insider blew the whistle about how its management 'accelerated' revenues, Xerox paid a $10 million fine that it hoped would settle the inquiries by the SEC into its accounting practices for leased products; agreed to change the treatment of revenues amounting to $2 billion and to restate its financial results between 1997 and 2001 after allegations that it overstated revenues; and changed its auditor and its chief financial officer. It also changed its chief executive twice. But doubts continued even if the company:

- settled SEC charges,
- renegotiated loans, and
- restated five years of accounts.

James Bingham, the whistleblower whom the company sacked in August 2000, alleged that Xerox lied about its accounts to disguise a deteriorating trading record. The SEC said that this was part of a scheme to enrich managers. The restated accounts, which the company filed on 28 June 2002, showed that

- this 'misapplication of GAAP', as Xerox called it, overstated profits by $1.4 billion between 1997 and 2001, and
- the failure of creative accounting obliged the company later to restate $6.4 billion in revenues over five years.

The board itself was a mess. For a high-technology company, very few Silicon Valley experts were sitting on it; also there were few independent directors and too many insiders.[24] Some of the directors, including Allaire, sit on five other company boards. Indeed, one of them sat on 11 boards, leaving him very little time to really understand what Xerox was doing, let alone to evaluate its operations and its future.

All that happened in the late 1990s and the result was to bring Xerox to its knees. The accounting irregularities were revealed in the early years of the twenty-first century. In mid-June 2003, the Securities and Exchange Commission punished the same Paul Allaire for having manipulated company accounts by injecting non-existent profits into its books to the tune of $1.4 billion. Allaire was fined a trivial $1 million, but he was ordered to pay a record $7.6 million 'disgorgement' of the gains he made out of accounting fraud.

There is an irony in this story, and many other of similar nature. Because Xerox's bylaws indemnify its executives against all such charges, it is the company's shareholders who have been paying Allaire's $7.6 million disgorgement, as well as the losses suffered through a five-year ban on his serving as director or officer of a public company – Xerox has only a slim hope of getting that money back from its insurers. In a way, this sort of blank coverage is a moral hazard. Xerox's 'directors and officers' (D&O) insurance policy covers executives against the legal consequences of their business mistakes. But the insurers, who received premiums of $4.9 million from Xerox in 2003, resist the claim on grounds that it goes beyond the confines of normal operational risk.[25]

The way insurers look at this moral hazard is that policies do not pay up for fraud, and although the Xerox executives have neither admitted nor denied wrongdoing, the insurers argue that this is mere semantics. Either way, however, it seems that the wrongdoers will be going largely unpunished for a fraud that occurred when they were supposed to exercise prudential management duties.

With hindsight, Xerox found itself in the centre of accountancy scandal for the same reasons as Ahold (see section 2). But in this case, the Securities and Exchange Commission's civil charges pointed to personal accountability including not only former chairman Paul Allaire and former chief financial officer Barry Romeril, but other persons, too. Michael Conway, a partner at former auditors KPMG, was warned that charges are imminent and given a chance to respond before they are made public.[26]

KPMG, the company's former auditor, did not emerge unscathed over its responsibilities in the Xerox fraud. At the end of January 2003, US regulators came close to suing KPMG for its role in the multi-billion-dollar alleged accounting fraud at Xerox. On 22 January 2003 KPMG said it had learnt that the Securities and Exchange Commission might file civil charges against the firm, three current partners and one former partner.

In April 2003, the SEC stated that Xerox management 'approved, implemented and tracked' accounting actions that led to the company bringing forward equipment revenue and increasing pre-tax earnings in the years up to 2000. KPMG had audited Xerox in the years in question. The US Justice Department's criminal indictment of the Arthur Andersen firm has set the tone for such cases. The SEC also said it would be more likely to hold a whole firm accountable for the actions of its partners if there was a lack of cooperation.

Certified public accountants should take note that the years of light responsibilities associated with external auditing are gone. They should also appreciate that the aftermath of conflicts of interest, scanty attendance to accounts, or misbehaviour may take many years to uncover – but when this happens the penalties can be significant.

Here is another case, this time in the UK, where it took seven years to uncover a scam. At the end of June 2003 the news was that a former partner at Deloitte & Touche faced possible eviction from the accountancy profession after allegations that he acquired a car from an audited client but failed to pay the agreed price of £34,000 ($57,800).

The Joint Disciplinary Scheme (JDS), which is the UK chartered accountants' regulator, said that it had decided to convene a tribunal to hear allegations that in 1996 Stephen Ives failed to pay for the Range Rover of the company's joint managing director. Ives also faced claims that he attempted to obstruct the JDS's efforts to investigate the matter.[27] This is what happens when personal accountability is absent, and ineffectiveness assumes the driver's seat.

## 7.   The Bridgestone and Ford fiasco. A case study

This is a case study on failure of corporate governance in the auto industry and its suppliers. Within a short time after it started, in mid-2000, the first global product recall by Bridgestone and Ford spiralled into a fiasco for all involved parties. Everybody was blaming someone else, and no one could explain the true cause of the tyre problem and the inexcusable engineering troubles which hit some Ford cars more than others.

This scandal started with the initial reaction of some of the key players, which was to blame Bridgestone/Firestone, the Japanese/American tyremaker, for the deadly accidents. Indeed, with the recall of millions of potentially defective tyres in the US and elsewhere, Bridgestone faced its biggest crisis ever. Investors did not take it well. As shown in Figure 3.2, within a month half the company's capitalization evaporated.

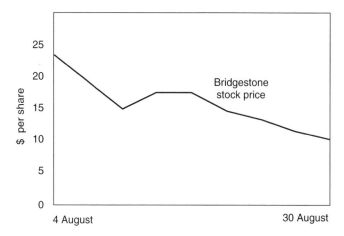

*Figure 3.2* The mid-2000 collapse of Bridgestone's share price, following the fatal accidents

Initially, the merger of Bridgestone and Firestone seemed to be effective. Since it acquired Firestone in 1988, Bridgestone saw its sales nearly double, making it the world's second-largest tyre company after Goodyear. By 2000 it had 50 per cent of the Japanese market and 20 per cent of the US. That is precisely when the troubles hit: investment experts suggested that the crash of the equity was certainly not the end of Bridgestone, but many questioned if that company was solely responsible for fatal road accidents.

The scandal of unreliable Firestone tyres exploded in mid-2000. Up to the end of September of that same year, at least one hundred Americans, forty-six Venezuelans, and more people in other nations were killed in motor vehicle accidents linked to faultily designed tyres. But it has also become clear that in two-thirds of the deaths, the Ford Explorer sport utility vehicle, and its tendency to roll over, was an equally strong cause of fatal accidents.

As it has slowly emerged, these accidents were caused by a combination of engineering errors. While most of the roll-overs occurred when the Explorer was equipped with tyres made by Bridgestone/Firestone, the motor vehicle itself had technical problems. According to what has been reported in the press, based on Ford internal documents,

- the carmaker knew that Explorer had a tendency to roll over, under certain speed and load conditions, as early as April 1989 – ten months before the first Explorer came off the assembly line,[28] and
- Firestone also knew that its tyres were shredding as early as 1996. Yet neither company made fundamental changes that were required to stabilize and make their cars safe.

The cars referred to, known as special utility vehicles (SUV) in the US and quatre-quatre (4×4, for 4-wheel drive) in France, are a babyboomer's craze in both these countries, and in others. They are basically a light truck with the cabin shell of a large station wagon grafted onto it. Practically every auto manufacturer makes SUVs because their profit margins are huge, ranging between $8,000 and $15,000 per vehicle. After all, an SUV is a light truck, which is the cheapest vehicle to produce, and automakers using the cabin shell charge double what they could get for a truck. But a heavy-duty *personal* vehicle and a light truck have different stability requirements. Beyond this, to save money, quality control does not seem to have been up to standard. On 20 September 2000, in a conference call with reporters, a Ford spokesman admitted that in 1989 his company did not test a finished product Explorer (the SUV), nor even a prototype. Instead, it tested what it called a 'mule', which was a Ford-150 pick-up truck, which was supposed to simulate the characteristics of the Explorer in the tests.

This proved to be a disastrons short cut with the most severe consequences. The Explorer and the Ford-150 truck have similarities but also a number of important differences. The use of 'mules' is supposed to cut costs, and bring the product to market as fast as possible. But that proxy may not even be close to the final product which is sold to customers.

According to reports, when in April 1989 Ford put the Explorer through tests at its Arizona test track, the vehicle exhibited very unstable behaviour. An article in the *Wall Street Journal* of 20 September 2000 disclosed documents in the possession of trial lawyers for plaintiffs who had sued Ford over accidents when Ford Explorers rolled over. One of them stated that during the April 1989 Explorer tests, the vehicle demonstrated a rollover response. The unstable behaviour seems to have been demonstrated with a number of tyre, tyre pressure and suspension configurations, under heavy load. But in a stunning display of irresponsibility, Ford's management decided on a quick and dirty strategy: deflate the tire.[29]

This was an irresponsible approach, representing the wrong engineering response to the fact that the Explorer had failed when equipped and operated with four Bridgestone/Firestone P235 all-terrain tires. These were fully inflated to a tyre pressure of a proper and safe level of 30 pounds per square inch (psi). The Explorer had also failed these same tests on Bridgestone/Firestone P235-AS, all-season tyres, and on Bridgestone/Firestone Firehawk tyres.

The Firestone tyre had its own design flaw. The freak event resulting from the combination of these two engineering errors increased the frequency of Firestone P235 tyre thread separation and potential blowout. The House Commerce Committee's Consumer Protection Subcommittee received documents showing that in 1996, Firestone conducted 10-minute-long tests, at which tyres were run on a test machine at 112 miles per hour.

- Of the 229 tires tested, 31 failed – a failure rate of 13.5 per cent.
- Of these failures, 20 were tread separations at the outside of the tyre.

It needs no explaining that two major design failures don't make a reliable product. Neither is there evidence that senior management in either or both companies was attentive enough to take immediate corrective action after the first sign of trouble – as they should have been. Yet there was plenty of evidence of that trouble.

While the first fatal accidents made big news, other less extreme failures which have been happening for years went largely unnoticed. This is best explained by a letter published in *BusinessWeek*[30] written by a person who rented a car with Firestone tyres back in 1974. The letter made reference to a rented GM motor home for a Christmas vacation from upstate Michigan to Florida. When two weeks later the family returned, not one of the original Firestone 500 tyres remained on this vehicle. All six had to be replaced, mostly due to tread separations while travelling down the Interstate 75.

However, the letter to *BusinessWeek* on Bridgestone/Firestone tyre blowouts also pointed out that, in contrast to several families' experiences with the Ford Explorer, no injuries or deaths occurred as a result of these thread separation troubles. The motor home did not flip over or go out of control when one of the Firestone 500s let loose. In consequence, a major engineering and managerial question is:

- Why have Ford Explorers experienced loss of control and serious roll-overs from similar tyre blowouts?
- Aren't modern vehicles supposed to be designed to survive adversity, or has something else has been wrong on management's side?

True enough, when these events took place Ford was undergoing a change in top management. But experts said Ford's musical chairs was only half of an excuse because it appears that the company's top management first learned of tyre failures on its vehicles in 1997 and 1998 in Venezuela, Saudi Arabia and Malaysia – while the change in CEO happened in 1999.

In fact, as eventually reported in the press, Ford's own documents have shown that Firestone was warning the carmaker against replacing tyres in Saudi Arabia because the companies might then be required to alert US regulators.[31] But Ford eventually moved forward with the replacement offer even though Firestone continued to insist there was no problem with the tyres, blaming:

- improper repairs,
- underinflated tires, and
- unique driving conditions in countries with extreme climates.

These excuses made Bridgestone/Firestone appear as if they were trying to avoid responsibility until the public outcry became too loud, and the failures too many to push under the carpet. Remember, however, that at least the claim of underinflated tyres had some truth in it. This was the fast and dirty way the then Ford management had found to ward off the damage.

Effective company management should be on the alert with the first signs of trouble, *before* failures become disasters. Instead, in a surprisingly large number of cases the response is not immediate control but cover-up. For instance, a cover-up of technical failures seems to be the case with Mitsubishi Motors (see the case study in section 8). The best advice is that transparency should be the golden rule of management in a service economy. Business reputation takes a long time to build, but it can be destroyed in a matter of hours.

## 8.   Cover-ups of management's ineffectiveness. Mitsubishi Motors

In October 2000 the daily press was full of reports that for two decades Mitsubishi Motors had covered up thousands of complaints about glitches with its cars and trucks. This was a surprising revelation about mismanagement at the daughter firm of a great Japanese engineering company, which in World War II built the famous zero fighter. It is also a good case study of the fact that in the longer run companies cannot continue hiding the facts.

The Mitsubishi Motors troubles came to the public eye when in late 2000 police in Toyo, where Mitsubishi Motors is headquartered, launched an investigation into allegations that the company was criminally negligent in covering up defects in its products. Mitsubishi declined to comment on the probe, but investigators told the Japanese press they had evidence indicating that serious car defects were secretly repaired at two Mitsubishi technical centres.[32] More was to come.

Disgusted with the unreliability of Mitsubishi cars after his Diamante auto lurched backward, hitting another car, Shigeo Toyoda set up a web site where Mitsubishi owners could report troubles affecting their motor vehicles. In just one month Toyoda received 1,000 reports of faulty brakes, engines that stop, and sudden acceleration. He also got visits from Mitsubishi executives, who were rude and implied he was a liar. But he remained undeterred. 'Someone has to stand up to Mitsubishi,' Toyoda said.

The handling of Ford Explorer, Mitsubishi Diamante and Bridgestone/Firestone tyres are cases of bad corporate management, which teach a precious lesson about the new economy and its pitfalls. Cover-ups are counterproductive. Using the global, instant reach of the web is an easy way to communicate among consumers – just as companies do to reach online suppliers, contractors and other business partners. The internet collapses time and space and saves money[33] – but:

- Is the company's top management effectively up to the task?
- Is the firm offering to the market a product of excellence, which benefits from propagation of news?
- Is the firm's internal control system ready to face the challenges? or
- Is management simply hiding lack of quality and managerial responsibility through misinformation and cover-up?

The cases of Ford, Mitsubishi and Bridgestone/Firestone are correlated. They all have to do with the *wrong kind* of corporate governance which has dire consequences for all stakeholders – from clients to the company itself, its shareholders, its bondholders, its board, its CEO and its employees. The top brass of every enterprise must appreciate that in the globalized market economy there is a trend towards market discipline.

This is true of all companies, not only of banks (see Chapter 2). The lessons from the Ford/Firestone case study followed in section 7, and from the Mitsubishi Motors case, are instructive. After the dust from the first unfavourable public reactions settled, auto industry experts went on to suggest that Ford's senior management was at fault because it did not rush to correct Ford's Ranger pick-up truck and the Explorer SUV rollovers. As for Mitsubishi Motors, legal procedures continue, as we shall see at end of this section.

- The market, including equity analysts, reacts negatively to low responses to responsibilities.
- Successive failures are a clear indication that management ineffectiveness plays a role in accidents, and statistics support the experts' thesis.

In the Ford/Bridgestone case, for example, according to US safety specialists and their analysis of auto deaths nationwide during the 1980s, 51 per cent of Rangers flipped over after a tyre-related accident, compared to 32 per cent of other light trucks in similar crashes. The Explorer performed even more poorly in a tyre failure: 93 per cent of these vehicles rolled over after a tyre blowout. By contrast, 67 per cent of other SUVs rolled over in tyre-related accidents – which itself is too high and completely unacceptable.

One of the ironies with auto safety is that motor vehicle manufacturers can forego it, because even if they are condemned, the penalty for concealing safety data is peanuts: a mere $1 million. Worse still is the fact that new regulations which passed the US Congress after the Ford/Bridgestone accident do not change the penalty issue in a significant way. The financial penalty for fatal failures has remained too low to trigger corrective action on the company management side.

Yet even if the money at stake is not big, many industry observers have suggested that Ford should have reacted proactively to save its image. The board should not have allowed the company's senior management to miss the warning signs. When the first fatal reports surfaced, corrective action should have been immediate – but at the time Ford was undergoing one of its many top management changes. The 'new' CEO, anyway, did not last long.

As for Mitsubishi Motors, it was a couple of years until it suffered a potentially serious blow to its already battered image. This happened on 26 October 2003, when police raided its offices to investigate a fatal accident involving an allegedly defective Mitsubishi truck in Yokohama – striking and killing a 29-year-old woman and injuring her two sons. Investigators said a broken wheel hub was the cause of the accident, and they have been considering bringing charges of professional negligence against the company and officials who perhaps were aware of the allegedly faulty design.

This investigation came at a particularly bad time for Mitsubishi Motors, which was struggling in the US market, with tumbling sales and a huge loss related to bad car loans. The probe also highlighted concerns about the quality of Mitsubishi vehicles. Fifty other cases of wheels suddenly separating from Mitsubishi trucks have been reported in Japan since 1992.

Readers should not that in 2003 Mitsubishi Motors, which Daimler-Chrysler controls through a 37 per cent stake, had yet to fully recover from the precipitous drop in sales in Japan that began three years earlier, when it acknowledged that it intentionally concealed information about vehicle defects from government regulators for decades, to avoid costly recalls.[34]

In the end, Mitsubishi recalled more than two million vehicles following the cover-up of 2000. The company's market share in Japan fell over the ensuing years, and though it has recovered slightly at 2.3 per cent, it is still too low – a level utterly inadequate to make a profit. This is a direct result of management's ineffectiveness.

In early May 2004, struggling Mitsubishi Motors suffered a new blow when Japanese police arrested seven former executives on charges of professional negligence and falsifying reports about a fatal truck accident two years earlier. The seven were held in connection with a 2002 accident in Yokohama that killed a 29-year-old woman and injured her two sons when they were struck on a sidewalk by a wheel flying off a Mitsubishi truck. After the accident, Mitsubishi Motors submitted a report to the government blaming faulty maintenance of the vehicle.

Police said the company failed to look into previous accidents stretching back to 1992 that should have indicated a design flaw was causing the wheels to pop off truck axes. In a hurriedly called news conference, the chief executive of Mitsubishi Motors bowed deeply in apology and promised to cooperate with investigators.[35]

In conclusion, damage control is never achieved through half-baked measures. The first question a management worth its salt should ask itself is: 'Is my strategy right?', followed by 'Am I in control of the firm?' and 'What are my alternatives?' The next serious step is a documented analysis of facts, including advantages and disadvantages associated with each option. Ford,

Mitsubishi and Bridgestone/Firestone don't seem to have had an effective management, and in the end they have been the losers.

## Notes

1. *Financial Times*, 23 January 2003.
2. In the US, Ahold also owns Stop & Shop and Giant supermarket chains.
3. *The Economist*, 17 May 2003.
4. *Ibid.*, 1 March 2003.
5. Chorafas, *Management Risk*.
6. *The Economist*, 1 March 2003.
7. *USA Today*, 3 October 2003.
8. *The Economist*, 15 November 2003.
9. *International Herald Tribune*, 5 September 2003.
10. In this case study the €/$ exchange rate is taken as of the end of 2003.
11. Contrary to everybody else who looked with dismay at the scandal, Italians took it stoically. Among bankers, the most persistent question was: 'Who pulled the safety net from under the acrobat?', the implication being that a political ploy ravaged the empire.
12. *BusinessWeek*, 12 January 2004.
13. *The Economist*, 20 December 2003.
14. *BusinessWeek*, 12 January 2004.
15. *The Economist*, 13 December 2003.
16. Freely translated: 'A banker with a heart is nuts.'
17. *The Economist*, 20 December 2003.
18. *Bloomberg*, 30 December 2003.
19. *Financial Times*, 30 December 2003.
20. *Ibid.*, 22 January 2003.
21. *Total Telecom Magazine*, July 2003.
22. D. N. Chorafas, *Outsourcing, Insourcing and IT for Enterprise Management*, Basingstoke: Palgrave Macmillan, 2003.
23. *The Times*, 25 June 2003.
24. Chorafas, *Management Risk*.
25. D. N. Chorafas, *Operational Risk Control with Basle II. Basic Principles and Capital Requirements*, London and Boston: Butterworths-Heinemann, 2004.
26. *Daily Telegraph*, 11 April 2003.
27. *The Times*, 25 June 2003.
28. *EIR*, 6 October 2000.
29. *Ibid.*
30. *BusinessWeek*, 9 October 2000.
31. *Ibid.*, 18 September 2000.
32. *Ibid.*, 9 October 2000.
33. D. N. Chorafas, *The Real-time Enterprise*, New York: Auerbach, 2005.
34. *Wall Street Journal*, 27 October 2003.
35. *Wall Street Journal*, 7/9 May, 2004.

# 4

# A Survival Strategy: Reinventing the Firm

## 1. Introduction

In 1992, NASDAQ made a study in Silicon Valley to identify the best survival strategy for its clients. By a large majority, the opinion expressed by cognizant high-technology company executives was that, to survive, a Silicon Valley firm must reinvent itself every two to two and a half years. It takes vision, resources and nerve to achieve that pace of renewal.

Companies are slow to change because they are made up of people and people mostly do not have the vision for 'U-turns', let alone the courage to implement them. Worse yet, some companies work on the principle that ignorance is bliss, and once they have reached the pinnacle of power in their industry, they think that they will stay there for ever. This is a belief totally devoid of realism.

The legendary watchmakers of Switzerland provide an example of what happens when a company, or a whole profession, stays put. Swiss watchmakers were so good at their craft, and so widely admired, that in the late 1960s, a quarter-century after the end of World War II, they controlled a remarkable 65 per cent of the world market for all types of timepieces.

But by 1980, just a dozen years later, the Swiss share of the global watch market plunged below 10 per cent. The Swiss had not suddenly forgotten how to make excellent clocks and watches. Nor did anyone boycott their products. What they were guilty of was failing to reinvent their watch industry. Others did it for them.

When an inventor suggested that quartz movement should replace the mainspring, the knowledgeable watchmakers of Switzerland scoffed. The Japanese listened, and companies like Seiko seized the market. This is a telling example of how the market looks at failures of vision and of guts, in changing the *status quo*, as unpardonable sins.

IBM in the 1980s presents another case of a company going down the drain because of management ineffectiveness. When it was the leader of the computer industry, IBM could afford to charge what it liked for its mainframes. But Japanese and other rival mainframers developed good reputation with lower prices, and they turned the tables on IBM. At the same time, mini and maxi computers decreamed the market.

By the early 1990s IBM found it difficult to sell its mainframe even at huge discounts. Its equity was battered at the New York Stock Exchange and the crisis cost its shareholders some $75 billion in capitalization while its employees were decimated, losing thousands of jobs. All stakeholders, from equity investors to employees, suffered from top management's ineptitude.

In the early 1980s, at least one part of IBM had tried to reinvent the company's product line. In 1981, Don Estridge, a middle-level manager, led a unit which launched IBM's first personal computer. It was a market success, and helped the whole company to announce record annual profits. This success story, however, did not meet with wholesale approval, and senior IBM executives became resentful of the amount of publicity Estridge and his 'baby computer' were receiving.

- IBM PC worked as long as the company's huge, cumbersome bureaucracy gave it free rein.
- But after top-level carriers were threatened, petty bureaucracy and internal politics reasserted themselves, and IBM's new foray into concepts was doomed to failure.

Over a couple of years, Estridge and his team developed a series of functionality improvements which could have proved invaluable. They attempted to build a home computer and wanted to incorporate a faster processor in the PC, but their efforts were wasted because of senior management's opposition and its support for the *status quo* – the obsolete mainframes.

What the company's top brass allowed in 1983 was the 'PC Jr', aimed specifically at the home market, as opposed to IBM's traditional business market. This was hopelessly inadequate. The machine was supposed to come out in July, in time for the Christmas season, but PC Jr faced many delays because IBM's top executives insisted on a number of changes which had an adverse effect on the product. In the end the PC Jr finished up as an inferior, expensive piece of equipment, and though intended for the home market, it was sold through the same outlets as mainframes, where kids and housewives never go.

The happy postscript to the IBM story is that it finally did manage to reinvent itself, but under totally new management. When Lou Gerstner took over, he made the necessary changes to the company's human resources, structure and product line; downplayed the mainframes, focused on software and services, and implemented a new strategy. By June 1994 the company had rallied. The disaster of 1990–92 was repaired, but no senior manager in any company should allow himself to forget this lesson.

## 2. Reinventing the functions of management

Reinventing our enterprise and reinventing the functions of management is by no means something that only supermen can do. When dealing with capitalism, we are dealing with an evolutionary process that involves organization, technology, and evidently human capital. Development of new products and opening of new markets are processes of industrial mutation that revolutionize the economic structure from within. They are destroying the old one and creating a new one, which has its own prerequisites in terms of adaptation and continuing renewal.

The development of a coherent organizational theory for corporations, on Darwinian evolutionary principles, which is built from the underlying mechanisms of mutation and selection, is far from complete. There is, however, plenty of evidence that the functions of management – forecasting, planning, organizing, staffing, directing, and controlling (see Chapter 1) are changing over time under the influence of:

- new challenges that management must confront, and
- innovative tools which become available, and help management in an effective manner.[1]

The first great development in terms of clarifying and restructuring the functions of management came in the mid-nineteenth century with the work of Henri Fayol, a French factory manager. Fayol was the first on record to attend to notions of authority, responsibility, discipline and unity of command. He established the essentials for elaborating and maintaining intersecting relationships for proper management, providing a process of adjustment but also promoting the hierarchical channel and the notion of span of control.

Today we recognize that the concepts behind these last two items contradict one another, because the more the intermediate steps of a hierarchy, the shorter is the *span of control* – meaning the number of managers reporting to a superior at a higher organizational level. New tools, however, help to reduce this contradiction.

In early twenty-first-century terms it should be appreciated that to avoid the effect of centrifugal forces, ineffective and information-poor industrial enterprises find themselves obliged to have many intermediate organizational levels. By contrast, enterprises supported by systems which work in real time and by knowledge artefacts (agents) dispense with several medium management layers, reducing overhead and greatly improving both effectiveness and efficiency (see Chapter 1).

While the work of Henri Fayol focused on management effectiveness, that of Frederick Winslow Taylor, Henry L. Gantt, Frank B. and Lillian Gilbreth and many others who lived in the first quarter of the twentieth century focused on efficiency. This has been the objective of time and motion studies, which revolutionized the work on the production floor – but not necessarily at senior management level, as Henri Fayol's contributions had done. Taylor's and Fayol's contributions started to converge in the 1970s and 1980s with management information systems (MIS) and knowledge engineering. Today management can benefit greatly from the work of both pioneers, as well as from the mid- to late-twentieth-century strides in technological advance. While it is not always the best technology that wins, other things equal this is the most likely. Technology acts as a catalyst in improving performance and in changing the environment to one in which there is more give and take between the company and its market, and among the different management functions within the company itself.

For instance, knowledge-enriched IT helps to obtain first-class results in internal control and auditing. This is a major area of concern, especially now, in the post-Enron era. To be rigorous and independent in its management control functions, the board requires vast improvements in information technology – a goal which cannot be met through the gradual, slow-moving IT approaches endemic in most companies.

Reinventing the functions of management and accelerating their pace is a 'must'. It is also an act of self-protection and professional survival, one which senior managers who care about their job can't afford to miss. In late 2003, a report by the American Enterprise Institute, a Washington-based think-tank, noted that only 16 per cent of the American public now thinks that corporate executives have 'high honesty and ethical standards', down from 25 per cent in 2001.

- Low technology hinders senior management's ability to detect new and old types of abuses.
- Worn-out systems and procedures inhibit the efforts of those managers who recognize in how deep a hole their profession is, and try to get out of it.

New tools and more effective systems are an integral part of reinventing the functions of management. Their development should fully reflect the fact that because business is based on confidence, compliance with high ethical standards is very important.[2] Such compliance is also a way to express management's effectiveness in being in charge (see section 3).

While necessary, ethical standards are not enough. Therefore, no one should underestimate the scale of effort needed to reinvent the functions of management with effectiveness, efficiency and business confidence as goals. Experts think that in the coming years CEOs and their immediate assistants will be much more cautious about what they do and say. In part, this may reflect a growing fear of legal risk, and of regulatory action, after the passage of the Sarbanes–Oxley Act and a series of shareholder lawsuits against boards and CEOs. But in part it also reflects the fact that market discipline is changing the rules of the game.

While most chief executives think the media have tarred them unfairly, they have taken note that things are no longer as they used to be. An article in *The Economist* takes as an example John Chambers of Cisco: 'In the Bubble years (Chambers) was always popping up to talk boldly and optimistically about almost anything – including how Cisco would generate revenues of $50 billion by 2004 and become 'one of the most influential companies in history'. By November 2003, when Cisco announced its highest quarterly revenues in three years and a 76 per cent jump in profits, Mr Chambers could manage only this rallying cry: 'While things are starting to look better, it is still fragile.'

Downsizing the ego is part of reinventing the functions of management, and this can have some unexpected consequences, not least that of lowering the executives' profile to a degree that is more comfortable for the market as well as within their own firm. Another likely consequence is to foster understanding between the company, its shareholders, judicial authorities and other public sectors.

For instance, to promote understanding between different professions, the Deutsche Aktiengesellschaft (DA) brings together people from German federal courts and from small companies to discuss rules and their practicality in day-to-day business. 'The judges must know how companies are organized and how they operate,' says Rüdiger von Rosen, DA's CEO. 'In Germany the new accounting rules, regulations and laws are a headache for the small to medium companies.' Taking care of that headache led to the process of:

- organizing and providing a platform of exchanges, and
- making sure that people from different professions do know and understand each other.

In a globalized economy, an integral part of reinventing management's functions is to close the gap that divides the world's main regions in terms of standards – including accounting standards. The US Financial Accounting Standards Board (FASB) and London-based International Accounting Standards Board (IASB) provide an example. Since October 2003, FASB and IASB have been working together to reach a convergence in general accounting rules between America and Europe, with the goal to create one set of global accounting standards. This will help to:

- deepen international capital markets,
- boost cross-border investment, and
- make life easier for multinational companies, who must currently report under a multiple of incompatible accounting standards.

Universal standards will help in much better understanding of financial statements and save time and money. But reaching them will not be easy. One of the main bottlenecks is executive stock options,[3] which are treated as an expense in Europe but not yet in America, though self-respecting US companies have decided to do so, even if the law is not yet explicit.

## 3. Malfeasance shows management ineffectiveness, not skill

The jury in the trial of Dennis Kozlowski, accused of looting some $600 million from Tyco, were shown details of where $30 million of the industrial conglomerate's cash went: on the former CEO's luxury flat. Furnishings included:

- hand-painted wallpaper,
- masterpieces by Monet and Renoir, and
- a $6,000 shower curtain for the maid.

The maid herself had been on Tyco's payroll at $70,000 per year plus bonuses.[4]

Finally Dennis Kozlowski, the former chairman of Tyco, and Mark Swartz, its former finance chief, went on trial in the second half of 2003. Both have denied looting the company of $600 million – as alleged by the prosecution.

Six months down the line, on 29 March, 2004, the judge in the corruption case against the two former Tyco International executives sent the jury back into deliberations, after declaring that the trial would not be dictated by the intense media coverage of bickering among jurors. Judge Michael Obus told the New York State Supreme Court that it be inappropriate to declare a mistrial, but on 2 April he did declare a mistrial citing intense outside pressure on one juror. Another juror, however, said the panel has been within an hour of delivering a verdict.[5]

The bad news for our society is that alleged swindling by CEO has by now reached unprecedented proportions. In the early phase of investigation of the Parmalat scandal (see Chapter 3) Calisto Tanzi, the company's founder and former CEO, had no difficulty in admitting that over the years of his reign he had taken €500 million of company money – overtaking Dennis Kozlowski (under prevailing exchange rates) in the race for the bigger scandal.

These are amusing but also tragic examples from industry, and they are far from isolated. A whole *bouquet* of management-made scams came out of the Elf corruption trials (Elf was the former state-owned French oil company). Looting by management had gone on for over nine years. Loik Le Floch-Prigent, Elf's CEO in 1989–93, Alfred Sirven, his deputy, and ex-'Mr Africa', André Tarallo, got prison sentences – respectively five, five and four years, a trifle given what had taken place. More prison sentences, some suspended, went to 27 other accused, as well as combined fines of about €20 million.

Le Floch-Prigent and Sirven were accused of operating and benefiting from slush funds to the tune of some €305 million – 'only 60 per cent' of what Calisto Tanzi admitted to have taken from his company's coffers single-handed. The two French businessmen insisted that they were operating an inherited *système Elf*, designed to further French oil policy and to benefit certain African leaders. But in the end such defences crumbled.

The Elf trial brought to public attention corruption, in the early 1990s, under President François Mitterand. But Roland Dumas, a Mitterand foreign minister and head of France's constitutional council, was cleared on appeal. By contrast, the case against his former mistress, Christine Deviers-Joncour, was sustained by the court.

The picture emerging from these cases is one of an extraordinary world of bribery and personal profit. It is not one of management effectiveness, no matter how 'effective' the crooks in hiding their wrongdoings over so many years. A similar statement is valid in relation to those who created the California energy crisis, where market manipulations, allegedly by Enron, played a key role.[6]

Neither are these examples of management ineffectiveness and disregard for both shareholder value and ethics one-off events. On 14 November 2003, a jury in Montgomery, Alabama, ordered Exxon Mobil to pay nearly $11.9 billion in damages after finding that the oil company had cheated the state of Alabama out of natural gas royalties, awarding:

- $63.6 million in compensatory damages, and
- $11.8 billion in punitive damages, a record in the state.

'We felt Exxon thought they were going to get away with this,' said the jury foreman, Joe King, a teacher. 'We wanted to send a message that they were not, and that this corporation can't get away with doing wrong.' An Exxon Mobil spokesman said the verdict was excessive and the company would appeal.[7]

It is gratifying to see that the law enforcement industry is not idle – even if, sometimes, it is very slow. Official investigations are still going on into Jean-Marie Messier, former head of Vivendi (see Chapter 7), who steered the French media conglomerate to the edge of bankruptcy in 2002. This subject has not faded from view, even if Messier agreed to forego a €20 million golden parachute in exchange for being let off the hook by the Securities and Exchange Commission.

Golden parachutes are themselves part of the problem because some executives consider them a sort of divine right, in spite of shareholder outrage. Investors' sharp reaction over the contract of Jean-Pierre Garnier, GlaxoSmithKline's CEO, forced some concessions. Garnier will still receive a handsome sum for heading the British drug company, but he:

- will face more rigorous performance targets, and
- will have to give up a highly controversial deal covering potential severance terms worth about £22 million ($37.5 million).

Exchanges, too, have become subject to much greater scrutiny, by both investors and regulators. In December 2003 the New York Stock Exchange faced allegations by CalPers, one of the world's biggest public pension funds, that its trading system allowed seven market-making firms to defraud investors of millions.

And there is the case of Mike Sears, Boeing's chief financial officer, and Darleen Druyun, an employee formerly with the US Air Force, both sacked for improper dealings over contracts for military aircraft. Druyun got a job with the aircraft-maker after involvement with negotiating a contract for tankers with Boeing. Sears has been accused of discussing future employment with her while the deal was progressing, but denies violating company policy.[8]

The message conveyed by these examples is that ethical values are an integral part of management effectiveness, even if they are not the only criterion by which to judge managerial results. The point to retain is that if the board's and CEO's ethical standards are *undemanding*, then the entity's culture is biased and the whole company will do questionable things.

The saying about Caesar's wife – that she should not only be virtuous but also be publicly appreciated as a virtuous woman – fits every CEO neatly. Virtue is effectiveness, if for no other reason than that ethical values make it possible to take difficult or unpleasant decisions in situations when business leaders often have to deal swiftly with conflicting demands.

Higher ethical values enable greater clarity and focus in executive decisions. They also permit creation of something that outlasts immediate day-to-day activities. Moreover, higher ethical values help to improve ability to judge other people – which is an essential prerequisite for management's effectiveness.

Ethical values promote a manager's emotional self-confidence because he or she knows that he/she cannot be accused of having done something morally wrong. Among the major advantages of self-confidence is that it allows managers to admit to weakness and ask for help without feeling defensive or inadequate for the job they are doing.

All these are traits of effective management which prove invaluable when things go wrong, as they do from time to time. Surviving a reverse calls for resilience, adaptability and flexibility, which are key ingredients in being able quickly to devise a completely different approach to a given problem than the one to which an executive has been passionately committed.

Each of the case studies we shall examine in the following sections has been a problem because the managers in charge have been lacking one or more of the characteristics outlined in this and in the previous chapters. This made it difficult if not outright impossible to turn misfortune into fortune by reshaping the problem and its challenges so that the company could survive.

## 4.   Standard Life, Equitable Life and Mannheimer Life Insurance

The downturn of three life insurers is the background of this case study. Standard Life, Britain's and Europe's biggest mutual insurer, has suffered greatly from plunging stock markets. On 21 March 2003, it revealed that one of its key investment reserves had lost 74 per cent of its value over the previous three years. The company's fund for future appropriations (FFA) stood at £3.2 billion ($5.44 billion) in November 2002, compared with £12.4 billion ($21.1 billion) at the end of 1999.

In all fairness to these three life insurance companies, it should be said that practically all insurers, life and non-life, have suffered greatly from plunging equity markets. The hardest hit have been those that allocated a major share of their portfolio to stocks. In Britain, the investment split among insurers has been loaded to the equities side, much more so than in any other major country:

- in 1999 about 50 per cent of insurers' assets were in equities and less than 15 per cent in bonds;
- moreover, there was an increase in equity holdings in 1999 over 1998,[9] which means that equity investments were made at the peak of the market and of the bubble.

In continental Europe, too, insurance companies leverage their assets, through equities, but at a much lower level – typically within a range of 25 per cent to 35 per cent. American insurance companies depend on equities at ratios below that, and therefore they have suffered less when the stock market goes into a tailspin.

Standard Life had invested in equities well above the British average. Shares were said to represent 76.8 per cent of its £31 billion ($52.7 billion) portfolio. When the market crumbled, that proved to be mismanagement of assets at the gambling level, as any investor loaded with equity risk was bound to suffer.

On 31 March, 2004, Standard Life announced that it has given itself two years to prepare for its long-awaited demutualization. Critics said that had the business gone public several years ago, the investment case would have been manifest given the entity's capital strength and its dominance in the with-profits savings market. But in 2004, this is a different company than at the dawn of the 21st century.

Sandy Cromble, Standard Life's new chief executive, admitted the company's business is capital constrained.[10] Its overcommitment to large equity holdings left it crippled by the bear market. Moreover, being a big market participant in with-profits products counts for less, because savers have lost faith in them. Therefore, Standard Life's board had little choice but to seek fresh capital from outside investors,

- Raising fresh capital, because its former investment case had been undermined badly, and
- Winning over investors by reinventing itself as a company with a more credible future.

Several moves pointed to the board's decision about restructuring, including cutting staff and suspending plans to expand in France. Critics said that while these moves were necessary, they were not enough. The life insurer also had to develop new business lines and this may require a distribution deal with a bank, plus a further retreat from recent expansion. Above all, to save the company senior management must develop a serious plan regarding its capital position and financial staying power. The only thing that could cheer up Standard Life's board members was that their company was not alone in facing strong headwinds in its investments policy.

On 4 September 2003, Royal & Sun Alliance Insurance Group, the British insurer that has had three years of losses, said that it planned to raise £960 million ($1.63 billion) by selling more stock to its current shareholders. The company has been offering one share for each share investors already own, at 70 pence, 55 per cent less than the stock's closing price on day of the announcement.

Similar to Standard Life, Royal & Sun has been hit in recent years by a slump in stock markets and a shortage of capital. Experts said the insurer may have to raise provisions for claims by as much as £800 million in the third quarter of 2003. Senior management has been selling businesses to increase capital depleted by asbestos claims and stock-market declines.

The British market did not react positively to the offer. The rights offer 'is an enormous dilution' to shareholders, said Richard Peirson, a fund manager at Framlington Investment Management in London, adding that 'all of the shareholder funds will effectively be going out again for the restructuring and provisions'.[11] Many other European insurers, including Germany's Allianz and Switzerland's Zurich Financial Services, have raised more than $10 billion in selling stock to existing investors in the 12 months preceding Royal & Sun's offer.

A short time before these events, figures from the Financial Services Authority showed that through some sort of creative accounting Standard Life had boosted its solvency ratio to 13.8 per cent by including future profits of £1.5 billion ($2.5 billion) for the first time. Excluding this, the ratio fell to 8.9 per cent from 18 per cent in 2002, as the life insurer suffered from its high reliance on equities.

Stockholders did not fail to notice that such a sharp drop in the mutual insurer's fortunes did not affect executive compensation, as should have been the case. On the contrary, Scott Bell, former chief executive of Standard Life, received *performance-related* bonuses worth £844,000 ($1.43 million) in 2002, while the group's with-profits fund sustained *losses* of £4 billion ($6.8 billion) from its equity investments. The bonus came on top of a basic salary for the year to March 2002 of £250,000, and the award of an extravagant pension worth £420,000 per year.[12]

In January 2004, Iain Lumsden quit as chief executive of Standard Life. Analysts said the entity had fallen foul of new methods for calculating its capital-based introduced in the wake of the near demise of Equitable Life in 2000. The insurer announced that:

- it would raise £750 million ($1.3 billion) of new capital, and
- it was ready to abandon mutual status in favour of stock market flotation.[13]

One of my professors at the University of California taught his students that it is always difficult to say where human stupidity ends and conflict of interests begins. Most troublesome is the fact that executives who, through their decisions and actions destroy shareholder value – and leave other stakeholders, like insured people and pensioners, high and dry – are rewarding themselves with millions. With management accountability a salient problem, the damage is done to business confidence and to the market as a whole. It is not only that insurers and pension funds at large depended so unwisely on heavy equity investments and were devastated by the falling stock prices; there is also the case that unloading the equities portfolio in the most inappropriate moment, these same entities fed the bubble and contributed to procyclicality.[14]

The Financial Services Authority has estimated that insurers alone sold a net £25 billion ($40 billion) of UK shares during the whole of 2002. Their sales evidently had a depressing effect on the stock market – and that may well be the reason behind the fact FSA let it be known that it would waive its existing rules on minimum solvency margins until they were recast in a more generous form.

Pension funds have followed the same unwise policy in asset allocation. Indeed, to add to the gloom, an analysis by Morgan Stanley has suggested that, if upcoming accounting rules persuade pension funds to cut their equity content even to 50 per cent of their portfolios, they will still have about £48 billion ($81.6 billion) more of UK shares than they should. This is tantamount to saying that pension funds would take over the stock market's undermining role from insurers, either by selling shares, or by failing to put in new money.

The case of Equitable Life goes a step further from where the Standard Life case study left off. On 26 March 2003, an Equitable Life policyholders' action group accused the mutual's former management of running the insurer like a pyramiding investment scheme, and claimed that its with-profits fund had sustained £1 billion ($1.7 billion) of decline throughout the 1990s, hidden from the policyholders' view.

In a document submitted to the Penrose Inquiry into the insurer, the Equitable Members' Action Group (EMAG) claimed that the reported values were consistently shown to be worth £1 billion more than the fair value of assets. According to this report, the insurer was already in deficit before the House of Lords forced it to honour pledges to holders of guarantees, which in turn meant a writedown of £1.5 billion ($2.5 billion) in its finances.

EMAG was demanding compensation from the government for policyholders' losses, because the Treasury and Ministry of Industry were responsible for regulating Equitable in the 1990s. That role was then inherited by the Financial Services Authority in 1999. The Equitable Life Members' Action Group also alleged that the insurers were making overly generous payouts to customers who retired or transferred.

These generous payments were funded from the money invested by newcomers, which is a typical Ponzi game: the new victims of a fraudulent investment scheme support the hefty returns made to the early investors until the money runs dry. The result of Equitable's alleged practice was the aforementioned $2.5 billion hole in the with-profits fund, which the company is said to have concealed over a long period of time.

Worse news for stakeholders was to come. In the last week of June 2003, the Equitable Members' Action Group published a report claiming that the black hole in the insurer's finances reached not £1.5 billion, as originally stated, but an impressive £3.3 billion ($5.61 billion) at the time Equitable Life closed to new business.

There is still one higher level of mismanagement which can hurt the stakeholders even more deeply, and this is the insurer's outright bankruptcy. In the last week of June 2003, a thorough investigation by BaFin, Germany's financial regulator, sent Mannheimer Lebensversicherung, a life insurer, into insolvency. Mannheimer was the prominent medium-sized insurer in the German Federal Republic – and up to mid-2002 it was generally considered to be quite dependable.

Following the insolvency, the assets and liabilities of the life insurance unit of Mannheimer were transferred into *Protektor*, a German insurance industry safety net set up in 2002 to safeguard policyholders' investments. But for the insurer's policyholders, the likelihood of insecurity associated with *Protektor's* funding cast further doubt on the survivability of their investments, annuities and pensions. *Protektor's* founding capital, of just €6.3 million (which is a triviality), was put up by only ten of Germany's insurers. According to experts, there is no firm commitment from all 120 German insurers to hand over up to 1 per cent of their assets to *Protektor*, which would amount to about €5 billion.

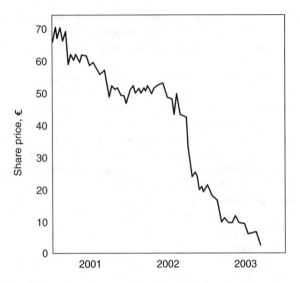

*Figure 4.1*   Mannheimer's equity nose-dived a year before its failure

How did things reach that point? Mannheimer's bankruptcy came in the aftermath of a year-long drop in its equity, as shown in Figure 4.1. Its slide and fall have opened up the prospect of other life insurer failures – while experts estimated that Mannheimer's bankruptcy would trigger a write-down of at least €25 million for Munich Re, which had a 10 per cent equity share in Mannheimer.

As one piece of bad news never comes alone, according to analysts, the failure of months-long rescue efforts by Mannheimer and GdV, the insurance industry association, was also a big disappointment for the German government. The life insurer's bankruptcy has negatively affected the government's plans to persuade the public to invest for their own retirement, rather than rely on state pensions. Private pensions are largely practised in the US, the UK and a few other countries like Chile. But they don't yet have any standing in Germany or France, and failures of insurance companies and pension funds do not promote public confidence.

Basically, the idea of diversifying the social safety net through a mix of private and public pensions is not bad. It is a natural evolution in an ageing society which can no longer look to its retirement through the prism of social security solutions worked out in the 1930s. But as the case studies in this section demonstrate, the downside is that investors who are concerned about their old age are exposed to huge mismanagement – which leaves stakeholders exposed to all sorts of risks.

## 5. Imperial Chemical Industries

All the board members and everybody in a management position is accountable for the way the company is – good or bad. Likewise, everybody in an organization is responsible for operational risk control, which includes everything from management risk to execution risk, fraud, information technology risk and legal risk.

Management risk and legal risk are correlated, as we have seen in the case study on Xerox (see Chapter 3). Both have a great deal to do with mismanagement which permits – if not outright promotes – creative accounting and other swindles. But mismanagement can also happen because of ineffectiveness and inefficiency, as the case study in this section documents.

On 26 March 2003, after a profits warning because of problems in its operations in North America and the Netherlands, Britain's formerly prestigious Imperial Chemical Industries (ICI) saw its shares drop by almost 40 per cent. At that level, experts suggested, ICI could be ejected from the FTSE 100 index of biggest companies, and the old standard-bearer of the chemicals industry in the UK might as well become somebody's takeover target.

While, according to some opinions, market reaction could be seen as overdone – after all, ICI said that first-quarter 2003 profits would be £50 million ($85 million) – experience demonstrates that a nervous market holds many surprises in the downside. This was compound by serious problems at ICI's food-and-flavours operations in the Netherlands (whose boss promptly 'resigned'), and its American adhesives and food starches division. Both the Dutch and North America operations were at the core of the company's growth strategy, and both were badly hit by poor management at the corporate helm, which brought other woes.

To a significant extent ICI's problems were not too different from those of Marconi (the former General Electric Company of Britain), which unwisely got out of older, traditional but profitable lines into newer, perhaps more exciting but definitely unstable and highly risky ones. In both cases, Marconi and ICI, the switch in product focus was made at the most inopportune time, while the company was overpaying for new acquisitions and letting poor governance ruin the business prospects.

More precisely, in ICI's case, after spinning off Zenaca, the company's drug division, in 1992, ICI's CEO sold another basic unit, the relatively low-margin but stable cyclical chemicals business at a rock-bottom price. With the money, he bought some specialty chemicals. The price-tag for the new businesses was high: £4.9 billion ($8.33 billion). This happened in 1997 and thereafter highly ineffective management loaded the company with debts that reached £4.2 billion ($7.14 billion), and then issued £800 ($1.36 billion) million of new shares to reduce its indebtedness by a notch.

Equity analysts did not fail to notice that by late March 2003 ICI's market capitalization was only about £1 billion ($1.7 billion) – which provided evidence that its strategy had not been at all successful. 'Patently incompetent,' is how one analyst described Brendan O'Neill, ICI's most recent chief executive, who made his name running Guinness, a brewery. As another analyst commented on ICI's strategy, 'There are no synergies between the sticky bits at National Starch paints, and the smelly bits at Qwest.'[15]

Chief executives still contemplating making a name through high stakes should take notice. All told, today's remnants of Imperial Chemical Industries are a far cry from the industrial giant and national champion it once was. Even compared to its recent past, ICI's results are dismal. Its 2002 turnover of £6.1 billion ($10.37 billion) was less than two-thirds that of the 1998 comparable figure. Moreover, after the aforementioned share price plunge, ICI's equity hit its lowest point since 1974, and investors who supported ICI's £800 million deeply discounted rights issue saw shares fall almost to half the 180 pence they paid in 2002.

Nor are the company's future prospects looking any better. As these lines are written, analysts expect the dividend of Imperial Chemical Industries to be cut for a third year, and they are very sceptical about top management's claim that it had transformed the firm into a specialty chemicals group. These are the fruits of mismanagement and of incompetence. Investors beware.

## 6. The second downturn of Canary Wharf

Readers will probably recall how, in the early 1990s, Canary Wharf, the lead investment of Olympia & York (O&Y), went under, pulling the too-big-to-fail Canadian construction company down with it. Banks lost a great deal of money; some, like Swiss Bank Corporation, also lost their AAA credit rating by independent agencies (see Chapter 2). The first time Canary Wharf crashed, 91 creditors of Olympia & York went to court to try to recover something of the remains. These divided into two groups: the secured and the unsecured.

The secured included banks, insurance companies and pension funds, who loaned money to the Canadian developer against a specific security, such as a mortgage on a building owned by Olympia & York. Paul and Albert Reichmann, the brothers who ran the company, were known to be very secretive about their financial accounts. Before the first crash of Canary Wharf, critics had said that 'secured loans' did not really represent any great security, because O&Y had managed to pile calamity upon catastrophe – and yet be able to survive up to a point.

To their credit, the Reichmanns were innovators. They were not afraid to try new departures. But their fast rise to fame came about through high leverage, and this made their empire unstable, particularly when the crisis hit.

O&Y's road to prosperity started in Toronto, migrated to New York, and ended in London with Canary Wharf.

If Toronto's First Canadian Place was one of the Reichmanns' early achievements, New York's World Financial Center (next to the ill-fated twin towers) was their high-water mark. Post mortem, it could be seen that Olympia & York followed sound building principles since the World Financial Center building held up well in the huge turmoil of the crash of the World Trade Center, the twin towers, on 11 September 2001.

After New York's docklands development with the World Financial Center came London's docklands, and there began the road to Waterloo, with the One Canada Square skyscraper and other toll buildings constructed by the Reichmanns. A basic problem was that this office space could find no tenants. Then Prime Minister Margaret Thatcher helped in Olympia & York's downfall by (correctly) insisting that a private enterprise must find its way out of its own mess. But maybe Thatcher extended the free enterprise principle a bit too far by asking that private money be spent for construction of the Jubilee Line Underground.

The in joke in London at that time was that the Reichmann brothers, and the banks financing them, were building a business centre in the middle of nowhere. The original idea was to attract tenants from the nearby City, which was chronically congested and where rents were very high. But the turkey did not fly. Tenants were moving out of O&Y buildings faster than they were moving in, and billions went down the drain in 1992. The rest is history.

Within half a dozen years Canary Wharf bounced back. Paul Reichmann and his nephews carved out a new role for themselves. But in March 2003, shares of Canary Wharf Group (CWG), which owns much of the real-estate development under the same name, took a tumble. The market's reaction brought back memories: the Canary Wharf project went bust in 1992, and this precedent made investors nervous that it might happen again.

Having peaked at over £5 before the terrorist attacks on the World Trade Center on 11 September 2001, CWG shares traded at about £1.50 as the first quarter of 2003 came to a close. This was a major loss in volume, yet Canary Wharf had changed a great deal since 1992. By early 2003, the estate contained 13.1 million square feet of office space, and many big-name companies, particularly financials, established their offices there, lured by reasonable rents as compared to the City.

Some analysts have even suggested that CWG's finances seem to have improved over time. Following a prudent policy, for some years CWG generally built to order; many of its existing rents have been fixed for 25 to 35 years; and its funding has come from issuing long-term bonds. Through the bonds, these rents are simply passed on to investors. Moreover, with real-estate assets securitized, the buildings have been largely off Canary Wharf's balance sheet.

Why, then, the downside? Most probably it is due to the change in real-estate development policy. In April 2003, Canary Wharf completed another tower block which had few tenants, making it a more speculative venture than past buildings. This came at an inopportune moment, as financial firms and associated industries have been feeling the pinch of market downturn, and demand for office space has fallen sharply.

Another negative aspect to emerge is that at least three tenants – Lehman Brothers, Clifford Chance and Skadden (the latter two law firms) – have the right to hand back a great deal of space to CWG, which would then be forced to pay the rent on this space to bondholders. If so, the company's cash flow would come under stress.

Some experts have also pointed out that, like O&Y previously, Canary Wharf is highly geared. Its debts are twice its equity, though the amount it has securitized might provide a cushion, at bondholders' expense. Competition also proved to be a threat. British Land, a property company, has been developing a 400,000 square foot (36,000 m$^2$) site in Gresham Street in the City. This has the potential to lure back to the centre of London some of Canary Wharf's tenants and prospects, further reducing demand for the empty space – which an unwise policy change in CWG produced at great expense.

Taking note of the fact that Paul Reichmann, Canary's executive chairman, was awarded a package of warrants when he floated the company in the mid-1990s, some analysts suggested that with the fortunes of the company nose-diving his options are worthless – despite a promising start. At the time these options were issued, they were estimated to be worth £250 million ($425 million).

By late August 2003 it became known that Paul Reichmann was plotting a management buyout of Canary Wharf. The other potential bidders were Morgan Stanley; Whitehall, the property fund managed by Goldman Sachs; and Brascan Corporation, heaven forbid, a Canadian conglomerate. Brascan already owned 9 per cent of Canary Wharf, but it was thought that Morgan Stanley remained the front-runner despite Whitehall's late interest.

On 3 October 2003, Paul Reichmann said he would turn the auction for the company he founded into a three-way fight with plans for his own bid. He also hired Lehman Brothers to advise him on a potential bid for the property developer, which owns Britain's tallest building. Any offer was to be made through IPC Advisers, a company owned by his family.

Reichmann had previously indicated that he would accept a trial offer pitched at about 310p ($5.27) per share. Analysts, however, expressed scepticism at the prospect of his tabling an offer for the company, saying that his intervention was merely a tactic to bid up the price. Financial analysts also suggested that Canary Wharf could be worth little more than 240p ($4.08), based on net asset value per share minus tax and debt – but surely not 310p per share. Moreover, Canary Wharf reported a pre-tax loss of

£13 million ($22.1 million) for the year to 30 June 2003. Yet Reichmann's bid strategy seems to have worked, since on 15 January 2004 Morgan Stanley said that it was upping its bid.

## 7. The European air transport industry is losing altitude

The bankruptcies of Swissair, Sabena and AirLib (including that of AirLib's predecessors) are looking like the tip of the iceberg in the shakedown of the European flag carriers and other air transport companies. Debt continues to be a feature of the different national airlines. In the first quarter of 2003, Lufthansa lost €356 million, KLM €252 million, SAS €208 million, Alitalia €198 million, Air France €98 million, and Iberia €51 million. As if to combine their losses, later on in 2003 Air France and KLM merged. Alitalia tried to join the merged company but it was rebuffed – advised, instead, to put its house in order.

These debts are not even surprising, given that all the flag carriers in question are very poorly managed. Operating cost at Ryanair, a low-cost carrier, are 60 per cent less than those of Lufthansa. Something similar is true of easyJet. Both easyJet and Ryanair are examples of reinventing the air transport industry. Costs matter greatly in the P&L statement, particularly when competition is fierce, as there is huge overcapacity with flag carriers and other airlines: Western Europe today features 14 different airlines, and the forecast is that by 2010 only three or four will have survived.

Like many American air transport companies – PanAm, TWA, USAir and several others – the Europeans have weakened themselves through steady mismanagement. Overstaffing, overpaying, overcapacity and other sure signs of ineffectiveness provide evidence for this statement. Runaway costs kill a firm. With air carriers, as with other industries, *management risk* is endemic.[16]

Too weak, if not outright pitiful, corporate governance has been made worse through repetitive and irrational strikes. In Europe, the strikes of pilots, air stewardesses, mechancis and other personnel are legendary. This has disgusted the travelling public, which has looked for alternatives. It has also deprived some of the flag carriers, such as Air France, of many of their formerly loyal clients – particularly the profitable business customers.

Keeping in mind the US precedent, though, welcome deregulation of the air travel industry is sure to precipitate the plethora of carriers which, given irrational state subsidies, continue limping on. But subsidies are not going to be for ever. Not only has the formerly massive and steady financial support by European governments finally started drying up, but European air traffic deregulation, announced in early June 2003, means that air carriers from any EU country – including low-cost – can serve the routes exclusively reserved so far to national flag carriers.

With deregulation, for example, Alitalia's monopoly on routes such as Rome–New York or Milan–Miami will be gone. British Airways (BA) can provide exactly this service, siphoning off the most lucrative clients. It is not that BA has found the elixir of life but, on the whole, it is better managed than Alitalia and many other flag carriers.

Note that BA, too, had its ups and downs, leading analysts to comment that even the most prestigious companies can go under very quickly if they are mismanaged and/or their industry is hit by major adverse events. This was the case with Swissair, which sank in 2001. That same year, British Airways, which was flourishing in the 1990s, had its name added to the sick list.

After severe job cuts in 2000 and in early 2001, by December 2001 British Airways was again shedding 7,000 staff, but still went into the red in that year. Credit rating agencies downgraded the airline's bonds to junk status. To gain altitude, at about that time British Airways also confirmed that it was planned to sell its 767 fleet, as it switched to smaller Airbus planes.

The fact that British Airways had, relatively speaking, better management than other flag carriers is shown by the fact that it avoided blunders like that of Iberia's acquisition of Aerolineas Argentinas, which proved to be an unmitigated disaster. But it did make the error of acquiring Air Liberté, which it had to disinvest after heavy losses.

Iberia's is an instructive case on the fate of takeovers, which is worth bringing to the reader's attention. The Spanish national airline acquired Aerolineas in 1990 in one of the first privatizations in Argentina. In 1990, as in 2001 and on so many other occasions, Argentina had struggled to control its public finances, pay at least the interest on its huge debt, and prevent an outbreak of hyperinflation. Privatizations were part of that 'solution'.

For historical and sentimental rather than for economic reasons, the Spanish government took a political decision to support the Argentinean government to get rid of bad assets. As a result, it ordered its then state-owned companies to buy Argentine government equipment which was put up for sale. Basically, this whole business was flawed:

- politicians on both sides of the Atlantic complained of irregularities during the sale negotiations, and
- Argentineans were concerned that Iberia lacked the capital and management skills to turn Aerolineas around.

For once, the politicians proved to be right. Within a short timespan, a mismanaged Aerolineas Argentinas sank into the red, accumulating a huge debt on Iberia's back. This sale has been characterized as one of the worst-executed privatizations in Latin America, which says a great deal. The huge debt forced everybody to rethink the strategy of buying privatized 'assets' left and right.

Because Iberia itself was sinking due to the ineffectiveness of its management and colossal accumulated losses, its own and Aerolineas, the Spanish government came to the rescue in a covert way. It took control of Aerolineas, injecting liquidity into Iberia. Nothing, however, could stop money from going down the drain, and a sale of Aerolineas did not attract any interested parties.

Only after years of trying, SEPI, the Spanish government's industrial company, managed to unload Aerolineas Argentinas on to Grupo Marsans, a private Spanish tour operator. This deal, made in October 2001, marked the end of the Spanish government's long years of involvement with Aerlineas. It was also a 'first' in the sense that Aerolineas has been privatized twice: once by Argentina, and a second time by Spain, which pumped nearly $2 billion into the sinking airline between 1990 and 2001.

Analysts said that while SEPI may have walked away from Aerolineas Argentinas, the troubles for its new owner were only just beginning. Not only is the international aviation industry in a slump, and the relatively busy routes to the US and Europe face heavy competition from some of the world's biggest airlines, but also Aerolineas, like Iberia, Portugal's Tap, Belgium's Sabena and so many other airlines is an entity in which nepotism is rampant and mismanagement is the rule.

This mini-case study of Iberia and Aerolineas has many imitators; and the same is true of the deadly effect of personnel strikes which make a very poorly run company much worse. It is indeed curious that neither the labour unions nor the airlines' own base appreciate that in an environment where financial weaknesses are widespread, striking airline employees are practically cutting off the branch on which they sit, as protected markets open up, injection of funds dries up and corporate privileges disappear.

Practically all national flag carriers today are publicly quoted and the market is voting with its money for the survivors. Right after the announcement of air traffic deregulation in the European Union, the shares of easyJet, Ryanair and British Airways went up. Those of Air France, Alitalia and other flag carriers went down.

Analysts drew parallels with the American precedent after deregulation. Top names like PanAm, TWA and Eastern Airlines are gone for ever. United Airlines, US Airways and many others sought protection from creditors under Chapter 11, to avoid outright bankruptcy. The US air transport industry has also provided an example of how, with deregulation, the aftermath of strikes becomes more affordable to the traveling public. As a result the number of strikes in the US has diminished, while the offer of alternatives made it possible to fill the gaps in air travel at the expenses of the strikers.

What all this means, in essence, is the end of an epoch in which air transport cartels pulled the strings, and the employees of these cartels were taking the passengers as hostages. In the future both weak corporate governance and unacceptable industrial practices, expressed through *employee risk*, will be punished by the market through greater loss of jobs than the 400,000 employee slim-down in 2001–2003 through bankruptcies and restructuring in the air transport industry.

## 8.   Will the integration of 'ten' accession countries be effective?

Mistakes having to do with lack of appreciation of the real situation happen at all levels, including that of national governments. The 2003 expansion of the European Union by ten new members is a good case study. Malta is one of these countries. I asked a senior banking executive from the small island democracy, 'What are the disadvantages?' She gave me four good examples:

- Foreigners may come and take our jobs.
- We risk losing our sovereignty.
- Competition will be tough for our companies.
- Foreign exchange rates do not give the island headway.

The knowledgeable executive added that there may also be other disadvantages. My next question was 'What are the advantages?' Here the reply came slowly, and somehow it carried less conviction. Two items were stated:

- The funds we will get.
- Foreign studies we can do to improve our jobs.

The funds that Malta, and the other nine new members of the EU, will get are, to say the least, questionable. Germany, which used to shower new comers to the EU with money is at this point in time the sick man of Europe. A recent article in *The Economist* called Gerhard Schröder, the German prime minister: 'Sick man walking.'[17] As for studies abroad, no country needs to be an EU member to have access to EU schools and universities.

- Even if one thinks that there are only advantages to a change in status, the facts of life can turn such hypothesis on its head.
- Disadvantages are always the other side of the coin; the need to do risk and reward analysis lies in this simple fact.

A country-by-country critical evaluation of this largest leveraged buyout ever made in many aspects of national sovereignty would have been a wise policy, leading to avoidance of future troubles. With the exception of the very small countries, such as Slovenia, the Baltic states and the two islands (Cyprus, Malta), there are major risks embedded in the fragility of the East European economies which have the greater weight in the enlargement of the European Union. Hungary provides an example: its economy used to be rather good, but in the expectation of its entry into the European Union, hedge funds directed huge amounts of money into the country. This boosted the foreign exchange value of the forint, Hungary's currency. To keep up Hungarian exports, the government exerted pressure on the National Bank to devalue its own currency. A reluctant central bank followed up on this demand, but reduced its target for the forint/euro rate by just 2.3 per cent. What followed was a crash of the forint by 7 per cent.

To right the balance, in mid-June 2003, the National Bank of Hungary reacted with a big increase in interest rates from 6.5 per cent to 9.5 per cent. Experts felt that this might be just the beginning of a much more severe currency crisis which will hit Hungary, then travel transborder to Poland, the biggest of the 'ten', whose economy is not on a sure footing.

The good news for Hungary, so far, is that only some short-term-oriented hedge funds have sold the forint. But once the larger hedge funds start pulling out, the situation will become critical for the Hungarian currency and the economy as a whole. This is particularly true as the current account deficit reached 5 per cent of gross domestic product (GDP) in 2002, while the government budget deficit is almost at 10 per cent of GDP. Both these statistics – the 5 per cent and 10 per cent – are way out of range with EU targets (more on this later).

Many analysts believe that events such as these will postpone by several years Hungary's and other countries' entry into euroland, currently planned for 2006 to 2008. Some even think that with political union in the future, even the 'old' 15 members of the EU will be facing serious problems whose origins lie in sovereign ineffectiveness. The failure of the December 2003 EU summit in Brussels has proved these sceptics to be right.

Yet, on the positive side, some of the 'ten' have advantages compared to the European Union's current members, particularly in regard to what is prescribed by the Growth and Stability Pact. As shown in Table 4.1, inflation in

*Table 4.1*  GDP Harmonized Index of Consumer Prices (HICP), government deficits, and consolidated gross government debt in EU accession countries in 2002*

| | GDP (€ billions) | HICP (inflation in %) | Net government borrowing deficit in 2002 | Government consolidated debt as % of GDP |
|---|---|---|---|---|
| Estonia | 6.8 | 3.6 | (1.3)** | 5.8 |
| Latvia | 9.0 | 2.0 | 3.0 | 15.2 |
| Lithuania | 14.7 | 0.4 | 2.0 | 22.7 |
| Poland | 200.0 | 1.9 | 4.1 | 41.8 |
| Slovakia | 25.2 | 3.3 | 7.2 | 42.6 |
| Slovenia | 23.4 | 7.5 | 2.6 | 28.3 |
| Cyprus | 10.8 | 2.8 | 3.5 | 58.6 |
| Hungary | 69.9 | 5.2 | 9.2 | 56.3 |
| Czech Republic | 73.9 | 1.4 | 3.9 | 27.1 |
| Malta | 4.2 | – | 6.2 | 66.4 |

* ECB, 'Bond Markets and Long-term Interest Rates in EU Accession Countries', Frankfurt, October 2003.
** Estonia was the only country with net government lending in 2002.

Latvia, Lithuania, Poland and the Czech Republic is below 2 per cent, a statistic darkened by 7.5 per cent inflation in Slovenia and 5.2 per cent in Hungary. Moreover, with the exception of Malta, consolidated government debt is below 60 per cent. In fact, in Estonia it is just a one-digit number.

Overall, this compares quite favourably with comparable statistics for existing EU members, particularly in terms of government debt. Better still are the statistics on debt securities by resident industrial and financial entities in the 'ten', in per cent of gross domestic product. Among the European Union's current members, only Irish companies have a relatively low gearing taken as a percentage of GDP. This quickly rises from 67 per cent in Spain (Malta is at about that level) to 198 per cent in the Netherlands. Compare this to Estonia's 3 per cent and Latvia's 9 per cent, as well as the other statistics shown in Table 4.2, and it can be seen that many busy-bodies from Western Europe and the US are getting ready for a round of leveraging.

As these statistics demonstrate, the 'ten' have something more to offer to the EU than the abstract notion of 'enlargement'. Maybe they also have something to lose. In euroland's case, for example, a crucial issue in a list of disadvantages is *uncertainty* about how long the EU itself might last. In an interview with the *Financial Times* in the first week of June 2003, Dr Milton

*Table 4.2*  Debt securities by resident industrial entities in EU accession countries in per cent of GDP, as of end 2002*

| Accession countries | Current EU members |
|---|---|
| Estonia | 3 |
| Latvia | 9 |
| Lithuania | 16 |
| Poland | 33 |
| Slovakia | 34 |
| Slovenia | 47 |
| Cyprus | 39 |
| Hungary | 55 |
| Czech Republic | 57 |
| Malta | 68 |
| Ireland | 17 |
| Spain | 67 |
| Greece | 84 |
| UK | 90 |
| France | 107 |
| Germany | 119 |
| Italy | 131 |
| Netherlands | 198 |

* ECB, 'Bond Markets and Long-term Interest Rates in E.U. Accession Countries', FRANKFURT, OCTOBER 2003.

Friedman, the Nobel Laureate and well-known economist, made the claim that the euro 'won't last' that long.

In the background of Friedman's bold statement is that he thinks that within the next 10 to 15 years the eurozone will split apart. Though Dr Friedman was careful to offer the proviso that sometimes he has been wrong, he followed his statement with advice to the British government to stay out of the euro. The EU and the euro are not the same thing, but membership of the former is supposed to lead to monetary union. Management which does not think of the longer term condemns itself to failure. Sovereign governance, like corporate governance, is not like selling watches from the back of a van.

## Notes

1. Chorafas, *The Real-time Enterprise*.
2. Chorafas, *Management Risk*.
3. Ibid.
4. *The Economist*, 29 November 2003.
5. *The Wall Street Journal* website, Saturday April 3, 2004.
6. Chorafas, *Corporate Accountability*.
7. *International Herald Tribune*, 15/16 November 2003.
8. *The Economist*, 29 November 2003.
9. Statistics from *Sigma*, No. 3/2003, Swiss Re, Zurich.
10. *The Wall Street Journal*, April 1, 2004.
11. *International Herald Tribune*, 5 September 2003.
12. *The Times*, 23 March 2003.
13. *The Economist*, 17 January 2004.
14. Chorafas, *Economic Capital Allocation with Basle II*.
15. *The Economist*, 29 March 2003.
16. Chorafas, *Management Risk*.
17. *The Economist*, 20 December 2003.

# 5

# Management and Mismanagement in the Telecommunications Industry

## 1. Introduction

It has been a deliberate choice to focus most of the case studies in this book on the telecommunications industry, the ineffectiveness of its management, and the downfall of big and mighty companies in the years following the boom of the late 1990s. This is the theme of all six chapters in Part Two. Before going into specifics, however, an overall perspective of the telecommunications domain is offered, because this will help to explain what has gone wrong with the different telecoms and their suppliers.

The best paradigm, as a start, is the similarity between telecoms and air travel. Specifically, we can contrast the transport of physical goods, people and merchandise by airlines (see Chapter 4) to the transport of non-physical goods – voice, mail, image – by means of wired and wireless media. Readers will notice that the main object of both airlines and telecoms is that of serving routes in a global network. There are also other similarities:

- both industries have been, over the years, more or less ineffectively managed, and
- both were characterized, at least in Europe, by state-owned monopolies that have been privatized only up to a point.

Another similarity is that market liberalization has led to new and more cost-effective entrants, with incumbents jealously guarding their 'inherited' access rights. A classic example in telecoms is local-loop copper lines and other discriminatory 'rights' which have the nasty habit of working to the disadvantage of those who hold them.

But there is also a clash in business interests between airlines and telecoms, which can be briefly expressed in the motto: 'Communicate, don't commute!' This contradiction in business interests between two sectors of industry is made worse by the fact that both are characterized by massive overcapacity in many of the links they feature, with empty seats on planes and underutilized fibre-optic cables, in some cases, by 90 per cent or more.

With similarities outnumbering the differences, which, after all, are commercial-type conflicts, it is not surprising that the struggling telephone companies are now looking outside their industry for 'lessons,' and air travel seems to provide some good examples. One of them is that incumbent airlines have been undermined by the new wave of low-cost carriers, such as Southwest Airlines and JetBlue in the US, and Ryanair and easyJet in Europe (see Chapter 4). These low-cost airlines are more profitable and, in terms of social services, more valuable than the incumbents. They have low overheads and they are innovative. In addition, they offer:

- freedom from bureaucracy,
- freedom from political nepotism,
- tickets on-line and freedom from assigned seating,
- new markets, and
- a single aircraft type to cut maintenance costs.

A big question is whether the telecoms industry is ripe for similar transformation. Several experts think the answer is positive, particularly because the telcos have started to face the effect of new competitors with a disruptive power analogous to that of the low-cost airlines. There is money to be made from such disruption of chronic ineffectiveness; however, there is scope for a frontal attack on the telecom incumbents.

During the late 1990s some newcomers in the telecommunications industry tried to act as suggested in the previous paragraphs, and they failed. Their strategy, however, was limited to broadband for the long haul, which is only part of the market. Global Crossing is an example (see Chapter 9). The new game in town, however, is not bigger and bigger broadband for the long haul, but voice over internet protocol (VOIP) – a pervasive low-cost application (see section 4).

As shown in Figure 5.1, based on statistics by Total Telecom, incumbents still hold the upper ground in annual national/international minutes of use. This, however, may not last for long. In terms of international traffic, VOIP is expected to overtake time division multiplexing (TDM) before the end of this decade; some experts think it may happen as early as 2007. In this connection, the Ryanair of telecoms may well be Teleglobe/ITXC; others will follow.

## 2. Irrational exuberance in the telecoms industry

The late 1990s and first years of the twenty-first century have witnessed an irrational exuberance connected with the future of the telecommunications industry and the prospects of its companies and their stocks, as well as those

(a)

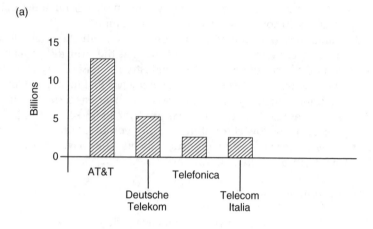

(b)

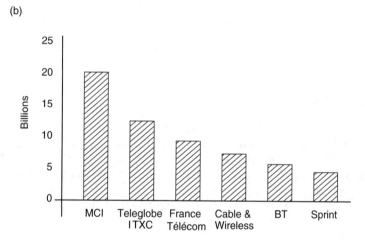

*Figure 5.1* Billions of international minutes of use by top telecommunications companies in 2003* (a) National minutes of use only (b) International national minutes of use
* Statistics from *Total Telecom Magazine*, January 2004.

of its suppliers. Spending big money was no problem, because the banks were happy to advance any kind of loan on demand. Few if any questions were asked if there was a market for the produce of these huge investments and, by consequence, if massive loans of billions of dollars could be served.

All this changed radically by late 2000, seven to nine months after the collapse of the NASDAQ. Then, as 2001 came to a close, not only telecommunications but also information technology spending generally all but disappeared, even if according to different surveys business managers still viewed computers and communications as their spending priority.

Another indicator of a downturn in technology in general, and telecommunications in particular, was that in the United States venture capital investing dropped nearly 80 per cent to $18.6 billion in the first half of 2001 compared to the same period in 2000. (Note, however, that this figure was still above the $17.5 billion raised in the first half of 1999.) Yet, not everything was negative. Telecom Italia, for example, said that it planned investments of $22 billion over the 2002–2004 timeframe, with a good deal of that money to be deployed in the mobile sector.

With hindsight, this and similar pronouncements were overoptimistic. A major recession saw to it that spending plans were on time. Instead, the market's attention was attracted by bad news connected with huge losses by telephone companies and their suppliers (see Part Two). Both sectors of the economy were experiencing a recalibration on a global scale characterized by:

- corporate losses
- debt defaults
- large layoffs
- tumbling stock prices, and
- rumoured hedge-fund catastrophes.

Not only were poor financial results the after-effect of management ineffectiveness, but also the failure to see through original investment plans as well as a rising number of scandals led to loss of market confidence. Analysts said that the fact that banks all of a sudden became prudent with the huge exposure of telecom operators was sure to delay a reasonable level of usage of the huge bandwidth being built in practically all regions of the world.

Added to the credit crunch has been market sentiment against equity in the telecommunications industry, compounded by the fact that European banking regulators expressed concerns that banks were overexposed to debt from the telecommunications industry. In many cases, the challenging questions were:

- which service provider would keep which accounts, and
- whether corporate customers were getting lower-cost deals, further wounding companies already in trouble.

As negative statements mounted, the market started to believe that companies which had invested in plenty of bandwidth were not so likely to recover their investment. A number of reasons underpinned this major change in the way the market looked at telecoms, their questionable business plans and their mountains of debt.

- Lending has been accelerating over the late 1990s, with the big operators going on the acquisition trail.
- Alternative operators have been building out new networks largely through vendor financing.
- A great deal of money was spent on third-generation (3G) mobile licences, with the whole 3G business getting out of hand (see Chapter 10).

Cooler heads suggested that high-speed data services must be re-examined from the bottom up: where is the market? the content? the market interest justifying the expense? '3G does not have the kind of value connected to the cost,' Dr Gordon Bell aptly suggested. Therefore, spending $250 billion on licences is really ridiculous. Contrary to some of the examples we have seen in Chapters 3 and 4, huge money spent on 3G was not corruption; it was plain incompetence.

The market did not fail to take notice, and the message, judging from the equity nervousness, is that, in all likelihood, practically every carrier and every telecom equipment supplier will be hurt. With bandwidth prices going down by around 95–97 per cent in 2000–2002, pan-European operators had to make a return on investment with just 3 per cent of previous income. Only a miracle or two could achieve this. Short of a quick turnaround, which proved unlikely, the whole telecom sector was sinking in a vast amount of debt, and Credit ratings across the telecommunications industry were falling accordingly (see Chapter 2).

Some experts said that for most credit institutions which underwrote the telecom industry's expansion, this was a moment of truth. Others suggested that there may be an even worse scenario – that of major telecom operators falling into the ownership of creditor banks, because the latter simply cannot afford to write off the loans, while at the same time they will find themselves obliged through government pressure to convert unpayable loans and accumulated interest into equity.

In retrospect, we know that nothing like that took place. What has happened is a different type of worst-case scenario – that of a prolonged slump among telecom operations and their suppliers. Some heads rolled, but in general the incumbent CEOs held their own, while there has been no U-turn, at least so far, in the telecom industry's fortunes.

As usual, those most badly burnt were the small shareholders, and in several cases they expressed in a colourful manner their displeasure. Apparently the annual stockholder meeting of Alcatel, held on 17 April 2003, at the Palais des Congrès, in Paris, was characterized by whistles and cries from the floor.[1]

Particularly targeted was Serge Tchuruk, Alcatel's CEO, who seems to have gratified himself with 40 per cent of options during 2002 – a dreadful year for this company and its stockholders – to the tune of 500,000 stock options. One of the stockholders asked: 'The value of my Alcatel equity dropped by 90 per cent. Why did your wages and benefits did not drop by the same proportion?'

Alcatel's CEO answered this query: 'Last year Serge Tchuruk reduced his salary by 43 per cent'. Cries came from the audience: 'Numbers, numbers!' Alcatel's CEO answered: 'My salary was €1.5 million ($1.5 million) in 2002.' Just imagine being paid €1.5 million for having brought Alcatel and its shareholders to the abyss! Is this a scandal? I leave readers to answer this query, just remarking that 2002, like 2001 before it and 2003 a year later, was a period in which lust and greed dominated the business headlines, while shareholders lost billions.

## 3.  Evolution of telecommunications services

Telecommunications entities have two major groups of clients: companies and consumers. In the early years of the twenty-first century, both continued spending on communications services, but not at the extravagant pace the carriers had projected as an upswing. To a significant extent, the telecom crisis of the first years of the new century was a direct result of irrational exuberance by the operators and the impact their deception had on their earnings.

From 1990 to 2003 household spending on telecommunications in the Group of Ten countries has increased by an impressive 65 per cent to 70 per cent, ahead of spending on health and education, which grew by almost 50 per cent. By contrast, consumers reduced drastically their expenditures on food and clothing which, over the same period, shrank by nearly 20 per cent.

Contrary to consumers, however, industrial companies and financial institutions have concentrated on ways to cut communications costs. This has partly been counterbalanced by the policy of moving back-office and other white-collar operations overseas, which means adopting telecommunications technologies that can interconnect far-away offices securely. There has also been a visible growth in mobile telephony, which siphons part of the market off from fixed-line communications.

With these trends in mind, in spite of the lows in capitalization and in investments in the first years of the twenty-first century, it is not possible to say that the telecommunications industry has really been in a depression, even if some sectors of it fared badly. Other statistics, too, are interesting. As 2003 came to a close, telecommunications industry revenues reached about $1.37 trillion for the year, for services provided by:

- a fixed plant which consists of 1.2 billion lines, with 670 million people having internet access, and
- a distributed, mobile network with an estimated 1.3 billion people – more than 20 per cent of the total population – carrying mobile phones.

Contrasting to this positive picture has been a big negative. This is the number of companies, among the telecoms and their suppliers, that have gone bankrupt, and those that found themselves just at the edge of the abyss because of their management's ineffectiveness.

Big money has gone down the drain, and overleveraging through a torrent of bank loans has affected the telecoms in a very negative way. To appreciate the level of investment plans which lost touch with reality, it should be remembered that telecommunications is an infrastructure-intensive industry:

- the cost of this infrastructure is high,
- the plant takes a long time to build, and
- telecommunications firms and their suppliers have to gamble on the level and nature of future demand.

Management ineffectiveness means that such gambles can go dreadfully wrong, as happened with internet infrastructure. When this is the case, the telecom operators are in deep trouble. The last five years have seen not only the internet broadband fiasco, but also the ridiculous licences to operate third-generation (3G) mobile networks. To get them, telecoms took on a huge pile of debts which have to be serviced.

At the same time, the expected unprecedented proportions of a data communications market were never realized. This is one of the curious errors in prognostication that telephone companies are prone, if not outright happy, to repeat time after time. Since the late 1960s when data traffic started to take off with what was, then, elementary 1.2 kilobit per second (KBPS) lines, telcos have not been hesitant to announce that 'data traffic will overtake voice traffic within the next five years'.

In the late 1970s, packet switching and the X.25 protocol (based on a layered architectural structure and the internet protocol, IP) gave rise to more irrational exuberance about data traffic and a new telecommunications world. The Japanese government decided that X.25 should become a sort of national symbol. One of the ironies of technological advances is that those who don't understand them become the standard-bearers.

True enough, some technological advances change our concepts and methods of doing things. Providing channel capacity is a case in point. Advances in technology at the end of fibre lines, essentially feeding and extracting signals into and from fibres, have helped to increase transmission capacity of each strand of fibre 100-fold (more on this in section 4).

The result of digital subscribed line (DSL) and other developments has been that total transmission capacity with existing plant has grown, but at the same time it is no less true that increase in demand could be accommodated by existing telecoms networks. The better-managed telecom operators have learned a lesson from the débâcle of overinvestments they made in the

1998 to 2000 timeframe, and they are now concentrating their spending on three areas:

- equipment to provide services and new sources of revenues, such as high-speed internet connections,
- means of simplifying their overcomplex networks, with a view to better management and cost reduction,
- software and operating support systems, allowing them to implement new income services more efficiently and quickly.

A good part of the simplification procedures revolves around new, more efficient protocols. An example is multi-protocol line switching (MPLS), which permits multiple old-fashioned network services, including voice, frame relay and asynchronous transfer method (ATM), to be carried over a single modern network based on internet protocol. MPLS is so attractive as an integrator because it has special traffic-management features giving priority to some types of communications traffic over others, thereby ensuring the smooth interleaving of different services. At a premium is the ability to collapse several formerly self-standing service networks on to a single aggregate. For this purpose, multi-service platforms are used to translate traffic to and from various formats and protocols.

The solution that recent technology offers is to make such a transition invisible to end-users. This is not only a welcome integration strategy, but also part of a policy of keeping complexity out at the edges, to allow simplification of operations and greater customer satisfaction. Knowledge-enriched software enables telecoms to offer new, more sophisticated services based on their existing infrastructure. At the same time, smart billing processes enable operators to introduce special offers and competitive tariffs.

Effectively managed telcos have also done their homework through post mortems, and have found that of the $1 trillion of money thrown at 'the problem', by themselves and their competitors, about $125 million went on unnecessary 3G licences, while $150 billion was spent building equally not needed telecom networks in America, with another $50 billion spent for the same reason in other parts of the world. These and many other unwarranted expenses have been at the origin of the telecoms boom and bust.

'History teaches that men and nations behave wisely only once they have exhausted all other alternatives,' Abba Eban once said. Within this perspective 2003 has seen two contrasting trends. The one focuses on financial restructuring and the other on market expansion. The better-managed telecoms operators are concentrating on:

- restructuring debt,
- cutting costs,

- backing out of bad investments, and
- cleaning up their balance sheets.

At the same time, they have started to rethink their policy on investments as demand increases for broadband internet access, which offers a new market for fixed-line operators once they have upgraded their existing telephone plant to broadband (see section 4). In parallel with this, mobile broadband and next-generation services call for advanced equipment at the edges of telecoms networks.

It might not seem so, but this is a major change from the emphasis placed in the late 1990s on more capacity in network lines, which is where so much unnecessary investment was made during the bubble. It needs no explaining that the new strategic choices have changed priorities in infrastructure spending. Today and for the next few years, the best prospects are for vendors at the network's edges, not at its core.

Moreover, the new business opportunities that seem to be developing require different skills than those services the telecoms have been traditionally offering. Designing, selling and maintaining sophisticated telecommunications support calls for a much higher degree of know-how than that demanded by barebone pipelines of voice and data signals.

- Leading-edge applications must be steadily developed and they must be customer-sensitive.
- The days when the telecoms wondered about the single *killer application* that would persuade users to adopt mobile data are gone; now the need is for a whole range of applications.

In conclusion, the telecom market is in a process of fairly radical change, and the company that stays put is lost. In the US the former Baby Bells – essentially the incumbents – are watching fixed-line voice revenues decline by 7 per cent a year. Some experts project that this is likely to get worse, as far as raw transmission power through old plant is concerned.

Neither have the old telcos any pricing power. By raising line-rental charges incumbents risk prompting people to give up their fixed lines altogether. To survive, new and old telecommunications companies must be able to exploit the business opportunities which are opening up. This means challenging the obvious, getting rid of obsolete concepts, abandoning old-fashioned telephones, and putting plenty of money in research and development (R&D).

## 4.  Voice over internet protocol

Gillette replaced the cut-throat razor with the safety razor in 1903. One hundred years later, the safety razor is still around, but its usage has undergone very significant evolution thanks to R&D. By contrast, telephone companies kept their twisted pair at subscriber premises (local loop fixed-line) much the same for more than 80 years. This may now be changing.

On one hand, telecoms and their suppliers have to face the uncomfortable reality that R&D budgets are attracting the scrutinizing gaze of accountants. On the other, while R&D expenditures are no longer an automatic upgrade in budgetary planning, financial strategy meetings emphasize that the industry will not get out of the telecommunications slump without new departures.

Voice over internet protocol (VOIP) is one of these new departures, and it looks quite promising – so promising that some of the incumbents have lost no time in launching the service. In the meantime, however, alternative networks, the newcomers, have taken away part of the market. Not only is VOIP growing in popularity in the US and Europe, but also – in terms of voice traffic – VOIP equipment is cheaper than traditional phone solutions. It can also be adopted easily by cable companies who want to offer voice services. Internet protocol also lowers the cost in rolling out new services such as video calls, and in instantly acquiring a second or third line.

Given these advantages, at the end of 2003 incumbents such as Verizon, BellSouth and SBC Communications launched VOIP services in 18 US cities for medium-sized enterprises. The companies said they would extend these services nationwide in 2004. Verizon adds that it is getting ready for a mass-market consumer VOIP service; and so does BellSouth.

Cable companies, too, are keen on VOIP technology. Time Warner Cable announced that by the end of 2004 it would roll out VOIP to its 10.8 million subscribers from New York. Some cable operators have done so already, and other cable companies are expected to follow. One firm charges $39.99 to customers who agree to a bundle of services. Some estimates talk of phone services accounting for $4 billion in new revenues for cable outfits.

A few days after Time Warner made its December 2003 announcement, AT&T said it would roll out IP phone service in up to 100 markets in 2004. But both big companies are really following the lead of small pioneers such as Vonage Holdings and Net2phone, which allow their customers to make unlimited local and long-haul calls over the internet. Other advantages of VOIP include:

- improved capabilities, such as instant teleconferencing with up to nine people together on a call, and
- simplicity of connection since, to get started, users plug their regular phone into a cable box equipped with phone jacks.

In the longer term, the deployment of VOIP technology will most probably change the way networks are designed and operated. Today, carriers have separate networks for regular and wireless phone service, as well as various forms of data traffic. In the future, carriers may have a single integrated IP network over which voice, data and wireless calls are sent and received.

But VOIP also raises new regulatory issues, some of them because it bypasses the local-phone network and, with it, many of the levies that phone companies use to help offset the cost of telephony for low-income customers as well as areas with sparse population. This may not be a major problem now, as VOIP accounts for fewer than 150,000 lines – a small fraction of the US total of 180 million lines; but it may become a problem in the future. On the other hand, with IP integration the aforementioned examples on subsidies may well become obsolete.

Perhaps more important in terms of pending or forthcoming regulatory action is the fact that regulators don't want to be left out of the picture. In 2003, the Federal Communications Commission held a forum to discuss regulatory issues around IP telephony. This forum preceded a more formal rulemaking process that is expected to follow soon.

To appreciate the most likely impact of VOIP solutions, it is wise to recall that the fixed-line telephone company is in the process of being transformed into a new mainstream service combined with the internet. Like packet switching for digital signals services (the IP principle) VOIP handles voice calls as packets of digital signals, allowing them to be transmitted like data internet traffic. This technology can be used in four ways:

- by telecom operators to carry calls inside their networks at lower cost;
- by other companies to save money by replacing separate voice and data networks with a single convergent solution;
- by international calling card outfits to keep prices down, and
- by consumers to profit on tariffs pioneered by startups like Vonage.

Using a small adapter box to connect an ordinary phone into broadband internet makes it possible to send and receive calls in the usual way. The fact that they are handled as packets across the internet is nearly transparent to end-users. This makes feasible not only lower costs, but also growing new services, for example:

- integration of voicemail with email,
- web-based logging and billing, and
- global portability of the same phone number, provided the phone is plugged into a broadband link.

The reference to web-based billing brings into perspective the telecoms equivalent to online ticketing in the air transport industry (see section 3). Other advantages open up new vistas in communications services. One example is Telmore, a Danish mobile operator which, like many low-cost airlines, deals primarily with customers over the web and offers a basic service. Telmore has no shops, nor does it own a network. It resells on very favourable terms channel capacity on a network owned by TDC, Denmark's incumbent.

There are no subscription fees or paper bills with Telmore. Customers check their balances via text messages. Since its launch in 2000, this newcomer has captured 7 per cent of the Danish market, with a model so potentially advantageous that TDC bought a stake in the firm in early 2003. Other new operators, too, offer low-cost calls routed over broadband internet connections. For instance, Vonage provides unlimited calling within American and Canada for $34.99 per month. It keeps costs down by outsourcing and partnering where possible, and handling billing, voicemail and other services online.

Net2phone is another start-up working along similar lines. One of the difficulties faced by low-cost alternative networks is that incumbents still own the wires that run into homes and offices. The traditional telcos are supposed to provide access to their local loops to competitors, but most find defensive legal, procedural and technical reasons for being slow about it.

Low-cost airlines got around the lack of landing slots by flying to and from secondary airfields. Mobile telephony might be an answer for low-cost telecoms, but fixed-wire connectivity is also important. The telecoms incumbents are very defensive because they find themselves unable to respond to new challenges – they are run by bureaucrats who lack vision. This puts them at disadvantage in:

- jump-starting new services,
- cutting costs, and
- moving towards convergence.

Another reason the former state monopolies are falling behind and feel threatened is that they are unable to translate laboratory discoveries into marketable products as quickly as their smaller rivals. One of these rivals, indeed the biggest VOIP upstart, is ITXC: Recall from Figure 5.1 the company's impressive market share.

To become one of the world's biggest VOIP carriers, ITXC capitalized on the fact that the number of international voice minutes carried on IP backbone networks is growing at an estimated compound rate of about 177 per cent per year. Led by Tom Evslin, its CEO, ITXC is the nearest telecom model to a low-cost airline, epitomizing cut-price phone operations and wafer-thin margins. It is giving the telecoms of the old school a lesson in integrating separate networks and in capitalizing on convergence towards IP infrastructure. Through its merger with Teleglobe International Holdings, Canada's former monopoly in international service (and a nearly bankrupt entity), the resulting company will claim No. 3 position in the international carrier business, behind market leaders MCI and AT&T.

Because there is pressure in the marketplace to converge on an IP infra-structure, Teleglobe/ITXC expects IP traffic to take more than half all international traffic by 2007. With plans for next-generation services in voice, data, IP and mobile communications, the company hopes to give the current leaders a run for their money.

Telecoms incumbents might avoid the fate of their airline counterparts if they learn how to move faster in development of services, in market appeal and in becoming low cost. The start-ups are not the only threat to them. AT&T's launch of VOIP services is a way of avoiding the access fees that it has to pay Baby Bell, the local network operators in the US, to route calls over their lines.

For AT&T such fees represent an estimated $10 billion per year. No such fees apply to VOIP calls, which are unregulated. The hinge is that VOIP service can only be offered to households with broadband. But with over 22 million American households already connected, there is a big poten-tial market. Today, North America is the world's largest market for broad-band, accounting for 45 per cent of revenues. But Europe is expected to have the highest growth in the coming years, probably at 30 per cent per year.

This potential market may become particularly impressive as broadband access gives not only VOIP telephone service, but also videoconferencing, movies on demand, and more. It also brings up the question of what happens to *the last mile* of telephone cable that everyone still counts on. Despite progress with fast modems and the rolling out of asymmetrical digital subscriber line (ADSL, see section 5) technology, we are still stuck with a plain old telephone service (POTS) wiring. This is not the ultimate solution, but technological developments may give it new life.

On the other hand, in the years to come, home area networks may see to it that the 'last mile' becomes an intermediate link rather than the end of the line. More and more devices and applications within the home will require high-speed networking. While the next-generation internet (NGI) will carry high-speed data to and from home and office, devices within the home will continue the high-speed connection with wired or wireless local area connectivity.

In this connection, a wireless gigabytes local area network (WiGLAN) project seeks to develop a wireless LAN that will transmit data with a 5.8 GHz carrier frequency at rates approaching 1 gigabit per second (GBPS). Data are transmitted by a network controller, which also measures the signal-to-noise ratio (SNR) to optimize the rate being transmitted.

Finally, to connect to network(s), various devices and gadgets within a home will require adaptation. Today the available devices typically work at different data rates, since they have been designed to operate as stand-alone. Networking changes all that, bringing in requirements for real-time transmission and quality of service.[2]

There are also some contradictory requirements which need to be addressed. Interactive video demands high data rates for real-time transmission, while voice may necessitate low power transmission because of issues connected to battery life. Moreover, since many home devices will be portable, they will need low power design approaches at the circuit, chip architecture and system levels – which brings our discussion back to the importance of investments in R&D.

## 5. Challenges with digital subscriber line

Businesses and homes, in short, the whole world of telecommunications users, have been wired and rewired many times for electrical and electronic applications. The first wiring occurred in the mid- to late nineteenth century for the telegraph. Morse invented it in 1843, but it took a while to extend a network of wires across the different countries.

The telephone of Alexander Graham Bell came along in 1876, and within a few years the western countries were wired once again for phones. Actually, both the telegraph and telephone wiring pre-date electrical wiring; Edison produced the light bulb in 1880, and the new invention brought along electrical power wiring on a grand scale.

It is therefore only reasonable to try to get extra mileage out of the existing wire networks, for instance, by turning the telephone wires into fast broadband, using digital subscriber line (DSL) technology.[3] For telcos, this provides a valuable new revenue source. In most western countries, DSL is in process of becoming the dominant means of providing broadband access to homes as well as to small and medium enterprises (SME).

Over the last few years, interest in DSL has grown massively in the business market. Small and medium enterprises are ditching ISDN[4] and dial-up, looking for more cost-effective ways of wiring branch offices and remote work sites. But more attention to a new process should also breed increased scrutiny. It is, therefore, only reasonable that those buying into DSL are demanding:

- more functionality over those connections, and
- better quality of service.

Today incumbents provide an estimated 70 per cent of the lines for high-speed internet connections in Europe, only 5 per cent assured by local loop unbundling, says a report from the European Competitive Telecommunications Association (ECTA). This report predicts that the UK, France, Germany, Italy, Spain and the Netherlands will have broadband penetration of 51 per cent by 2007.[5]

To face up to the new realities, telecoms have to make some tough choices. For instance, if they are trying to kill two birds with one well-placed stone, offering DSL and protecting other parts of their business – such as ISDN, which costs much more than DSL – then they will spread their management attention and investments thinly, while at the same time undercutting their own products.

A sign that this poor business practice may be changing is the fact that the old telecoms in Europe are starting to turn the promise of television over DSL into services. This is a strategic move, because it gives them the chance to surge ahead of cable operators who are also after VOIP in their efforts to persuade consumers to switch from their familiar service providers.

Take France as an example. In 2003 television offerings through DSL services were announced. In December 2003, Free became the first French service provider to launch a television over DSL with around 100 free channels. The incumbent France Telecom said it would offer TV over DSL in the Lyon region, and LDCom is also promoting a TV over DSL service.

Experts think that television and video over DSL will most probably make headway in countries where consumers are used to receiving digital television through a set-top box. The UK, France and (to a lesser extent) Germany and Spain are examples. By contrast, in Switzerland, Belgium and the Netherlands, where there are fairly dense cable networks providing low-cost access, consumers are not going to pay more for DSL connection.

Moreover, as far as competition is concerned, cable operators have an advantage over telcos in terms of putting together voice, television and internet. They already have agreements with content providers, which is one of the barriers telephone companies have to overcome. On the other hand, it is no less true that the European cable market faces difficulties. Despite the restructuring of NTL in the UK and UPC in the Netherlands, its financial troubles are not over and in many countries the cable market remains splintered.

The challenges cable operators are facing may make the telcos feel more comfortable with their offer of DSL services, but the die is not yet cast. Like ISDN, DSL addresses itself mainly to the local loop level, and it faces headwinds in bringing together two opposing forces:

- The demand by business, industry and banking for high bandwidth and reliable but low-cost solutions, and
- the telcos' own internal conflict, which is fuelled by economics: a low-cost DSL risks killing the cash cow of the current subscriber base.

Associated with the challenge posed to the old telcos by these two points is the issue of local loop unbundling. Since the late 1990s, in most of the Group of Ten countries alternative networks (the telcos' competitors) have been asking incumbent telecoms to share their fixed lines. This process is known as *local loop unbundling* (LLU). The incumbents camplain that this is threatening their core business.

Most regulators of the telecommunications industry do not seem to buy this argument. On the contrary, they believe that by allowing competitors to lease or resell lines, they can foster competition in both telephony and broadband access. But the former state monopolies have political patronage supporting their objections to unbundling. One such objection is that while it may promote competition, it inhibits investments that telecoms might otherwise have made. Essentially this argument says that while unbundling boosts competition in the short term, it makes it less likely that a competing infrastructure will be built, renewing the network. This argument rests on weak foundations. Another objection is that unbundling requires close and continuing regulatory oversight of wholesale prices and other issues. Part of this argument is that though it is often described as deregulation, unbundling may end up by meaning more regulation. This is a tricky issue. What is quite certain is that LLU will lead to legal challenges as incumbents try to slow down the unbundling process. For instance, disagreements over America's unbundling regime, known as UNE-P, have twice gone all the way to the Supreme Court. Incumbents in other countries have also resorted to the courts to oppose unbundling.[6]

An alternative to unbundling is technically known as structural separation. Since each incumbent telco owns its network, one strategy is to split this incumbent into two firms, the so-called *LoopCo*, owning the local loop, and *NetCo*, offering the services – from raw capacity to sophisticated solutions. This is a strategy that has been followed with railways, but the results have not been so good that repetition is warranted.

Because the telecoms industry is changing so radically, some of the clearer-eyed telco executives are seeing the problems that lie ahead. Therefore they are commissioning task forces to predict changes in the market that will ultimately damage the phone company. But in general the top brass still cannot bring themselves to make the necessary adjustments.

The main reason for the telcos' resistance to change is partly complacency partly brought about by big egos. A superiority complex leads unavoidably to dubious decisions. ISDN has flopped for mispricing and technical reasons, but who can tell whether DSL will be a success? Technically speaking, cable operators have an advantage when it comes to offering VOIP because their networks:

- have low latency,
- feature a high downstream capacity, and
- support quality of service for upstream traffic.

Moreover, for cable operators voice offers significant revenues. Take Spain's ONO as an example; it offers free voice calls between its customers, claiming that its pricing strategy encourages customers to take at least two products. ONO's broadband access, TV and telephony costs €60 per month, whereas broadband access alone costs €39. Of ONO's 600,000 customers, 18 per cent take three services and 69 per cent take two or more.[7]

The case I have just outlined presents important competitive advantages working against the incumbent, Telefonica, and against DSL. Moreover, the pitiful strategy of stonewalling by some incumbent operators works against a service orientation of the old telcos. By contrast, newcomers:

- analyse their future customers' needs,
- design and implement new systems,
- write custom software, and
- manage the client's relationship in an effective way.

This kind of system service has traditionally been offered by large information technology firms such as IBM and Unisys, or by consultancies such as EDS and Accenture. But as the overlap between computers and telecommunications grows, some telecoms are getting in on the act too, in an attempt to increase their margins and strengthen customer loyalty. They hope for an IBM-type turnaround, but defensive policies mean that this is far from being a 'sure thing'.

## 6.   Wi-Fi wireless technology and its limits

Discussion of another telecommunications subject will help the reader appreciate some of the issues behind the case studies in Part Two. This is *Wi-Fi*, or wireless technology, technically known as 802.11B. It provides mobile workers with high-speed access to the internet and, through the internet, to corporate networks and computers. Wi-Fi is a technology that is still unproven, and which is sure to have limits.

To start with the good news, with mobile connectivity becoming increasingly pervasive, wireless data might develop into an attractive opportunity in the communications market. Vendors are developing Wi-Fi chips and modules to be incorporated into products. All major PC manufacturers seem interested in this subject – particularly low-cost, high-performance 802.11B approaches, as well as a roadmap to deliver multi-mode, high-speed solutions as demand gains momentum.

A further application to note is R&D combining 802.11 and subscriber identification module (SIM), to enable user authentication and billing for wireless access services. The aim is to make laptop wireless access as commonplace as cellphone calls, but we are not there yet.

One of the applications under study is installing Wi-Fi base stations to allow engineers at different sites to work more productively, because they can review and revise complex plans on their laptops without having to return to the office. In the background of this and similar cases is the wish to improve site communications, gambling on the probability that freedom from wired internet connections will redefine:

- how many people can effectively work together, and
- how they use computers and other electronic equipment in the office and in the home.

Connecting a computer to the network involves plugging in a small wireless adapter. Wi-Fi, allows people to use a laptop anywhere in the house, office or campus for communication. But it does not amount to a revolution. There are currently an estimated 30 million Wi-Fi enabled laptops, but few users carry their laptops around all day, and there are also significant infrastructural prerequisites to be met.

Some companies build Wi-Fi hotspots in public places such as airports, conference centres and coffee shops to cater for laptop travellers. Establishing Wi-Fi networks involves setting up and connecting a small base station to the broadband internet. Within 50 metres, Wi-Fi-enabled laptops can then connect to the internet wirelessly, via the base station.

IP wireless base stations are mounted on existing mobile-phone masts. These cover the same sort of area as a standard mobile-phone base station, or about 10,000 times larger than a Wi-Fi hotspot. Perhaps the greater importance of Wi-Fi comes from the fact that it provides a preview of potential wide-area wireless-broadband technology, seamlessly working beyond small hotspots.

Under present conditions, within the coverage area, Wi-Fi competes with incumbent operators offering voice and broadband over copper telephone networks. Users generally suggest that this is an interesting service, provided several prerequisites are met – both technical and commercial, the latter being intimately related to what the market demands.

This is precisely where some of the limits lie. Critics say that while Wi-Fi can be a useful solution for specific networking requirements, one should not forget that there are concerns about its wider employment, particularly in public hotspots. Therefore it is important for service providers and their customers to fully understand and appreciate the limitations of this technology. For example, most Wi-Fi networks operate in a spectrum that in urban areas is already congested. Like any other communications channel, Wi-Fi networks have to compete for bandwidth, making it difficult if not impossible to guarantee that a connection will work consistently. In rural areas, congestion is not a major issue, but wider connectivity is a problem because broadband is not always delivered over fibre or cable. There are also security issues of which users should be aware. Users frequently fail to activate encryption algorithms, thereby allowing anyone nearby to scan the network, read messages, upload illegal material and so on. Moreover, even when encryption is enabled, Wi-Fi has a weak algorithm and therefore additional security measures may be needed.

In addition, Wi-Fi is a developing and still imperfect technology, which must compete with other solutions and interface with wider networks. A case in point is third-generation wireless services (3G, see Chapter 10). Contrary to 3G, Wi-Fi is cheap, fast and, as we have seen, it works with base stations popping up in homes, offices and airports. However, wireless operators all over the world struggle with the transition to third-generation cellular networks, and it is not certain that they will divide their attention to heed the needs of another wireless technology, like Wi-Fi, which uses unlicensed radio spectrum to share an internet connection.

Moreover, the precedent provided by other interim solutions is not positive. Wireless access protocol (WAP), a rather crude form of web browsing designed for mobile phones, was introduced by operators in 1999. Originally, WAP was described as a mobile version of the internet, when in fact it was not so. WAP has been a failure for several reasons. One of them is the time it took to establish a connection to a WAP phone and download any of the limited content available. Also, the tiny monochrome screens of mobile handsets further heightened users' frustration with WAP services.

Yet, even if WAP was a deception, the telecoms went on promoting it, pushing a technology rather than creating useful services by employing it. Experts who remember this chaos are not impressed by general statements such as 'Wi-Fi capability is fast becoming a standard feature of laptops' or 'Entrepreneurs are building large Wi-Fi networks.' They note that so far such efforts have fallen into two camps, and neither has yet shown convincing solutions:

- top-down networks, built in the traditional way by network operators, who then charge fees for access, and
- bottom-up networks, built by loose federations of enthusiasts who offer free access to all.

Both approaches have problems, though some of the start-ups promise to solve them. To do so, they act as aggregators with log-on and authentication software providing a wrapper around existing networks. In this way users might access all of them by means of a single account. Other start-ups aim to increase the number of Wi-Fi hotspots by providing a commercial incentive for people to set up new ones. All these are interesting efforts, but it is still too early to say whether they will succeed, though with 3G in the doldrums they might have a chance.

## 7.   Liquidity, indebtedness and external rating risk

The objective of this section is to complement the technical discussion on new telecoms products and services with a financial viewpoint which will make the case studies in Part Two more understandable. At the same time, the emphasis on liquidity, and the lack of it, as well as on the role of independent rating agencies, brings back into the picture the theme of external rating risk which was introduced in Chapter 2.

Following the liquidity crisis which ravaged internet companies and telecoms, seeing to it that even the biggest carriers fell from grace, credit ratings agencies suggested that they would give more frequent commentary on *liquidity risk factors*. This is indeed a way to keep misinformation at bay. Some telcos might tell investors that they are doing a lot of trade, but their liquidity might suggest they don't have the cash flow to face the obligations resulting from their indebtedness.

Like 'democracy' and 'freedom', however, 'liquidity' is a word with several meanings. There are four definitions of liquidity of which the reader should be aware. One is the amount of money in the market, essentially the money supply, which is the product of the monetary base and the velocity of circulation of money. Monetary base and velocity are monetary policy targets established by the reserve bank.

The second definition of liquidity, as Dr Henry Kaufman aptly suggests, can best be described as the 'feel of the market'. This has a great deal to do with market psychology. The third definition of liquidity relates to the cost of money expressed through interest rates. Basically, interest rates are the pricing of the money supply needed by companies to accomplish the missions described by their charter – or, sometimes, by their fancy.

As with all commodities, when the cost of money is low, it is more sought after and there is greater liquidity in the market. The correlation between mortgage rates and the health of the real-estate industry is an example. This leads to the fourth definition of liquidity most pertinent to this discussion: the cash flow and liquid instruments, or assets, timed to correspond to assumed obligations.

Liquid assets include cash, balances due from banks and other counter-parties, as well as short-term investments. The latter are assets that mature within the next three months and should be presented in the balance sheet at fair value – not through creative accounting gimmicks. These short-term assets are precisely what the telcos examined in this and in the following chapters have been missing.

Statistics on a company's liquidity plus information on used capacity versus unused but available capacity are vital in appreciating an entity's (even an industry's) ability to survive, as well as its quality of governance and the effectiveness of its management. Taking submarine cables as an example, Figure 5.2 demonstrates that since the sharp take-off in 1996 it has become clear that:

- unused capacity had become a high multiple of used capacity, and
- it made no sense to put money into building more channel capacity until demand could catch up with supply.

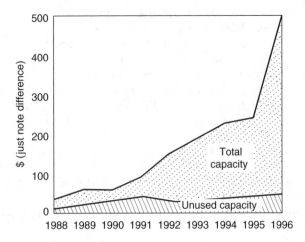

*Figure 5.2*   Submarine fibre-optic cables and their utilization

Given these facts, an effective management would have lost no time in taking corrective action, rethinking capacity planning in appreciation of the fact that such a great imbalance would lead to a financial earthquake – which it did. Yet, in spite of that evidence, not only telcos kept on investing in 'more channel capacity', but also leading international banks continued lending huge amounts of money to new and old telcos. They wanted to get a piece of the action in future telecoms independently of their:

- illiquidity,
- lack of profitability, and
- lack of creditworthiness.

The prevailing hypothesis at that time was that telecoms were surely inheriting the earth. On the contrary, all available evidence indicated that the communications industry was losing the battle to manage its own resources, including its existing networks, as new technologies were introduced. It did not take long for a tsunami of negative watches and credit downgrades to hit the shore. Rating agencies questioned the creditworthiness of overextended, underfunded carriers who were encumbered by debt and had no sign of income and liquidity justifying further funding.

The liquidity crisis of 2004 led to the unravelling of Vivendi (see Chapter 7). On the heels of the winter of telecoms funding, independent credit rating agencies downgraded several telecoms companies. Credit rating risk (see Chapter 2) helped to redefine what interest rates a company would have to pay its long-term lenders and its bondholders.

Effective management would have appreciated that the sensitivity of ratings to the pace of debt increase reduction has crystallized the need for management teams to rebalance priorities. On the contrary, however, some telcos, such as British Telecom, were reported to be considering allowing their credit rating to fall as they struggled to find ways to deal with their debt mountain – probably forgetting that a company whose credit rating is downgraded finds itself facing an increased interest bill.

The right rebalancing act would have involved many tough choices on the part of a company's board and CEO. The salient question is: Which is the preferable option? Mounting what would effectively be a firesale of 'this' or 'that' asset or division or paying more for outstanding debt? The choice is not easy, as both shareholders and bondholders are affected by it, but that's why senior management is paid so much money: to find effective solutions.

There is indeed a fine balance between stakeholder interests and strong credit ratings. Therefore management has to walk between the constraints of reducing debt and concerns that it might give away shareholder value. Choices become intriguing because the telecom industry has operators with very high leverage that only a few years ago did not carry anything like the debt profiles they do today.

* The financial risk profiles of some operators are much weaker than their business risk profiles would suggest.
* Bringing that discrepancy back into alignment is a challenge few telcos are equipped to face.

In the absence of a book of rules, even in some cases of precedent, the senior management of many telecommunications entities has found out the hard way that, though necessary, special care over credit ratings detracts from gaining control of the underlying business. Therefore some of these companies timidly suggested that investors need to be more concerned with business fundamentals than credit ratings – a statement which is less than half true.

Some analysts have expressed the opinion that if 'more debt' has been the way telcos funded their businesses for the past eight years, without the mounting debt funding their business plans would have fallen into distress long ago. Other analysts, however, were of exactly the opposite mind, saying that precisely because it is a main way of funding, debt should not be overused, because eventually comes the downgrade, which can be a killer.

The latter opinion is well supported by the fact that debt levels have adversely affected the telecom industry's weakest players – and this in the most negative way, which many experts see as unprecedented. Another view is that credit analysts have always been more sceptical about the telecoms sector than equity analysts. Credit analysts and ratings agencies are more focused on the indebtedness of the telecoms sector than shareholders, but when the equity market becomes sceptical, the result is that credit and equity analysts are on the same wavelength.

One opinion I heard on Wall Street is that a crucial factor in bringing credit and equity analysts together has been the fact that some of the telecom companies also came under scrutiny for their fraudulent accounting practices. The cases brought to public attention included not just Enron Broadband Services, Global Crossing and WorldCom, three of the most spectacular 2001–2002 failures, but also KPN of the Netherlands, a former PTT.

In KPN's case a shareholder group says that it has shown an inflated balance sheet with at least €10 billion ($10 billion) in doubt. Another similar example is Optus in Australia. Singapore Telecom, its parent company, wanted some costs previously hidden on the balance sheet moved on to the trading account, where they really belonged.[8]

In light of these facts, both equity analysts and credit analysts agreed that the near future for telecoms is not bright, even for those entities which have not been cooking the books. The hopes of telecommunications companies, and their suppliers, based on double-digit revenue growth, have not been met – and practically nobody now believes they will be met in the near future (more on this in Chapter 6).

Beyond all that, WorldCom's woes have created an invisible hand that tends to pull other entities into the abyss. And the telecommunications industry's troubles have rippled far beyond that industry's sector. Banks, insurance companies, pension funds and hedge funds have bought huge amounts of telecoms bonds, gambling that this business is healthy even if its stock continued to fall. But weaknesses in equities did not go away, and accounting scandals hammered the telecoms bonds.

Scams brought it into perspective that credit risk management did not pay due attention to the ripple effect and its aftermath. This should be done through stress testing.[9] Historical scenarios can help. For instance, in 2002, in the wake of Adelphia Communciations' woes, cable stocks tumbled, with highly leveraged companies such as Charter Communications and Cablevision down by roughly 70 per cent.

In conclusion, by 2002, widespread mismanagement turned the telecoms industry into one that had lost control of its future. The hope is that in the not too distant future this will change – but no industry, no company, and no investor can live on hopes alone. This is one of the lessons to be learned from the case studies in Part Two.

## Notes

1. *Le Canard Enchaîné*, 23 April 2003.
2. Chorafas, *The Real-time Enterprise*.

3. The number of DSL lines worldwide grew by 78 per cent in 2003, to 63.8 million. Revenue from DSL shipments increased by 59 per cent to $5 billion from 2002. China has been the leading broadband market by number of lines, ending 2003 with 10.9 million lines, compared with only 2 million at end of 2002 (*Total Telekom Magazine*, April 2004).

4. Originally, ISDN stood for integrated services digital network. From the start, because of cost levels implied by telcos, it was nicknamed 'I See Dollars Now' (see D. N. Chorafas, *Local Area Network Reference*, New York: McGraw-Hill, 1989).

5. *Total Telecom Magazine*, December 2003.

6. *The Economist*, 11 October 2003.

7. *Total Telecom Magazine*, January 2004.

8. *CommunicationsWeekInternational*, 18 February 2002.

9. D. N. Chorafas, *Stress Testing. Risk Management Strategies for Extreme Events*, London: Euromoney, 2003.

# Part Two

# Case Studies in Management Effectiveness in the Telecommunications Industry

# 6
# Big Telecommunications Companies Brought Themselves to the Edge of the Abyss

## 1. Introduction

British Telecom's (BT's) Sir Peter Bonfield, Deutsche Telekom's Ron Sommer and France Télécom's Michel Bon have all lost their jobs because of mismanagement, including their inability to decide about what are and are not a telephone company's (telco's) core assets and primary business. Another major decision issue on which all three CEOs, and their companies, have failed is how they should go after *their* chosen telecommunications services and market, rather than spreading themselves and their entities too thinly in too many fields – at home and abroad.

It is not just the equity market's downturn which saw to it that in 2000/2001 European telecoms shares suffered a disaster, though this has been a factor to which the telecoms themselves contributed a great deal. The real reason runs deeper. The big telecommunications companies have spent huge amounts of money on:

- Unwise acquisitions at exorbitant prices, and
- third-generation (3G) wireless licences bought from various European governments.[1]

As their excuse for spending big money without control left, right and centre, the big telcos said 'they felt they needed' both the acquisitions and the 3G licences, the latter, among other things, to enable them to offer internet access from mobile phones. The sums the telcos have spent on 3G licences may well turn out to be the largest 'investment' in the shortest time by any sector in history – as well as the poorest large investment ever made. Indeed, this is a monument to:

- miserable corporate governance, and
- management ineffectiveness.

The final tally is yet to come, but the big telephone companies, and most of their smaller brethren, like Finland's Sonera, already know that whatever they spend on the licences, they will have to shell out once again on building the 3G infrastructure (see Chapter 10). As we shall see in this and the following chapters, total spending might add up to over $600 billion.

It is not at all surprising that with the ill-conceived acquisitions and the unnecessary 3G licences the telecommunications companies' debts have sky-rocketed in just two years. Their leverage shot up tremendously. Figure 6.1 shows the telcos' debt in January 2001. Less than a couple of years down the line, at the end of 2002, both France Télécom and Deutsche Telekom had managed to catch up with AT&T, the debt-laden leader at the $65 billion to $71 billion level (more on this later).

It is superfluous to add that when debt reaches that height, it is devastating. For example, at the end of 1998 Britain's BT had debts of $1.5 billion. Two years later, those debts have risen to $30 billion, sending its debt-to-equity ratio soaring to 190 per cent. As many other incumbent telecoms also run themselves down, investors finally appreciated that nobody – on the telcos' side – really knows whether consumers will want to use their mobile phones to surf the internet, or, if they do, whether competition will allow any telco to make money.

What hit the big telephone companies on the head, in the first years of the twenty-first century, was more than a cyclical downturn. What the telecoms have experienced, and their top management failed to perceive, is a full-blown industrial depression because of overleveraging and overexpansion in practically all sectors of the western economies. In the US market alone,

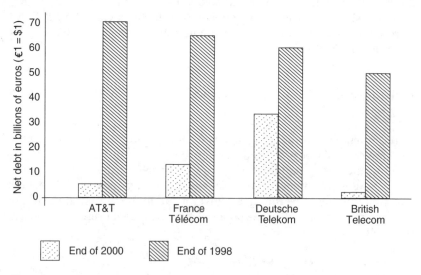

*Figure 6.1*   What a difference two years make in telco superleverage!

the downturn wiped out half a million jobs and trillions in market value, while turmoil in the global telecoms industry is still on going.

The seven biggest telecoms companies outside the United States and Japan – Deutsche Telekom, France Télécom, British Telecom, Vodafone, Telecom Italia, Telefonica (of Spain) and the Dutch KPN – have between them an unprecedented short-term debt which they can hardly service. At €71 billion, France Télécom's indebtedness exceeded that of the whole state of Portugal. The telecoms sector worldwide has been crushed under its debt.

Since misfortunes never come singly, to the telephone companies' sorrow consumers have refused to collaborate in being ripped off for pie in the sky. Industrial, financial and commercial companies took the same attitude. After the lunacy, cost control has gained the upper ground. By the start of 2004 something became evident that is embarrassing to the big telcos: the key online service is still *email*. For the rest of the new services the dust has not yet settled. So why can't the telephone industry get it right?

## 2.  Ineffective managers spend other people's money

The common phrase among asset managers in the late 1990s when it seemed as if there were no limit on the market's rise was *shareholder value*. The events which followed the market crash of 2000 have demonstrated that, rather than being a leitmotiv, shareholder value was just an excuse for unwise investments and general mismanagement.

As has been proven post mortem, assets managers and CEOs of many companies had only one thing on their mind: higher and higher leverage to get more and more in commissions based on paper profits. Finally, it is the shareholders and bondholders who paid the bill through bankruptcies, near-bankruptcies and unprecedented downgrading of the companies in which they had invested.

Having spent their investors' money in the most ineffective way, telcos, including the big ones, found themselves in the middle of this near-bankruptcy and downsizing spiral. To get their huge debts under control, they had to sell assets at firesale prices. Even so, they did not raise as much money as they had hoped, if only because the operations they wanted to unload had become much less valuable than they were when they bought them.

Since the sale of assets alone, at rock-bottom prices, proved to be no solution, telecoms have had to turn to bond investors and banks, only to find that those potential saviours had become much more reluctant. When bond investors and credit institutions refused their support, the only way left has been bankruptcy – or the classical *Deus ex machina*: the taxpayer.

A good example is Elektrim, the Polish telecoms and utilities operator. It filed for bankruptcy in September 2002, in the largest collapse of a listed firm in Poland's history. Just two years earlier, in 2000, the company had a market capitalization of $1.5 billion, but aggressive expansion plans, particularly in the telecoms market, depressed its market value to just $24 million – way below its liabilities.

Another of the dramatic cases among the telecom operators was the Dutch KPN. In 1999, KPN was a high-flier, the darling of investors. But in early 2001 its stock fell more than 60 per cent in just four days. If the Dutch taxpayer had not come to the rescue, KPN would have defaulted on its €23 billion ($23 billion) debt.

As money gone down the drain through bankruptcies and near-bankruptcies demonstrates, the telecoms bust is ten times bigger than the better-known dot-com crash. Experts say that the rise and fall of telecoms might well qualify as the largest bubble in history, taking this dubious honour away from the Mississippi Bubble and the South Seas Bubble – both of the early eighteenth century.

The shareholders of the big European telcos were not the only investors who got burned. Very unpleasant surprises awaited their bondholders, since their debt became little better than junk. For their part, banks were up to their necks in telecom debt, and did not want to take on more, if only because regulators have been urging them to reduce their exposures.

Having fallen from the height of glory to the abyss of a financial depression, because of greatly defective corporate governance, telecom companies had to pay much more for urgently needed cash. They also had to offer extra inducements, such as guarantees that If they are downgraded, then they will increase the coupon on their bonds.

It is not just the European telecoms that were in trouble. In America in January 2002, Global Crossing filed for bankruptcy protection (see Chapter 9), then in mid-2002 WorldCom went bust (see Chapter 8), while Sprint and AT&T, the other two large US long-distance carriers, have been downgraded.

Some experts said that the fault behind these bankruptcies and near-bankruptcies laid in deregulation, which has led to a huge increase in competition. For instance, by 2000 there were 500 long-distance carriers in the US alone, and their profits were falling fast. To make up for this shortfall, they have tried to get into other areas, such as mobile phones, and obtain economies of scale through mergers.

Neither has been the miracle solution. First, and foremost, competition kills only when top management is ineffective. Then, as historical evidence has proved time and again, mergers and acquisitions (M&As) bring along with them a mare's nest of cultural, product line and financial problems. In business and industry, M&As are by no means the 'miracle solution'.

Moreover, M&A activity is typically accompanied by rising debt, whose impact grows while, because of market downturn, some of the entities resulting from mergers have a very rough going. This affects M&A activity. The pattern from first quarter 2001 to first quarter 2003 is shown in Figure 6.2. The reason for the surge in M&A at the end of this histogram is Olivetti's

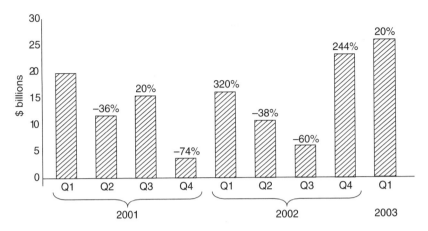

*Figure 6.2* Volatility in M&A activity of European telecoms, 2001–2003

$15.7 billion acquisition of the remaining 45 per cent stake in Telecom Italia and Vodafone's $6.8 billion acquisition of equity stake in Cegetel.

Both deals have added to the telecoms' indebtedness, while the market for mobile telephony and mobile data did not respond in the big way the telecoms had projected. As noted earlier, email is still the preferred mode of communication for most businesses and consumers. With the market for mobile telephony and the data market refusing to take off in a big way, the telcos are right to ask: what company can afford to rest on its laurels and continue to work the same way it did 30 years ago? The answer to this query is, to a large extent, like the chicken and the egg puzzle: where are the tangible benefits from 3G broadband mobile which would justify the users' costs and leave a decent profit?

On the basic technical side, there is little doubt that telecommunications is a vital component of the global business engine, and will continue to play an expanding role. But one-sided approaches don't pay off. A telco's combination of assets in the local, long-distance and wireless domains provides an opportunity to develop integrated telecommunications products and services. The challenge is not in technology. It is in:

- the financial overleverage of the telcos,
- the high cost of customer acquisition in new services, and
- the blurred picture of cost-effectiveness in this new services arena.

For these three reasons, financial markets are worried that there is no revival in sight for telecommunications companies' profits, as traditional business lines' profits are falling rapidly, while profits from new lines are rising slowly, if at all. Neither should the customer acquisition costs be discounted.

The great euphoria of the late 1990s saw many telephone companies acquiring customers at negative margins, with the intention of improving their cost structures over time. This supposedly one-off cost per customer varied depending on factors such as:

- the telco's business model,
- its sales channels,
- its mix of services,
- whether the telco had just started its customer acquisition campaign, and
- whether the customer had direct access to the company's own network or was acquired off-net.

Many telcos made things worse for themselves by waiving or heavily discounting charges for customer premise equipment, and/or by forgetting to take into account customer profitability. In Europe, some telecoms used as a sales tactic the offering of domestic services free of charge to win pan-European contracts. This has been instrumental in creating an unquantifiable loss of cash flow, at a time when overleverage required a very healthy and steady cash flow.

Moreover, the lack of cost control has been proverbial, even if in the latest period it has been replaced by a new priority – that of reducing cash-burn. All these are manifestations of mismanagement on the telcos' side. They are compounded by the lack of metrics that provide management with an analysis of results, allowing them to take decisions in a factual and documented manner – which is one of the pillars of effectiveness.

## 3.  The bubble of European telcos, credit exposure and write-downs

Enron's bankruptcy and problems connected to its financial reporting have drawn attention to accounting issues, and highlighted the financial risk from off-balance-sheet obligations. This brought under even more scrutiny the fact that as of 1 January 2002, nearly a month after Enron's downfall, Europe's carriers owed creditors a staggering $285 billion and this amount was growing by leaps and bounds.

The bulk of this $285 billion, spent so unwisely, came from loans. Nobody among the European telecoms' top brass seems to have really understood that these loans had to be repaid with interest, while the companies' cash flow was wanting. Top management is accountable for this plight. To cover the facts, different accounting gimmicks have been invented, and up to a point they were able to hide the massive debt.

For instance, telecommunications companies have been writing down billions in assets. This, however, does *not* reduce debt. Taking sharp cuts in the value of acquisitions and 3G licences only helps an entity to do a sort of artificial clean-up of its balance sheet.

- Write-downs do nothing to reduce loan payments.
- Responsible accounting practices dictate that assets be carried on the books at a reasonable value.

Contrary to what the different telcos and telecom equipment manufacturers hoped, write-downs made borrowing more expensive by slashing the available asset base against which companies can collateralize their loans. Management took no measure worth talking about to make the telecoms financial picture less bleak.

- Creative accounting is concerned with only the king on the cake.
- But in business what really matters is the substance, and the substance remained rotten.

Theoretically, large write-downs are a sign of financial prudence. By reducing annual amortization and depreciation charges companies say that they are cleaning up their books. Practically, highly leveraged enterprises find write-downs the easy (but fake) way to deleverage, in an attempt to return towards net profits, which most often prove elusive.

For example, through a combination of asset sales and spin-offs, British Telecom managed to cut its debt in half. But if this was dexterity, then the dexterity of other telcos did not get them that far. France Télécom and Deutsche Telekom rapidly exhausted the easy moves. They continued selling off a few assets here and there, but mostly they have been waiting for equity markets to develop a renewed appetite for stock issues, since unhappy investors have pushed share prices down for both companies more than 80 per cent from their peaks.

KPNQwest, a leading pan-European data network services provider, which was a joint venture of KPN, the Dutch telco, and Qwest, crashed in June 2002. This first alarmed the markets, because other telecom companies were also heading out of control. On all the evidence, very little could be salvaged from KPNQwest assets, and the crash raised the question whether internet protocol, as a technology, can give returns to major telecom carriers who smashed the pricing of data circuits, with the result that voice may be subsidizing the cost of data transmission (see Chapter 5 on VOIP).

Mispricing of services to gain market share, and the bad news that followed on return on investment (ROI), may well have been in the background of KPN's decision to write down the value of its assets in KPNQwest after it booked charges of €477 million relating to its 40 per cent stake in the company. This came after KPN announced a goodwill impairment charge of

€12.4 billion on the value of its holding in German mobile phone company E-Plus, in March 2002.

Very few of the companies that practise creative accounting and other financial alchemy realize what it takes to rebuild their balance sheet, let alone to regain customer confidence. Recapitalization is no easy business in a depressed market, particularly when so many companies try to issue new stock and investors continue to fear that they will be taken for a ride.

Experts say that even if governments feel no constraints in subsidizing their former telephone monopolies, the chance of survival of several of the wounded telecoms is slim, because while the market is depressed their debt stands at record levels. This does not mean that in North America things look any better. According to investment advisers, the exposure to telecoms debt of the US economy is almost as large as its combined exposure to the savings and loan crisis in the late 1980s, and the junk bond failure of the early 1990s.

No creative accounting can cover this huge amount even if telecommunications and other companies are turning to 'new ways' for funding. Capitalizing on low interest rates of the first years of the new century, in growing numbers they are raising long-term bonds to pay off short-term debts and more costly bank borrowing. The debt, however, remains, and in basic economic terms this is counterproductive:

- Short-term securities, commercial paper issued by companies to fund day-to-day operations, find no buyers when the company issuing them has a low rating.
- On the other hand, to find investors for long-term finance, a company must be able to show that it is not overdependent on short-term debt and its creditworthiness is high (see Chapter 2).

One of the cash mechanisms on the rise in the telecoms market is receivables financing, based on the receipt of sales to customers. Enron tried this gimmick with its *prepays*,[2] with the result that the bank which engineered them as well as their insurers landed in court. By providing financing based on accounts receivables, factoring companies help an operator speed up its cash flow, but at the same time deprive the recipient of its future cash flow – and, moreover, this practice can turn into a scam.

Another one of the quick fixes being used in some cases and contemplated in others is a capital markets version of prepays. It consists of securitizing assets, such as the accounts receivable from fixed-line phone accounts, selling them in the market. France Télécom hoped to raise $880 million this way, but it has not happened yet. Deutsche Telekom has been talking of $1.8 billion. The capital market seems to be unconvinced.

This is a different way of saying there is no such thing as a free lunch. One of the major concerns with the different gimmicks in policing rotten balance sheets is that because paying off debt soaks up too much cash, telcos don't have enough money to invest in new infrastructure. Neither do they seem to have ideas about how to develop and market new revenue-generating services, including the 3G which is not expected to be rolled out in any meaningful sense until some years down the line (see Chapter 10).

Before the hard facts of financial life obliged them to be more realistic, European telcos were hot on 3G rollouts, not only because of their huge investments in licences, but also because they hoped to capitalize on Europe's mobile telephony penetration rates. These were said to be as high as 80 per cent versus 61 per cent in the US. Some independent observers, however, were suggesting that the wireless penetration argument was false, and rates in Europe had been overstated for years.

- European carriers counted customers as subscribers even if they had not spent money on wireless service for months, and
- subscribers were often double-counted if they bought from two different carriers a subscriber identity module (SIM) card, and a computer chip that stores wireless minutes.

According to these same sources, if one accounted for these two factors, then European penetration would be in the middle to low 60s percentages. Under these conditions, the gloomy statistics on the profitability of American mobile telephony carriers would apply to their European counterparts. It seems that, of the six US wireless providers – Verizon Wireless, Cingular Wireless, AT&T Wireless, Sprint PCS, Nextel Communications and Voicestream – only the first two made any profits, while the other four have been in the red.

Notice that the smaller of the American 'big six' also had the worst losses. Deutsche Telekom's US subsidiary, Voicestream Wireless, has the smaller number of US subscribers, less revenue per subscriber than its competitors, and huge debts. No wonder Deutsche Telekom has been trying to sell it, but all it could get is 30 per cent of the money it paid to buy it in the heyday of the telecoms boom.

### 4. The negative net worth of France Télécom

Among all the telephone industry's former state monopolies which run themselves to the ground, critics condemned most severely France Télécom (FT) and Deutsche Telekom (DT), with two others coming right behind: British Telecom (BT) and KPN of the Netherlands. This section looks in greater detail at the troubles of France Télécom, section 5 focuses on Deutsche Telekom, and section concentrates on British Telecom and NTL.

The first big puzzle to every analyst is how France Télécom, still majority-owned by the state,[3] was allowed to run up a debt that outstrips the GDP of every African country except Egypt and South Africa. If the company's CEO and his bureaucrats could not see what they were doing, somebody in the French government should have had a cooler head.

People who like to fabricate excuses say the companies France Télécom bought could have been worse in failure terms. At least Orange, the optimists say, has millions of real customers. However, given the choice, French taxpayers would have spent in a wiser way the money that Equant, Mobilcom and other non-entities have cost – for instance, on schools, which require urgent upgrade.

Moreover, the deep pockets of the state have biased the French telecoms market. Alternative operators repeatedly complained to a European Commission inquiry that in addition to the share purchase, France Telecom has been receiving several billion euros of soft financial aid from the government. The fact that France Télécom has state backing means that it pays lower interest rates on its debt.

There are further curious things taking place in regard to ineffectiveness and poor corporate governance. To reduce its €70 billion debt, FT planned a record-breaking €15 billion rescue rights issue, launched on 24 March 2003. In April 2003 it was said that France Télécom would pay €180 million in fees to banks to underwrite its issue, and 21 banks were fighting over this €180 million pot of fees.

In Paris analysts said that France Télécom was planning to divide the fees, depending on how much underwriting capacity each bank could raise, pitting income-starved investment banks in a competition. Eight banks among the 21 have been leading the issue: ABN Amro Rothschild, BNP Paribas, Crédit Agricole, Crédit Lyonnais, Deutsche Bank, Goldman Sachs, Merrill Lynch and Morgan Stanley. These have been supported by seven lead managers and six co-leads.

About a year before the issue, by the end of June 2002, France Telecom's market capitalization had shrunk to just $10 billion, with its shares trading at one-third the market price of its public offering in 1997. Small investors, who were early subscribers and kept the stock, lost 66 per cent of their assets. Another irony was that this $10 billion in France Télécom's capitalization was $7.5 billion less than the 84 per cent stake it owns in wireless operator Orange. The market ascribed negative value to the company's:

- $42 billion in annual revenues,
- 90 million customers, and
- estimated $31 billion in physical assets.

Like Deutsche Telekom in Germany, which took the country's small investors for a ride, France Télécom is the most widely owned stock in the French Republic. Its rapid fall has been dragging down the entire Paris Bourse. Beyond that, the company's debt wounded the banks which extended credit, and its weak financial position held back development of broadband access to 3G wireless systems, for which it paid a huge amount of money. Two more factors must be kept in mind in evaluating FT's position. One is that up to and including 2002, the debt of France Télécom, like that of Deutsche Telekom, has been rising very fast, at 39 per cent in one year. This is shown in Table 6.1. The other is that even these statistics on rapid debt growth are understated, because they do not reflect all the liabilities the carrier has assumed. As shown in Table 6.2, adjusted for these liabilities the debt of France Télécom grows to €77.5 billion, 10 per cent higher than the Table 6.1 figures.

Some experts have suggested that to get out of a debt spiralling past €71 billion – or €77.5 billion, according to your lights – France Télécom might try to sell off Orange. Other analysts, however, have said that Orange would probably fetch far less than the $40 billion France Télécom paid for it in 2000. Neither can it be forgotten that for its parent company the wireless carrier was the source of:

- 92 per cent of its revenue growth, and
- 28 per cent of its operating profits in 2001.

*Table 6.1* Throwing good money after bad. The debt of mismanaged companies increases very fast

|  | In billions of Euro | | % increase in 16 months* |
| --- | --- | --- | --- |
|  | June 2001 | October 2002 | |
| France Télécom | 51** | 71 | 39.2 |
| Deutsche Telekom | 43 | 60 | 43.4 |

\* Which corresponds to 30 per cent per year.
\*\* When these accounts were made, the $/€ exchange rate was at 0.985, nearly parity.

*Table 6.2* France Télécom's net debt rises because of other liabilities

|  | € billions |
| --- | --- |
| Estimated net debt, October 2002 | 71.0 |
| Adjusted net debt, with consolidation of Mobilcom debt | 74.3 |
| Approximate rating agency view of debt for property sales, leaseback and sale of receivables | 77.5 |

Under these conditions the €15 billion bond issue in 2003 was practically a last-ditch approach because, like its kin in other European countries, France Télécom did not have many options, apart from letting the French taxpayer become the lender of last resort. What FT has done is no different from the strategy of other European telecoms.

Banks have been afraid to throw good money after bad, as the telecoms are struggling to face up to their past obligations. Moreover, the fact that many telcos are badly treated by the stock market does not help. Therefore, capitalizing on low interest rates to contract long-term debt and get out of some current liabilities has been a commendable strategy, except for two factors. First, since most of the money was contributed by shareholders, it is the French taxpayer who paid the bill, since in 2003 France Télécom was still majority-owned by the government. This is a risky strategy under European Union rules, particularly so if it is repeated. As should be recalled, in December 2003 the European Commission ordered Electricité de France (EDF) to repay some €900 million ($900 million) to the French government for unfair tax breaks given to the nationalized power company in the 1980s and 1990s.

The French government also agreed to phase out guarantees that give EDF and Gaz de France easier access to private funds in the bond market. Basically that's what has been the motor behind the capital market's interest in France Télécom's long-term bonds. Bonds, whether their timing is long or short, are part of a company's leverage – like bank loans. Therefore the indebtedness remains, and so does its aftermath.

The statement made by the new CEO of France Télécom, that in 2003 the company was able to cut its debt by €20 billion, is inaccurate. What happened was that FT changed the chapter in which the €15 billion have been written, from outright bank loans to bonds – and these bonds have to be serviced, because bonds *are* loans.

More worrisome, to its shareholders, is the fact that France Télécom seems determined to continue adding debt. In September 2003, it bought out the remaining shareholders in its mobile subsidiary Orange, in an all-share deal valued at €7.1 billion. This gives the French incumbent a greater grip on Orange's cash output. An estimated 40 per cent of the telco's free cash flow will now be generated by Orange, but the €7.1 billion adds to FT's debt.

## 5. Deutsche Telekom's creative accounting

Deutsche Telekom is another example of a company which cannot find its way out of the mess into which it has got itself. In late August 2001 the equity price of Deutsche Telecom hit €16, only slightly above its price of issue in November 1996, with DT's privatization. Then by August 2002 it went below €10, while since then it has been hovering in the €12 to 15 range.

Similarly to France Télécom, the other privatized big telco, the capitalization of Deutsche Telekom made a huge inverted U-turn after having sky-rocketed.

The only consolation to its shareholders is that, taking other equities as an example, it might have been even worse. For instance, Eurotunnel went from Fr. 35 to Fr. 129 before falling to Fr. 10 (correspondingly $5.2, $19.2 and $1.5).

Moreover, in another piece of bad news, in 2003, the European Commission fined Deutsche Telekom €12.6 million for overcharging competitive operators to access its local loops (see Chapter 5). Independents are obliged to use Deutsche Telekom's circuits since the former monopoly controls 95 per cent of domestic fixed and broadband connections.

Being, like any other company, in need of liquidity, in 2003 Deutsche Telekom used a different way to serve itself with cash. It used creative accounting and, apparently, stock exchange regulators have been looking the other way. Although everyone talks about a European Union, capital markets in different countries are far from having the same standards or enforcing the same rules.

In late February 2003, Deutsche Telekom's mandatory convertible bond, at €2.3 billion, was the biggest of its kind. Doubts were rekindled about the wisdom of a type of issue that French regulators have already called into question following similar deals from two well-known companies in 2002. In December 2002, commenting on the mandatory convertible issues from Vivendi and Alcatel, the French Commission des Opérations de Bourse (COB) said that the potential consequences of these deals are still difficult to gauge, whether it the effect on the secondary market of the issuer's shares, or the ability of the public to take part in transactions that are inherently complex.

Subsequently, the COB has banned further issues of the mandatory convertible type, where the coupon on the bond is paid in advance. It also expressed concern at the high level of hedge-fund interest in such instruments, which reflects a common feeling that, in the longer term, shareholders are losing out as companies go in desperate search of a quick capital fix.

Basically, the case of Deutsche Telekom, which in Germany was allowed to go ahead with the issue, is no different from that of Vivendi and Alcatel, which was forbidden in France. There is no doubt that with over $60 billion of debt, Deutsche Telekom is under pressure to raise capital. But *mandatories*, which are quite common in the US with a broader investor base, are seen in Europe as a desperate measure.

The main concern of regulators is whether this type of issue is fair to existing equity investors. A hint is given by the fact that Deutsche Telekom shares fell almost 10 per cent on the day of the bond issue. For another example, in early 2003 another big corporate issuer of mandatories was Japan's Sumitomo Mitsui Banking Group, with an issue almost as big as Deutsche Telekom's. Its shares fell 26 per cent on the day of issue.

Many financial analysts have been critical of *mandatories*. They say that these amount to a huge value transfer where money belonging to existing shareholders is being taken out of their pockets and put into the pockets of hedge funds and some banks. Indeed, one major reason that shares of Deutsche Telekom and Sumitomo Mitsui fell is because hedge funds buy the mandatory and short the underlying stock as a hedge. With shorting, they sell shares they do not own in the hope of buying them back later at a lower price to make a profit. This is resented by big long-term shareholders of Deutsche Telekom, which include the likes of Merrill Lynch Investment Managers, Fidelity, Deutsche Asset Management and Dresdner Allianz – plus a long list of minor investors.

As Mark Lovett, head of investments at Dresdner Allianz, said, 'I'm uncomfortable with a strategy that refinances the balance sheet at the expense of equity shareholders. Any convertible has to be part of a long-term strategy rather than a short-term opportunistic move.'[4] Lovett is right, except for the fact that companies which overleveraged themselves and reached the edge of the abyss don't have the luxury of long-term strategies. If they are alive tomorrow, it's enough for them.

These companies may, however, have high-placed friends who see to it that good money runs after bad. This is the case of Kreditanstalt für Wieder-aufbau (KfW) and Deutsche Telekom. On 8 July 2003, KfW, a bank originally founded to aid in German post-World War II reconstruction, issued the world's biggest-ever convertible bond. Its objective was to cash in part of its stake in Deutsche Telekom, seeking €4.5 billion that might help to:

- Support tax cuts by the German government, and
- Provide the government with income to trim its deficits.

It is not easy to unravel the complexity of this multi-party deal which aims to kill three birds with one well-placed stone, except to say that it falls outside KfW's charter. Neither is it that easy to penetrate the veil of creative accounting around it. What is certain is that such moves further dilute Deutsche Telekom equity as the bond could convert into about 5.8 per cent of Deutsche Telekom's share capital – cutting KfW's stake in the telco to 6 per cent, and the total government stake to 37 per cent. On the news, Deutsche Telekom stock fell 2.9 per cent to €12.87.

Proof that creative accounting is no long-term solution can be found in the fact that, as 2003 came to a close, Deutsche Telekom proposed a 10 per cent wage cut for around 100,000 German employees to save money. The incumbent operator said that this reduction in salaries and wages would take some €500 million off its payroll, and could save up to 10,000 jobs at the company.

No proof has been given on how this latter miracle would happen; as for payroll savings, DT's employees are being taken twice to the cleaners. Because nearly all of them are Deutsche Telekom shareholders, with the mandatories they have lost part of their equity. Then, they are being asked to give up 10 per cent of their salaries and wages for the common good.

In the meantime Deutsche Telekom continues buying other companies, thus spending rather than saving money. In October 2003, it was in the process of purchasing the 51 per cent it did not already own of PTC, Poland's top mobile operator. Cash-strapped DT was scheduled to pay current owners Vivendi Universal and Polish bankrupt conglomerate Elektrim – two companies also thirsty for cash – €1.1 billion for the stake.

Having failed once the big way, Deutsche Telekom's management should have been more prudent with the taxpayers' and shareholders' money it spread around. The company lost €364 million ($434 million) in the fourth quarter of 2003, after a short period of recovery following the loss of €25 billion for 2002, the largest ever by a European company. Management was quick to blame charges at Toll Collect – a consortium that has tried but so far failed to develop a satellite-based road-toll system for lorries for the government,[5] but both Toll Collect and all other losses were proof of DT management's ineffectiveness and incompetence.

## 6. Management ineffectiveness at British Telecom and NTL

British Telecom (BT), also a formerly state-owned telecoms monopoly, has been another basket case in management ineffectiveness. It dug itself into a hole by buying stakes in overseas telecoms, without the benefit of a solid strategic plan and rigorous study of their equity, and by paying billions of pounds for licences to operate 3G mobile phone networks – and we know what has happened to those pipe dreams.

As with France Télécom and Deutsche Telekom, this expansionist strategy has not worked well for British Telecom. Experts say that adversity hit for two reasons. The first is organizational. The company has a split personality in its product line, with different divisions offering fixed-line, mobile and data services to businesses and consumers in competition with one another. Moreover, these divisions don't offer solutions; they only compound customers' problems.

BT's second failure is that though it has bought minority stakes in overseas operators, management has repeatedly failed to turn those minority stakes into controlling interests, where a unique global strategy can be implemented. Over the years, BT controlled small mobile operators in Germany, Ireland and the Netherlands, in addition to Cellnet, the British operator. It also had small stakes in telcos operating in Japan, India, Malaysia and eight other far-away countries – spreading itself too thinly.

Before being thanked for his services, Peter Bonfield, BT's CEO, proposed splitting the telecom up into eight divisions and floating off minority shares in some of the, presumably, more profitable bits. The plan called for 25 per cent of BT's wireless division, BT Wireless, to be sold off in a share offering which was expected to raise £10 billion ($17 billion) to go towards the debt. Selling off selected minority holdings in overseas firms was expected to raise

*Table 6.3*   The escalation of British Telecom debt shows that management had lost control of the company's fortunes

| | |
|---|---|
| • September 1999 | £4 billion |
| • December 1999 | £7 billion |
| • March 2000 | £9 billion |
| • June 2000 | £15 billion |
| • September 2000 | £18 billion |
| • December 2000 | £19 billion |
| • March 2001 | £30 billion |

another £5 billion or so. This emulated AT&T, which had floated a similar plan.

In neither case was the market impressed with these initiatives, or similar ones which followed them. Neither 'plan' did anything to fundamentally improve BT's position. Instead, analysts focused on the track record; particularly on the fact that BT's debt grew far too fast. The company had overleveraged itself with debt it knew it could not serve, let alone repay. Table 6.3 gives a glimpse at the escalation which took place in the 1999 to 2000 timeframe.

A crucial question is: what did BT and its shareholders get for all this debt loading? The answer is dismal. In the UK, British Telecom's market share fell below 60 per cent for call revenues, and below 70 per cent overall as mobile calls continue to substitute calls over the fixed network. As experts see it, these statistics can only get worse, because in the medium term there is the prospect of substitution by low-priced voice over internet protocol calls (see Chapter 5 on VOIP and its assets).

The trends now developing in telecommunications are poison for BT, which has exclusive ownership of a copper network built at the expense of the taxpayer. Also, one should not forget that British Telecom's historic debts were forgiven when the company went public in 1984. Since then it has managed to put plenty of debt back onto its balance sheet, including the huge amount of money accrued for 3G licences. In other terms, as far as BT's treasury is concerned, there is mismanagement left, right and centre.

The excuses some British Telecom insiders found are not too different from those of other incumbents, and altogether they have been ridiculous. An example is to say that in the US, too, telecoms debt also grew fast. This is unconvincing, even if between 1995 and September 2000 the debt of US telecoms quadrupled from $75 billion to $309 billion. In the UK, the US, Germany, France, the Netherlands and so many other countries telecoms debts were rising much faster than their sales, but the fact that other telecoms are not any better does not justify continuing mismanagement.

Investors who looked more carefully into British Telecom's finance pattern were dismayed when they found the negative correlation displayed in Figure 6.3. Analysts I spoke to in London in mid-2001, when BT was going under water, identified four main mistakes by the company's senior management.

First, it loaded itself with debt, as has already been discussed. Second, it followed a bifurcated strategy, unable to decide between land-based and wireless-only lines. This was unattractive to investors. Third, in a drive to become global, it took small but costly stakes in operators in 11 Asian countries, and some European, spreading itself too thinly. Fourth, BT had learned nothing from the other telcos' failures, for instance from the share offering by Orange (of France Télécom), which raised less than half as much as expected.

The negative lesson from Orange is important because, as the previous paragraphs stated, BT also planned to float off a chunk of its wireless operations in a declining market. Analysts who identified these four reasons for BT's malaise stuck to their opinion, and the market proved them right.

Other British telecoms and cable operations did not fare that brilliantly either. Two examples are mmO2, the mobile operator, and NTL, a US/UK company and Britain's largest cable operator. In 2003, mmO2 said it would take a writedown of £9.7 billion ($16.6 billion), including £5.9 billion related to its investment in third-generation licences. The company posted a full-year 2002 loss of £10.2 billion ($17.2 billion).

Roughly a year before the mmo2 shock, in early April 2002, the City of London has been bracing itself for Britain's biggest bankruptcy, as cable operator NTL prepared to file for protection from its creditors. NTL had run up about $20 billion of debts. At the time, this amount of money easily

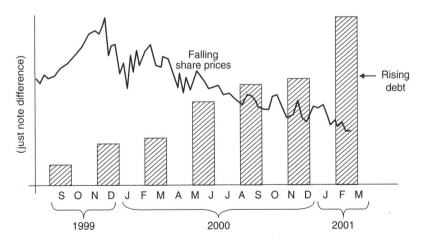

*Figure 6.3* British Telecom's correlation between rising debt and falling share price

exceeded the previous record-holder, Global Crossing, which, as we will see in Chapter 9, collapsed with debts of $12.4 billion.

Some experts said that the silver lining regarding NTL's woes was that, unlike Enron, the cable company could be expected to survive, provided the lenders agreed to exchange their loans and their bonds for new shares – giving them more than 95 per cent of the equity. Those who lost nearly everything were the shareholders. Worst hit were two companies already in trouble for other reasons:

- France Télécom, which had an 18 per cent stake in NTL, and
- Cable & Wireless, which had an 11 per cent stake, as part-payment for its UK cable operations, which it had sold to NTL two years before the bankruptcy.

At the time that particular deal was completed, C&W's NTL shares were worth $3 billion. After NTL's downfall they became practically worthless. NTL had a $12 billion loss in 2001 after an $8 billion impairment charge. But it also had 3 million customers in Britain, even if the company is based in New York, where its shares are also traded.

A few months after these events, on 14 November 2002, NTL admitted that its underlying earnings for the year had been overstated by up to £45 million ($76 million), following an incorrect allocation of expenses between the company's capital and operating budgets. This creative accounting disclosure raised doubts over NTL's ability to pull itself out of Chapter 11 bankruptcy protection.

Also in 2002, investors did not fail to link NTL's case to that of WorldCom. An improper allocation of costs between capital and operating budgets was, indeed, at the heart of the financial fraud that brought down WorldCom – when the company fraudulently booked $9 billion of ordinary expenses as capital items. Some experts said that the fact that telcos and cable operators lean towards creative accounting reflects the deeper issue their business is a margins game.

The wider economic slump of 2000–2002 had meant that operators were actively looking to beautify their balance sheet in an effort to maintain their market appeal. There is always a possibility of twisting financial reporting – and keep or, even improve, their margins through EBITDA (earnings before interest tax, depreciation and amortization) financial reporting.[6]

Easy fixes such as headcount reductions and theoretically slashed over-head costs may temporarily appease the bankers. Savvy investors, however, look at margins, and this raises the question of fraudulently beefed-up profit and loss statements. Sometimes, though by no means always, the trick works.

Having written off more than $2.3 billion of debt, by January 2003, NTL was out of bankruptcy. But even with this financial restructuring at the expense of its stakeholders, the company had to fight for its future. On the marketing side, NTL has lost significant ground to satellite operator BSkyB in the race to carve up the market for multi-channel television. The number of cable subscribers in the UK slipped from 3.6 million at the end of 2001 to 3.3 million by the end of 2002.

As most lost NTL customers switched to satellite, News Corp-controlled BSkyB, NTL's rival, stormed ahead, growing subscriber numbers by more than 400,000 to about 6.5 million (see also in section 8 the competition between cable TV and other providers). The UK regulatory environment had also gone against cable. It takes first-class corporate governance to turn to one's own advantage so many misfortunes, and this was precisely what NTL, and so many other telecoms, was lacking.

## 7. The double pain in telecommunications: slow data growth and falling prices

It will be clear by now that, following the 2000 downturn, the hopes of telecoms and their suppliers about continuing double-digit revenue growth have not been fulfilled. In 2002, revenue growth stood in the 0 per cent to 5 per cent per year zone, depending on the company and the market. In 2003 there was only a tiny improvement. The end result was a long way from the expected 25 per cent to 35 per cent increase in revenue on which most telecoms based their plans.

Analysts said that because of price wars, carriers and the telecoms equipment industry supplying them need *annually* 50 per cent to 70 per cent traffic growth just to produce *flat* revenues. Even with 30 per cent to 35 per cent traffic growth, revenues actually fall as the average selling price declines very fast. The law of the photon has meant that, in some cases, declines are by two orders of magnitude:

- In 1990 a unit of bandwidth cost, say, $100.
- In 2003, the cost of the same unit of bandwidth was below $1, declining at 3 per cent per year for most of the intervening period.

Technology's fast advances had made optimistic projections for the telecoms industry largely unreliable; and even the more realistic ones were questionable. 'Don't worry, data traffic is still growing,' has been a refrain often heard from the telecoms equipment sector and from the telcos themselves. But if one measures data growth in terms of dollars, one will not arrive at that conclusion. The fact that both revenue and income have become focal points in financial evaluations has changed the perspective of banks and investors. This is particularly true as:

- the whole telecoms sector has been sinking in a vast amount of debt, and
- credit ratings across the sector continued falling, with no hope that the curve would bend upwards in the near future.

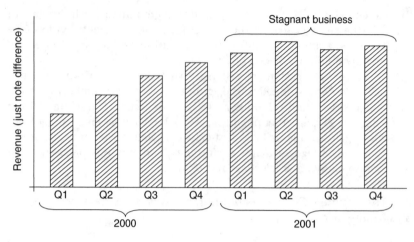

*Figure 6.4*   Revenue growth at a sample of major American carriers

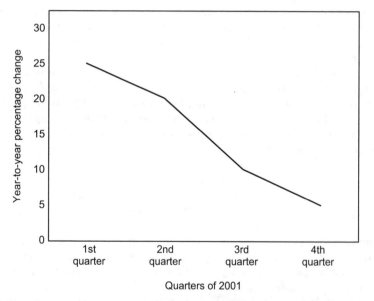

*Figure 6.5*   Year-to-year percentage change at a sample of American telecoms

Figure 6.4 shows the results of a 2002 study, at about the middle of depression, which covered the previous two years. The statistics reflect data revenue for a sample of major US carriers, demonstrating a worrying trend. The data in Figure 6.5 include revenues for Verizon, BellSouth, Qwest,

AT&T, Sprint, WorldCom and other telcos. Though these are 2000–2001 statistics, in 2002 and 2003 nothing spectacular was achieved in terms of market turnaround that would have a significant impact on the equities of telecoms.

What there has been is plenty of wrong judgement by telecoms, vendors and investors in regard to market potential, profit margins and future prospects. For instance, telecommunications operators and investors in global mobile personal communications systems (GMPCS) have committed the capital sins of:

- overestimating demand for services, and
- underestimating the profit and loss aftermath of technological improvements.

Part of what turned out to be an overestimate for suppliers of the telecoms industry was due to the disappearance of their clients. In May 2001, for example, analysts pointed out that customers such as WinStar Communications and NorthPoint Communications, which contributed 20 per cent of Cisco's revenues in the second half of 2000, were off-stage because of bankruptcy. At that time, Cisco itself suggested that its dot-com business could fall to less than 2 per cent, while it was originally expected to double, to near 10 per cent of its total sales.[7]

Two years down the line, by late 2003, some analysts said that telecoms and their vendors had now learned to respond to the need for greater financial realism as well as a sound business plan. This is not necessarily true, neither can anyone guarantee, at the present time, that the telecoms have found a path to greater profitability. It should be remembered that the market is in full change and criteria, as well as milestones, which were valid yesterday no longer make sense.

Not everything is, of course, bleak. Once they recognized their financial difficulties, the better-managed telecom companies, and their vendors, made adjustments to spending. For instance, investments shifted from long-haul network capacity, which was in overabundance, to servers at the edge of the newly installed networks. But even today the telcos' overall strategic plan has not yet been properly restructured, and there are long-term commitments to be serviced, which act as fixed costs.

High fixed costs can be deadly at a time when increases in information technology and telecommunications-related spending have practically disappeared, and customers are changing their spending priorities. Again, among the better-managed firms, in light of slowing revenue growth the focus has shifted to streamlining operations and processes. But to serve customers telecommunications companies need infrastructure, and that costs money to install and run. Also carriers need interconnecting and that costs money, too.

Slowly, even the former high-spending carriers have recognized the benefits of a low-cost operating model, but theory is the easy part. Being able to operate so as to improve cost-effectiveness is much more difficult, if not altogether elusive. Greater cost-effectiveness requires a strategic shift on the part of the telecoms. Squeezing assets inevitably affects everything:

* for the company itself, from a carrier's network operations to back-office systems and solutions,[8] and
* for the market as a whole, more effective strategies for customer acquisition, servicing and retention.

It comes as no surprise that the venture capital market has taken notice of the difficulties faced by the telecommunications industry and its vendors. In the United States venture capital investing dropped nearly 80 per cent to $18.6 billion in the first half of 2001 compared to the same period in 2000. This is one of the key sectors of the economy which experienced a recalibration, as it has been obliged to change business models. Since then the better-managed carriers are primarily interested in technology that:

* lowers their margins,
* reduces the cost of capital, or
* increases average revenues per user (ARPU).

The good news in early 2004 is that there are indications that operational and back-office improvements are starting once again to drive enterprise spending and provide product efficiencies. The goal of offering companies and consumers the benefits of technology at an affordable cost is coming back to life. At the same time, users are keeping an eye on the telcos' financial health, since responsiveness to business demand requires financial staying power.

Both facts mean that all sorts of companies are now going through a full examination of their suppliers' resilience to ensure they are in good standing. This is as true of telecommunications companies and their suppliers as it is of other companies which use telecom services. It is also a positive sign because it indicates that some measure of sanity has returned to the market.

## Notes

1. One of the problems with 3G is a profusion of 'standards' along with made-up terms that make it hard to compare different alternatives. A case in point is 3G and UMTS. While, at least in Europe, these terms are used interchangeably, they should not be. 3G is a generic term; UMTS is the European protocol for 3G. All UMTS is (or at least should be) 3G; but by no means all 3G is UMTS.
2. Chorafas, *Management Risk*.
3. Though in January 2004 the French government suggested it would privatize some of its holding, bringing its equity share in France Télécom below 50 per cent.

4. *Financial Times*, 26 February 2003.
5. *The Economist*, 13 March 2004.
6. Chorafas, *Management Risk*.
7. *BusinessWeek*, 21 May 2001.
8. Chorafas, *The Real-time Enterprise*.

# 7
# Mismanagement Led to the Downfall of Vivendi Universal

## 1. Introduction

Starting with a water company, the French Compagnie Générale des Eaux, which was formed under the reign of Napoleon III in the mid-nineteenth century, Jean-Marie Messier, the company's upstart CEO, built on sand a mobile-phone conglomerate. The drama has been played out in the setting of a globalized, industrial empire. After the crash, the fired CEO blamed his downfall on external factors such as:

- rivalries within the French business élite,
- the bursting of the dot-com bubble, and
- mistakes made by other people who could not share his vision.

All but forgotten was the fact that the company's liquidity crisis in 2002 led to its downfall. Vivendi Universal's chief executive who, at his time of passing glory was nicknamed J6M – Jean-Marie Messier, Moi-Même, Maître du Monde – mishandled not only the firm he led and its many wild acquisitions, but also the company's debt by taking on too many short-term liabilities.

As if to cover his own ineffectiveness and that of his immediate assistants, he held an exaggerated media profile. While Vivendi's stock was crumbling, he posed for *Paris-Match*, the French weekly magazine, ice-skating in Manhattan.

Seduced by his initial success in making a conglomerate out of a water and sewage utility rebaptized Vivendi, Messier failed not only in his planning but also in guarding against the possibility of things going wrong. He repeatedly overpaid for too disperse acquisitions, and he continued doing so even after the internet boom had bust. In the end, he left the company with a massive €19 billion ($19 billion debt), as well as write-downs of the assets he had so hurriedly acquired.

Videndi's crash amounted to the biggest loss in French corporate history, and even the rescue operation mounted on J6M's departure has not yet brought the wreckage out of the tunnel. Behind the rescue operation, some analysts said, can be found the hand of the French government which is making sure that key assets of floundering Vivendi Universal stay French.

In October 2002, the Group's $3.7 billion publishing arm was quickly, and not very transparently, sold off to France's Groupe Lagadère despite the fact that the integrated entity would enjoy near monopolies in textbooks and reference books in France. Shortly thereafter, a government-sponsored group took control of Vivendi's large utility and water unit – the original Compagnie Générale des Eaux rebaptized Vivendi Environnement – and renamed it Veolia Environnement.

Then, in spite of being debt-ridden, in early December 2002, Vivendi turned down a $6.8 billion offer from Britain's Vodafone for its 44 per cent stake in Cegetel, owner of the second-largest mobile operator in the French Republic. Moreover, French banks put up enough loans to allow Vivendi to pay an additional $4 billion so that it could control Cegetel.[1]

While these events were taking place, investors were crossing their fingers, hoping that Vivendi's new management would be able to salvage what remained of the industrial empire. Some of the people who lost their money went to court. In July 2002 American investors filed a securities fraud lawsuit against Vivendi Universal and its former CEO, Jean-Marie Messier, alleging that the ousted chief executive had inflated the value of the Group's shares by concealing a financial crisis (more on this in section 7).

While this story makes sad reading and adds personal arrogance to the many failures of mismanagement at Vivendi Universal, financial analysts at major brokerages which strongly recommended Vivendi were in no way blameless. They drummed up Vivendi Universal's stock until the last minute, and by doing so put many investors on the hook.

## 2.   Merrill Lynch rates Vivendi as 'strong buy' shortly before its fall

On 10 June 2002, Merrill Lynch characterized Vivendi Universal as 'strong buy' in the short term, and 'strong buy' in the long term. The reason for this was that Rupert Murdoch's News Corporation presumably agreed to pay Vivendi Universal €1.5 billion ($1.5 billion) for Telepiù, an Italian pay-TV company which until then had made only losses.

Here is how the analyst's report by Merrill Lynch tried to justify this euphoric, and misjudged, opinion: 'We view the announcement positively, as the transaction should help to allay investor and credit rating agency concerns over debt levels, while also enabling Vivendi to stem pay TV cash losses.' To say the least, this judgement was ultra-light. Telepiù accounted for some 10 per cent of the Canal Plus subscriber base in 2001; but it represented two-thirds of Canal Plus's cash losses. Was getting rid of that tiny piece of negative assets enough to make a short-to long-term 'strong buy' out of a vast conglomerate which was sinking under a mountain of debt? Why did the broker and his analysts overlook all other negative factors influencing on Vivendi Universal's survival?

True enough, in the late 1990s, analysts did their utmost to push selected stocks – selected on the basis of the amount of related investment banking business. The 28 April 2003 settlement with the SEC of ten Wall Street firms is explicit enough on this matter. In Vivendi Universal's case, however, we are in June 2002 and the analyst's euphoric statements continue to misguide investors.

Even the statistics did not add up. The aforementioned analyst noted that the deal was worth €1.5 billion for Vivendi. Taking as a base Telepiù's 1.5 million subscribers, this meant valuing each Telepiù subscriber at €1,000, much higher than the $600 that Messier had previously considered paying for each Stream subscriber (another money-losing Italian pay-TV he wanted to buy). In fact Murdoch was not unwise enough to throw out of the window all that money. He renegotiated and redimensioned Telepiù's price.

Neither is there any evidence that before expressing the 'strong buy' opinion the Merrill Lynch analyst took account of the fact that Vivendi had suffered successive downgrades, reducing its debt to virtually junk status. While the company did try to give an image of financial health through proforma reporting – its favoured scheme is earnings before taxes, interest, depreciation and amortization (EBITDA)[2] – independent analysts are not expected to be taken in by creative accounting. They must justify their opinion through facts.

For instance, in 2001, before the events referred to, Vivendi reported EBITDA of €5.04 billion, of which the telecoms holdings accounted for nearly half: €2.31 billion. This figure itself was misleading, because it integrated at 100 per cent Cegetel and its affiliate SFR – the mobile telephony arm of Vivendi Universal. If the true ownership level was reflected, then the telecoms EBITDA would have fallen to €807 million.

- Vivendi's EBITDA was therefore only around €3.5 billion, and
- its debt/EBITDA ratio was 5.1, much worse than the 3.8 under Vivendi's own creative accounting.

The Merrill Lynch analyst, and his pals in other investment houses, should have taken all that into full account. EBITDA and creative accounting generally mislead investors, and they end up by depressing the capital markets. Where they do help is in beefing up the bonuses of top executives.

Neither should the analyst have forgotten that in 2001 Vivendi Universal's huge loss included a €12.6 billion write-down in the value of assets bought during its acquisitions rampage. The biggest of Vivendi's write-downs was €6 billion against the value of Canal Plus, the pay-TV operation, which owned

Telepiù. There have also been twin bad management decisions by J6M and his immediate assistants:

- In 2000 Vivendi paid €12.5 billion to buy the 51 per cent of Canal Plus that it did not already own, and
- this unwise acquisition took place at a time when Canal Plus was making losses and had some €2.8 billion of debt.

Even a blind person with dark glasses could have seen that such investment should have been judged as accounting for the fate of other pay-TV companies in Europe, including KirchPayTV and ITV Digital, which have gone bust. Neither should Merrill Lynch have brushed aside the fact that by the beginning of 2002 the equity of Vivendi Universal was below 50 per cent of its peak in early 2000; and then, as Figure 7.1 shows, between January and May 2002 it lost another 50 per cent of its value.

The broker's analyst should have known that in the background of Vivendi's equity drift was a continuing swirl of negative news about the company. Vivendi's sorrows had joined the bad news of other former high-fliers in the Paris Bourse, clamping their stock to a five-year low. Investors were watching cautiously to see how France Télécom, whose share price had dropped

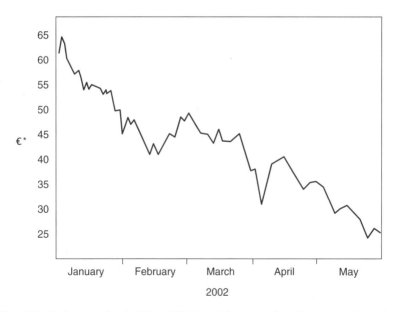

*Figure 7.1*  In five months, the Vivendi Universal share price lost 60 per cent of its value
* Taken as €1=$1

61 per cent, and Pinault-Printemps, which had lost 32 per cent of its value, were behaving. In other countries too:

- vaporizing valuations and balance-sheet carnage were hitting overleveraged companies like Vivendi, and
- revelations about disastrous corporate governance had demolished the tradition of creating national champions of industry.

Not only had Vivendi's Jean-Marie Messier, France Télécom's Michel Bon, and Pinault-Printemps-Redoute's François Pinault, and their people badly misjudged the markets, but they also miscalculated their own capacity and price sensitivity. Even the big banks did so. Vivendi's issuance of new equity in early January 2002 is a case in point.

Two years into the market blues, Vivendi came bursting out of the blocks with a €3.3 billion ($3.3 billion) share sale. Deutsche Bank and Goldman Sachs led the deal, and are estimated to have lost millions on this trade. In its financial results for the first quarter of 2002, Goldman said that revenues in its equities business plunged 76 per cent to just $105 million.

- Goldman attributed part of the decline to a one-off hit from the Vivendi trade, estimated at up to $75 million in debt.
- Deutsche Bank did not speak of numbers but analysts were of the opinion that it was likely to have lost more, as it underwrote 60 per cent of the unwise Vivendi equity issuance.

A colourful aspect of this financial disaster is that, on the morning of the equity sale, Vivendi took the unusual step of releasing a statement declaring that the issue was 'firmly underwritten with a pricing range of Euro 60 to Euro 61'. The Vivendi shares were eventually placed at $59.2 but down the line they fell to about €10. So much for shareholder value.

In the meantime, pressed for cash, Vivendi tried to find a buyer for one of its big units United Cinemas International (UCI).[3] Jointly owned by Vivendi Universal and Paramount Pictures, a division of Viacom, UCI is one of the largest operations of multiplex cinemas outside the US, with 1,091 screens in 120 cinemas in 12 countries, including the UK, Germany, Italy, Spain, Argentina, Brazil, Japan and Taiwan.

Another asset up for sale was Vivendi Universal's 49 per cent stake in Elektrim Telekommunikacja, which owns 51 per cent of Polska Telefonia Cyfrows (PTC), the dominant mobile operation in Eastern Europe (see Chapter 6 on Elektrim's bankruptcy and the involvement of Deutsche Telekom). This, too, was to be a firesale. While the stake cost around $1.4 billion when Vivendi purchased it, in 2002 it was thought to be worth around only €600 million.

With the liquidity crisis mounting, at its April 2002 meeting the board gave Messier until the end of 2002 to get Vivendi Universal back on track, though some board members made it known that they were not prepared to abide by that deadline. Among the worst hit were Edgar Bronfman Jr, along with other Bronfman family members. Following Messier's acquisition of Seagram in 2000, the Bronfmans owned 6 per cent of Vivendi, but the value of their combined stake was falling fast.

Other major shareholders, including executives of big French companies such as Saint-Gobain and the bank Société Générale, were hurting, too. 'Our patience is wearing thin,' said one of the Vivendi board members,[4] while Vivendi's market cap hovered around $27 billion, which was less than a quarter of its peak. That was in May 2002. Note that just a month *later* Merrill Lynch issued the short-term/long-term 'strong buy' for Vivendi.

Then, by August 2002, Merrill Lynch changed its mind. On 14 August 2002, Paul G. Reynolds, a Merrill Lynch analyst, wrote: 'We feel it is impossible to present a Buy recommendation on a stock which is capable of being declared insolvent within two months and for which we have no clarity on the prospective group structure and strategy. We therefore downgrade the stock to Market Perform[5] from Buy. We are reducing the target price to Euro 16 per share from Euro 30. Further downside cannot be ruled out until the liquidity issues are addressed.'[6] If Vivendi Universal stock was 'market perform', then the global equity market must have been in deep depression, worse than that of the 1930s.

## 3.  Analysts finally appreciated external rating risk

On 5 March 2002 Vivendi Universal registered a €13.6 billion ($13.6 billion) loss, the largest in French corporate history, to a significant extent due to the writeoffs of goodwill according to the new rules by the Financial Accounting Standards Board (FASB). Vivendi Universal may be a French entity, but it is also quoted in New York. The company took a €15.7 billion charge mostly linked to its $34 billion acquisition of Seagram and €12.5 billion purchase of Canal Plus.

Because the market was aware that mounting debt would affect the company's financial result, its equity lost 22.5 per cent between 1 January and 11 March 2002. Of this, a loss of nearly 4 per cent corresponded to one day only: 11 March. It is the creative accounting practised by a number of firms – some of which, like Enron, WorldCom (see Chapter 8) and Global Crossing (see Chapter 9), went bankrupt – which led the supervisory authorities in America to be very careful with financial reports.

- The statements of quoted companies to stockholders and the authorities, have been subjected to greater scrutiny than ever before, and
- this scrutiny has revealed that corporate accounting is much more a matter of art and of twisting numbers than of iron-clad rules.

In Vivendi's case external rating risk came by way of market discipline. Commenting on the downgrading of his company's equity by the capital market, Jean-Marie Messier, then Vivendi's CEO, said: 'Sometimes there is a confusion between write-offs and the creation and destruction of value. Given that the acquisitions were virtually (all) paid in shares, not cash, this non-cash charge does not represent any value destruction.'

This and similar statements made by CEOs and COs of other companies hit by writeoffs of goodwill, at best, are only half true. It therefore came as no surprise that both investors and analysts criticized the Messier statement that by paying in shares for acquisitions made at the peak of the stock market bubble, his company had avoided destroying shareholder value.

In the words of Grave Fan, a media analyst at Bank of America, 'That [Messier's statement] is completely wrong, of course. We are a long way from seeing Vivendi Universal earn its cost of capital. I expect it to earn a return on capital of around 3.5 percent this year (2002), rising to only 7.5 percent by 2005.'[7] Other analysts pointed out that even overvalued shares had an important *opportunity cost* to existing shareholders, as

- a company could choose to exploit any valuation bubble by issuing equity for cash, and
- it may be buying other overvalued assets which would fall in value, as there seems to be no end to 'creative ways'.

Even Messier had to admit that some of his acquisitions failed. For instance, the June 2000 purchase of Canal Plus had yet to prove a success, underscoring the decision to write off €6 billion from Vivendi's book value – roughly half this company's total acquisition cost. Canal Plus lost €374 million ($374 million) at operating profit level in 2001.

Vivendi also faced serious problems with the handling of its debt. In early May 2002 Standard & Poor's revised downwards its short-term ratings outlook, and moved its long-term BBB rating outlook, to negative from stable. Similar concerns were expressed by Moody's. Analysts indicated that any further downgrade from either agency would have refinancing implications. Both credit ratings agencies downgraded Vivendi Universal's senior unsecured debt to sub-investment grade on 13 August. S&P's downgrade was two notches, to BB; Moody's downgraded three notches to B1 from Ba1. Both ratings remained on a negative outlook.

As if external rating risk were not enough, the company was hit by stockholder woes. Reports about shareholder nervousness appeared to compound the uncertainty spread by Vivendi Universal's announcement that it would ask a French court to annul the results of voting at its 2002 annual meeting. The reason given was suspected tampering with a wireless electronic voting system. The company denied that it tried to quietly slip a stock-buyback plan past investors.

Bad news piling upon bad news, the negative market response, investor nervousness, and rating agencies' downgrade led to a vicious cycle. Both Moody's and S&P cited lower cashflow generation than forecast and concern that the company might not secure new bank financing as reasons for the downgrade. This was particularly true given that the existing lenders, of a €3.8 billion senior bank facility, can block new lenders from taking a preferred security position in Vivendi ahead of their loans. Two of the largest French banks, BNP and Société Générale, were major lenders to Vivendi, with several hundred million euros in loans.

In establishing their rating of Vivendi Universal, independent ratings also faced other challenges, for instance, variable credit rating in the same group. As of late September 2002, the credit rating of Vivendi Universal and that of Vivendi Environnement, its former fully owned subsidiary, diverged in a significant way. Vivendi Universal, which still owned 40.8 per cent, was rated as non-investment grade (junk), but with a stable business base Vivendi Environnement remained in the investment grade category.

Indeed, the spreads on Vivendi Environnement's bonds narrowed by 25 to 30 basis points, and there have also been suggestions by major market players that Vivendi Universal should return its 40.8 per cent stake in Vivendi Environnement to its shareholders. This was seen as preferable to a decision to sell it at a discount to a buyer in order to fill the gaping holes in the balance sheet of the parent company.

The foregoing paragraphs describe in detail the disastrous situation confronting the company's new CEO, Jean-René Fourtou in August 2002. With annual business of €30 billion, Vivendi had lost €12.5 billion in the first period of 2002, after losses of €16 billion in 2001. Even investors accustomed to bad news about Vivendi were flabbergasted.

As a result, Vivendi Universal's equity lost 45 per cent of its value in a few days – down to €9.3, at the Friday, 16 August 2002 closing. And besides being relegated to junk credit rating agencies, Vivendi must reimburse €2.4 billion before the end of 2002 and another €5.6 billion before March 2003 – a total of €8 billion.

The banks which up until then had financed Vivendi were not inclined to throw good money after bad, which those who might have done, probably under government pressure, put as a condition the firesale of the company's jewels. The new line of credit under discussion stood at €2 billion, which was too little too late, given the condition in which the company found itself. Finally, the French banks and the company's new management settled, on 18 September 2002, on a guarantee of €3 billion. With this, Vivendi's depressed stock jumped to €13.2.

The question of which of the company's jewels to sell was difficult to decide. Vodafone seemed interested in buying Cegetel for €4.7 billion. However, the new management wanted to keep Cegetel and make Vivendi a mobile operator. It was thought that the sale of Houghton Mifflin, the US publisher, might bring €2 billion; and another €2 billion was expected to come from the sale of USA Networks. But even if such sales went through at these prices, they would still not be able to restore liquidity, given the €8 billion that had to be reimbursed in cash.

Nobody can ever be sure how far the market can push the price of a firesale. On 23 October 2002, Vivendi Universal announced the sale of its European publishing operations to Lagadère, backed by US finance house Ripplewood Holdings. The price was €1.1 billion ($1.1 billion) against the €3.5 to 4.0 billion Vivendi was seeking for its combined European and US publishing operations.

Because the Houghton Mifflin unit was estimated to be worth about €1.5 billion, considerably less than the €2.2 billion Vivendi paid for it in June 2001, it was thought that the European publishing operations would fetch €2.0 to 2.5 billion. Vivendi Universal accepted the half-price Lagadère offer of €1.1 billion – or, more precisely, 40 per cent of the price it was seeking. That's the result of sale under distressed conditions.

While the capital losses in firesales were heavy, Vivendi had also to write off failed forays into business lines outside its core activities. An example is *Vis-à-Vis*, the internet content business unit which had cost a cool €1.0 billion to develop. On 30 August 2002, it was sold for €150 million, about one-seventh of its cost.

At the same time, financial analysts were distressed by the fact that Jean-René Fourtou was not coming forward with a strategic plan of action. As one expert was to suggest, at least with Messier (the former CEO) one knew that Vivendi Universal was a media group. With Fourtou (the new CEO) the market knows nothing. That investors do not like uncertainty needs no explaining; when to this is added €19 billion in unpayable debt, only storytellers could be euphoric about the company's future fortunes.

## 4.  Vivendi Universal and the conglomerization of the entertainment industry

Among other major issues brought to the fore during the 2000 to 2003 market blues is the growing list of problems that surfaced in the aftermath of the conglomerization of the entertainment industry. A key question is whether these lumbering conglomerates make sense and, if not, whether shareholders will gain more value by breaking them up and selling their pieces.

In the late 1990s, the conglomerization of the media business was built on the idea that there are big profits to be made by bringing all kinds of content creators under one roof: movie studios, record labels, theme parks and internet outfits. AOL Time Warner was an example; analysts developed this concept, and the market went along with it. Subsequently, these conglomerates began acquiring the channels through which they distribute entertainment to the public:

- TV networks,
- cable systems, and
- internet service providers.

Little thought has, however, been given to corporate governance, in particular, how to manage this sprawling mix of businesses, since each product channel has its own salient problems. For instance, there is continuing fallout from the attempt to run together entertainment and technology interests, as demonstrated by the pains of AOL Time Warner, Walt Disney, Viacom and Vivendi Universal.

Insiders say this combination of diverse products and business interests is full of conflicts. One of them is the conflict of interests, given that a cable operator and cable programmers are located within the same enterprise and compete for financing from the same funds. Key questions needing comprehensive answers are:

- how effectively can diverse units, with partly conflicting interests, be managed?
- what is the right economic strategy for merged media and technology firms?
- what does it take to fix the governance of these firms when they are not yielding synergies?

Creative accounting is no way to fix management ineffectiveness problems resulting from lack of synergy, because eventually the market and regulators catch up with it. Even so, some companies did try that path. In Vivendi's case, for instance, a $1.5 billion transfer of current expenses into capital budget has allegedly been found. It seems that the intention was somehow to reduce the huge 2002 financial losses. The French Commission des Opérations de la Bourse (COB) correctly rejected this creative accounting.

Other big names in the conglomerized media industry are said to have followed creative accounting practices. For instance, in late July 2002, investors aggressively sold AOL Time Warner equity out of concern about the way the company accounted for advertising revenue. The sale of equity took place despite swift denials by senior management that there was anything improper about the company's bookkeeping.

The amount in question, some $270 million, is small compared with the total revenues of the business, but analysts said that without it AOL would have missed earnings targets. Part of the problem was that AOL had other credibility issues with its financial supports. In May 2000, the company agreed to pay a $3.5 million fine to settle accusations by the Securities and Exchange Commission that it had capitalized marketing costs instead of counting the expense against earnings. Also, more recently, the reliability of its tally of 34.6 million worldwide AOL subscribers has been questioned, because the company accounts free-trial subscribers among its numbers, and this evidently affects its growth figures.

Apart from the alleged creative accounting exercise at Vivendi, Jean-Marie Messier drove the company to the rocks in pursuit of a grandiose but unsound vision: combining Universal's movie, music and TV assets with Vivendi's nascent telecommunications businesses in the vain hope that this would 'soon' allow consumers to download entertainment wherever and whenever they wanted.

What Messier and the other CEOs of the aforementioned entertainment and communications conglomerates forgot is that, behind the scenes, companies have to be effectively managed and to make profits. When they merge with a bigger firm and/or they diversify in different directions, they have to be governed even more carefully and wisely – and with much greater skill, which is most often missing.

Even undoing a sprawling, mismanaged entertainment and communications conglomerate proves messy. In January 2003, Jean-René Fourtou, the rescue chairman hired to replace Jean-Marie Messier, announced that he had completed disposals totalling €8.2 billion. The market was not impressed because a nasty habit of huge debt is that it keeps on growing as interests accumulate.

Vivendi's sell-offs might have temporarily resolved the Group's €3 billion liquidity shortfall, and could help to cut the Group's net book debt from the €19 billion that Fourtou inherited. But the new CEO's failure to articulate, let alone demonstrate, a coherent strategy for the Group, turning down the multi-billion offer from Vodafone for its minority stake in No. 2 French telecoms operator Cegetel – while selling its market-dominant European and US publishing interests – has left the market quite uncertain about Vivendi's future. Experts simply did not believe the new management knew where it was going.

By July 2003 analysts thought they finally had a slightly clearer picture. Bankers advising Vivendi Universal over the sale of its entertainment assets expected to receive bids of up to $15 billion at a New York auction. Just before this event advisers at Citigroup and Goldman Sachs were understood to have received a handful of offers ranging from $11 billion to $14 billion for the company's entertainment assets, which included Universal Pictures and Vivendi Universal Games.

The challenge was not only about who pays what. One of the hurdles for bidders was an indemnity given to the Bronfman family when Vivendi merged with Universal in 2000. If a substantial chunk of the Seagram assets were sold within five years of the deal closing, the Bronfmans could be liable for up to $2 billion in tax. Vivendi agreed to cover the liability, thus tying its own hands and underwriting more debt.

Experts said that Vivendi must keep some of its US entertainment interests long enough to avoid this large tax liability. It can either keep one of the divisions, or it can sell a majority stake in its entire US portfolio, but maintain a minority shareholding. Neither of these two options, however, quite fitted the policy of all-or-nothing sale by Fourtou.

The final battle for acquisition of Universal's properties was fought between two very different offers: a mostly stock merger by GE, and a cash-rich acquisition bid from the Bronfmans. The deal proposed by GE called for NBC to control the merged entity, tentatively named NBC/Universal. In return, Vivendi was supposed to get about a 20 per cent ownership stake and the opportunity to cash out completely in several years. The Bronfman group was bidding $13 billion for Universal, offering some $8 billion in upfront cash and debt assumption. That was thought to be enticing to Vivendi, which was still struggling with $14 billion in debt.

By 2 September 2003, the chips seemed to have fallen – tentatively at least – in GE's favour, as NBC and Vivendi Universal announced that they had entered 'exclusive negotiations' to merge the peacock network with Vivendi Universal Entertainment (VUE). The goal was to create an entity that will rival Disney, Viacom and AOL Time Warner, with revenue of $13 billion and earnings of about $3 billion.

The combined NBC Universal's assets were to include the No. 1 US TV broadcast network; a half-dozen cable networks, from USA Network to the Sci-Fi Channel and CNBC; as well as film and TV studios. To compensate cash-strapped Vivendi, NBC promised to give upfront cash of $3.8 billion and to assume $1.6 billion in debt at the closing. The benefit to NBC was that the deal would diversify its revenue base from 90 per cent advertising to a 55–45 per cent split between advertising and fees, taking a lot of volatility out of NBC's business.

The broad terms of the deal agreed on 8 October 2003 were unchanged from when the companies entered exclusive talks a month earlier. NBC emerged with 80 per cent of NBC Universal, with Vivendi taking a 20 per cent stake and $3.3 billion in cash. Vivendi could sell its stake in the new company from 2006 onwards, but the agreement included the option of floating its shareholding.

Jean-René Fourtou said that Vivendi's US entertainment arm – home to the Universal film studio, theme parks and the USA Network cable channels – was a 'risk asset', adding that 'These are major assets, risky and difficult to run from Paris.'[8] But if what Fourtou said was true, then Messier's acquisition at high cost of Vivendi Universal was a huge management blunder.

Fourtou could take comfort from the fact that the NBC agreement somewhat simplified Vivendi's corporate structure. The downside was that it left it as a ragbag of telecoms and media assets: a 70 per cent stake in Cegetel, France's second-largest telecoms group, and ownership of mobile phone operator SFR.

The sale of Universal also left Vivendi with the dubious asset of Canal Plus pay-TV network, a computer games unit, Universal Music unit, and stakes in unexciting telecoms companies including Maroc Telecom. Analysts were uneasy about the fact that Vivendi's CEO had not decided whether to split its telecoms and media assets. Another fly in the ointment, a remnant of Vivendi's USA expedition, was the 5.5 per cent stake in VUE held by media tycoon Barry Diller. Negotiations over the sale of the shareholding, and Vivendi's stake in Diller's InterActiveCorp, did not destabilize the NBC deal but they could be costly to Vivendi as Diller seemed to hold the upper ground.

## 5.   Competition in the borderline between telecoms, cable TV and the media

The case study on Vivendi Universal is characteristic of companies that have gone out of their way, and of their core business, to enter into products and markets for which they have had neither the inclination nor the skills to manage. It is therefore not surprising that, as far as these companies are concerned:

- management effectiveness departs,
- corporate governance turns into a joke,
- their equity becomes the subject of casino-type gambling, and
- their shareholders are eventually taken to the cleaners.

It is indeed surprising how many of the old and new companies have misjudged the market, its direction and its potential – also their own strengths and weaknesses. The media companies come right in the middle of these errors, but telecoms cable TV companies have also made similar mistakes. A case in point is mobile telephony entities which literally bend over to gain part of the action – and of the communications market.

The cases of poor governance which have been presented so far demonstrate that the 'plans' made by a number of firms for their own future leave much to be desired. To justify their overoptimistic projections, some of the media companies have said that they foolishly trusted the analysts' estimates and their inclination to mix entertainment and internet traffic. Beyond this, they insisted, they become victims of other people's errors and other firms' changeable policies. This is the subject of the present section. The argument is detailed because, in all likelihood, the way the telecoms market goes will be a core issue during the coming years, not just for terrestrial broadband lines but also, if not primarily, for third-generation mobile communications (see Chapter 10) on which Vivendi – or whatever is left of it – seems to be betting its future.

- Failure to define what may be *wanted* by the market, if anything like that exists, is at the top of the list of handicaps facing penetration by 3G.

- The next big issue is focus. Though cable TV and 3G have different content needs, there might also be a synergy which companies will surely try to locate and exploit.

Besides content and market focus, another issue of interest to companies with 3G licences, such as Vivendi, which can be studied through proxy, is the consolidation which will eventually take place in mobile communications. This consolidation is ongoing among cable companies, as seen by the merger of Comcast and AT&T Broadband and other similar initiatives.

When in July 2001 Comcast made a bid to buy much bigger AT&T Broadband, some analysts suggested that such a takeover could spark a wave of cable TV consolidation,[9] hurting major phone companies in the battle for high-speed internet customers. Behind this opinion lie the facts that:

- in the US market phone companies lag cable TV firms in offering broadband internet service, and
- according to some opinions, stronger cable TV firms, gaining huge savings by merging, could widen the aforementioned gap.

The pro-merger people have been saying that with increased financial and operational might, cable TV firms could roll out high-speed services faster, and possibly at lower prices. Also, newer companies may have an efficiency advantage over the older. With about 18,000 employees in its cable division, Comcast swallowed AT&T Broadband, with nearly 60,000 workers.

At this point, however, enters the issue of efficiencies and inefficiencies connected to mergers. Part of Comcast's plan was to improve the profitability of AT&T networks by slashing the overhead from $500 million annually to $50 million. Some experts, however, disputed whether the comparison was fair, though they admitted that even if this difference of an order of magnitude were significantly reduced, it could still remain impressive.

AT&T itself said that Comcast's figures ignored that it had made expensive investments in upgrading the cable systems it acquired in the late 1990s. Comcast responded that it, too, had made substantial capital investments in its network to the level that 95 per cent of it had been or was about to be rebuilt to handle modern services such as digital cable and high-speed internet access.

For obvious reasons, internet traffic is a sector of the market where cable companies and telcos clash. In the broader context of cable versus digital subscriber line (DSL) access (see Chapter 5), the larger companies in cable tend to scare phone companies. Still, the two are not the same. While their high-speed services are similar, cable and phone companies reach customers differently, in that cable firms use cable modems, and telcos use upgraded phone technology.

*Table 7.1*   Cable and digital subscriber
lines customers in the United States

| Year | DSL users | Cable |
|------|-----------|-------|
| 2000 | 1.9 | 4.1 |
| 2001 | 4.2 | 7.1 |
| 2002 | 7.0 | 9.8 |
| 2003 | 9.5 | 12.0 |
| Est. 2004 | 12.0 | 14.5 |

In the early years of the twenty-first century, cable has been ahead of DSL in terms of subscribers, as Table 7.1 shows. Another of cable's competitive advantages is that cable firms don't have to share their networks with rivals as much as phone companies do. This is one reason that regional Bell telephone companies have asked Congress for less regulation or else, they say, they won't have the economic incentive to roll out DSL at a fast pace; neither could they afford to drop prices.

This argument becomes more complex if content is brought into the picture. Section 4 explained the reason for this statement. The conglomerization of media has brought content providers closer to TV operators than to telephone companies, but mobile communications are an exception which brings into perspective the issue of fixed lines versus satellite communications – and, with it, alternative carriers and their financing (see Chapter 9).

## 6.   The choice of mobile telephony rather than water

'There is no logic holding Vivendi together. It is only a series of mistakes,' said Michael C. Kraland, a fund manager at Trinity Capital Partners in Paris.[10] Kraland had dumped his Vivendi holdings in the second quarter of 2002. This statement was made by a former investor at a time when the formerly mighty media and telecommunications conglomerate urgently needed to reduce its $19 billion debts.

In fact, Kraland was by no means the only disgusted investor. Others were more biting in their comments when, at the end of June 2002, Vivendi Universal shares were down nearly 75 per cent since the June 2000 merger with Seagram. This downfall made the company the worst performer in the French stock market after France Télécom – and worse was still to come.

Investors had already sent Vivendi Universal board members a clear message about their feelings concerning Messier's mismanagement. In spite of that, however, in late June 2002 Vivendi Universal board re-elected Messier as the company's tsar. 'Regardless of whether it's right or wrong,

Messier has lost complete credibility and it's past repair,' said an analyst at a London-based bank. 'There was surprise he did not offer to resign, but he is a tough guy. He knows he has made mistakes and failed to integrate the US and European assets, but he's not a weak person and he will fight,' suggested a boardroom insider. 'It's hardly news to him that the Bronfmans [the former Universal owners] are fed up.'[11]

There is no question that a huge debt of €19 billion both confused the management of Vivendi and reduced future prospects. The €19 billion was part of the free spending policy followed by Messier when he bought Seagram, Canal Plus, and so many other companies. Even in 2001, when the market had fallen, he ran up more than $25 billion debt with acquisitions such as USA Networks and Houghton Mifflin.

In the meantime, Vivendi's former chairman and CEO, Jean-Marie Messier, apart from having already been largely discredited for his ineffective management of Vivendi Universal, faced French prosecutors who launched an inquiry into the accuracy of Vivendi's financial statements during his tenure. These alleged accounting irregularities at Vivendi, in 2000 and 2001, surfaced after a complaint by a shareholder group.

One of the events which confirms how poor was Vivendi Universal's governance is that, as billions ran out of the company's treasury in a torrent, business planning and cash management had departed. The company's top brass was waiting for a miracle to happen, hoping that Canal Plus and French mobile phone group Cegetel would provide new outlets for Seagram's Universal film and music properties. But as we have already seen, Canal Plus was losing money and retreating from markets, and new mobile phone services remain a distant dream as a big income earner.

The surprise has been that Fourtou, and his new management team which took over Vivendi's wreckage from Messier, continued to believe in the pipe dream of making a fortune in mobile telephony through a relatively small company in the French market. Instead, they should have known that, loaded with billions of debt for 3G licences, mobile phone services have been in a depression and prospects for recovery were not very good. Therefore they should not have bet on Vivendi's mobile telephony future.

Vivendi should have bet its future on *clean water*, which after all was its origin and expertise, as Compagnie Générale des Eaux, where it had a great deal of know-how and therefore where it could leverage its skills worldwide. In fact one of the rare right moves Messier had made during his tenure was to buy water companies in the US and the UK. The former Compagnie Générale des Eaux could capitalize on these investments through technology transfer in water purification and distribution.

Rebaptized Vivendi Environnement, Compagnie Générale des Eaux possessed considerable skills in proper design of water systems, which eliminates the possibility of pollution presently prominent in many parts of the world. In fact, some experts have been suggesting that a water crisis will be the curse of the twenty-first century, and future wars will take place to control sources of clean water rather than for territorial and other gains.

By upgrading and marketing its expertise in water, Vivendi could have had the upper hand in a global water market – while it should have sold its mobile telephony operations to get out of debt. Instead, in late October 2002 not only Vivendi Universal rejected Vodafone's offer for its 44 per cent stake in Cegetel but also it created for itself further credit risk by asking and winning a bid for 41 per cent stake in Cegetel owned by SBC and British Telecom.

Analysts said that this sort of management choice, and the decision underpinning it, simply did not make sense. Cash-strapped Vivendi, with €19 billion of debt, wanted to hold on to Cegetel at all costs – while it was selling its water company Vivendi Environnement in bits and pieces to different city councils. Somehow the strategic plan of the new management left much to be desired.

The opinion expressed by experts who participated in my research was that clean water was a better future than the overleveraged and still dubious mobile telephony business. Some said that the choice of clean water as the company's main line would have been a return to Vivendi's origin – after a long nightmare. The 150-year-old water company would have concentrated on its most precious assets by disinvesting 23 controlled companies in media, telecoms and other sectors which, when bought, were worth $77 billion.

This would have also been a sound financial strategy as Messier's successor was under pressure from lenders to lower the debt level, particularly so by BNP Paribas and Société Générale, which stood out among French lenders to Vivendi debt. BNP Paribas is France's biggest bank by assets, and Société Générale the country's No. 3 bank. Both have been among Vivendi's main lenders, as well as part of the group of 18 banks that, in March 2002, extended the €3 billion credit line to Vivendi when the latter faced a severe liquidity crisis.

In conclusion, the salient problem facing Fourtou and his management team has never been whether or not to sell assets and reduce Vivendi's astronomic level of debt. Rather the question was: which assets? The answer to this set the strategy for the future because it identified what the company preserved and what it disposed of. Unfortunately for the shareholders, the new management's choice was not *water*.

## 7.   In the corporate world all bets are not equally effective

Those responsible for the wreckage that used to be Vivendi Universal made a profit. In 2000, Jean-Marie Messier had said in his autobiography, *J6M.com*, that executives should not get bonuses when they are being fired. 'These special payments are not justifiable for company executives.' However, with his own interests at stake Vivendi Universal's former chief executive officer has since changed his mind.[12]

After his departure, Messier was asking for as much as €20 million ($20 million), the same amount paid to Edgar Bronfman Jr when he resigned as the company's executive vice chairman in December 2001. This was in full contradiction with Messier's own pronouncement. 'When one is named to the head of the company, big or small, one knows that one can be removed at any moment by a decision of the board,' he wrote in his book. 'One is paid for that, and well paid.'

Here is another example on the same lines. In 2001 Jean-Marie Messier got a salary of €5,120,000, including a 250 per cent bonus paid a short time after the company announced *record losses* of €13.6 billion for the year. This amounted to a 250 per cent pay rise, despite the dismal financial results. It left him with net earnings of €2,377,000, while shareholders were running for cover. So much for 'shareholder value'.

Vivendi Universal's board ousted Messier after $77 billion of takeovers left the company with France's biggest corporate loss in 2001 and led (curious coincidence in numbers) to a 77 per cent share slide that year. The billions lost through ineffectiveness of the chief executive hardly deserved severance pay, besides the fact that Messier was already paid €5.1 million in 2001, while Vivendi lost €13.6 billion that year. Vivendi's board, led by Jean René Fourtou, the new CEO, refused to handover the €20 million. Messier went to court in New York, where he now lives, and the court decided that Vivendi should pay.

Neither was J6M's reign thrifty in executive options. Seemingly with the board's approval, it has been revealed that Vivendi Universal's executive management offered itself 'lavish guaranteed options'. This new species of options has been an ingenious move, because the payout is independent of results. Some analysts said its only sure aftermath was to make a mockery of 'stockholder value'.

When, because of superleverage, Vivendi shares fell to €13.90, it was said that the departing CEO and other executives had the right to exercise their options at €64, the stock price when they got them (!!). The badly wounded company was supposed to pay the difference. Experts, however, were quick to remark that these are handouts which may be bordering on fraud.

The fired CEO also wanted Vivendi to help him 'find a solution' to a $25 million loan he contracted two years earlier (in 2000) to buy 500,000 Vivendi shares. Two board members, who were not named, were strongly opposed to Messier's demands, which also included the right to use, until the end of 2002, a $17.5 million New York penthouse that Vivendi bought.

The New York penthouse was close to the ex-CEO's heart because Big Apple is precisely where J6M landed after having opened his golden parachute; and that is also where he faced his next challenge. Readers will remember the reference made in the Introduction to the securities fraud lawsuit against Vivendi Universal and its former CEO. This suit had been seeking class action status on behalf of investors who bought Vivendi Universal securities between 11 February and 3 July 2001.

'Messier orchestrated a scheme to conceal the severity of Vivendi's liquidity problems,' the suit alleged. 'Only days before his ouster, [he] caused the company to issue several press releases that falsely stated that Vivendi did not face an immediate and severe cash shortage.' In parallel with this, in mid-July 2002, the French stock market regulator, Commission des Opérations de Bourse (COB), raided Vivendi Universal's Paris headquarters to start a probe into its financial disclosures since January 2001.

Fourtou (correctly) was not about to pay the sums demanded by J6M's golden parachute. As a result, Vivendi got locked in a messy legal dispute with Messier who continued claiming €20.55 million in compensation following his boardroom ousting in July 2002. In mid-August 2003, a Paris court allowed Vivendi to withhold the money sought by Messier.

Moreover, in a first for French corporate history, the court authorized the company to sue Messier and his former No. 2, Eric Licoys, for the same amount, because they signed the 'termination agreement' without the board approval required by French law.[13] But in New York, Messier won an arbitration against Vivendi regarding this same golden parachute, and also held the upper ground in the appeals court.

In mid-September 2003, a state judge in New York ruled that Vivendi Universal must pay $22.8 million in severance to its former chief executive, Jean-Marie Messier. Marilyn Shafer, the Supreme Court justice, upheld the 27 June 2003 arbitration award to Messier and entered a judgment against Vivendi, which had challenged the panel's ruling, claiming it had made legal errors. Here we have precisely the same case judged in two different jurisdictions, a French and an American, which has ended in two contradictory results. So much for the globalization of justice.

Still resident in New York, Jean-Marie Messier had reason to feel honoured and happy, but that was without counting the results of the class action by American shareholders against him. On 23 December 2003 he had to decide what was the least evil (to him) between two bad alternatives: keep clear of wearing stripes and let go the golden parachute, or the other way around.

On that date, the Securities and Exchange Commission settled a court case brought against Vivendi Universal and two of its former senior executives: Jean-Marie Messier and Guillaume Hannezo.[14] According to the SEC, the two men undertook systematic fraud between 1999 and 2002, the year of Vivendi's near-collapse. While the alleged fraud at Vivendi Universal was less brazen than the scheme at Parmalat (which had collapsed a couple of weeks before that SEC decision), many of the mechanisms seem to have been the same:

- creative accounting,
- inadequate disclosure, and
- use of complex derivatives deals between controlled entities in a company's sprawling global operations.

Messier's choice seems to have been to give up his claim to a golden parachute of €20.8 million, in exchange for being let off the hook by the Securities and Exchange Commission for alleged misinformation of shareholders to beef up Vivendi's stock price. Contrary to most of the investments and M&A activity done while at the helm of Vivendi, this was a reasonable choice.

However, according to this settlement, Vivendi Universal must pay €50 million to its shareholders in the class action, for the financial damage they have suffered because of misinformation. To equity investors, this corresponds to a few peanuts per stock, but the cash-strapped company must put its hand into its pocket and come up with the funds as ordered. Quite probably, this €50 million will not be the only money paid in compensation, and therefore below the radar screen of Vivendi's debt.

As a post-mortem, the reader will fnd in the Appendix the new misfortunes of Vivendi.

## Notes

1. *BusinessWeek*, 30 December 2002.
2. Chorafas, *Management Risk*.
3. *Financial Times*, 10 April 2002.
4. *BusinessWeek*, 20 May 2002.
5. !!!
6. Merrill Lynch, *Equity News Note*, France, Media, 14 August 2002.
7. *Financial Times*, 7 March 2002.
8. *The Guardian*, 9 October 2003.
9. In financial terms, the deal, valued at $58 billion in stock and assumed debt when it was announced, made Comcast America's largest cable TV company, with 22 million customers – up from its pre-merger third rank with 8.4 million.
10. *BusinessWeek*, 8 July 2002.
11. *Financial Times*, 27 June 2002.
12. *Bloomberg*, 5 July 2000.
13. *The Business*, 24/26 August 2003.
14. *The Economist*, 17 January 2004.

# 8
# Lessons from the Crash of WorldCom

## 1. Introduction

Bernard J. Ebbers spent almost two decades building WorldCom into one of the biggest global long-distance companies and internet channels. The market applauded as he was able to snowball Long Distance Discount Service (LDDS), a small telecommunications venture, into a company competing head on against AT&T and Sprint.

WorldCom is an excellent case study not just for its own fortunes and misfortunes, but also in what has happened to the telecoms industry at large. The story starts with the US Telecommunications Act of 1996, which created plenty of opportunity for competition. Ebbers and his (then) small company wanted to compete with the incumbents on more than just price.

- Through 70 or so acquisitions, WorldCom tried to get a stake in every domain of telecommunications services.
- The company's market drive addressed both business and residential customers, anywhere there was profit to be made.

In his efforts to become one of the leaders in the telecommunications industry, past those entities already well entrenched, Ebbers exploited every opportunity offered by the deregulation of the telecommunications industry in the US. His strategy was to build capacity and pay attention to costs, the second goal differentiating him from other empire builders.

Through deal-making, WorldCom's CEO showed that it was possible to undercut AT&T in the long-distance market and still make money. But the dynamics of industry change, and the downturn came when Ebbers overplayed his hand, bringing himself down by wounds that, to large measure, were self-inflicted.

There have also been number of alleged scandals both personal and corporate, the latter involving creative accounting. When Ebbers resigned as CEO of MCI WorldCom, he personally owed the company more than

170

$366 million for loans and loan guarantees to cover potential losses on his stock speculation, as the company's share price plummeted. Also, WorldCom became the subject of a continuing investigation by the Securities and Exchange Commission, which has been scrutinizing its accounting practices and the financial relationship with its animator and boss.

The crash did not happen suddenly. For more than a year there were signs that, as practically all telecoms companies, WorldCom was in trouble. But top management repeatedly tried to hide the facts. Just two months before the company's bankruptcy, WorldCom's senior executives from around the globe gathered at the company's headquarters in Clinton, Missouri, to hear CEO Bernard J. Ebbers reveal his grand vision for resurrecting a company mired in huge debt, sluggish growth and rising controversy over its accounting practices.

WorldCom has also been under intense scrutiny for the sizeable six-figure retention bonuses paid out to executives in 2001. With those bonuses due to expire in July 2002, WorldCom's bond rating has been downgraded to junk status by Moody's Investors Service, with the company's shares falling to around $1.20 from a high of over $64 in June 1999. This is another example of external rating risk.

All this was known when the aforementioned top-level meeting took place, but in spite of all the talk about 'resurrecting', or at least 'rescuing', no policy was announced to cut the fat bonuses. Instead, Ebbers said that from then on his executives would follow a checklist of priorities referred to as 'Bernie's seven points of light'. One of them was to count coffee bags, another to make sure no lights were left on at the end of the day, and so on. In short the grand strategy was reduced to shaving pennies.[1]

WorldCom's problem, however, was not pennies but billions. After net income rose 18.1 per cent in 2000, it fell 21.8 per cent in 2001 and was expected to drop a further 30.1 per cent in 2002 if all went well. Analysts were suggesting that combining WorldCom financial results with those of MCI, which Ebbers had acquired after a long battle, earnings could decline 40 per cent in 2002. However, some of the the more daring analysts were predicting that WorldCom had no alternative but to file for protection under Chapter 11.

## 2. A quick glimpse at the WorldCom saga

Reference was made in section 1 to the fact that LDDS, a small discount telecoms entity, built itself into a giant in that industry through more than 70 acquisitions. With them came slivers of market share, products, skills and a message to the market that Ebbers's company was on the rise. The market took note.

At one time, what was to become MCI WorldCom had some of the best talent and assets in the telecommunications industry. UUNet, which Ebbers had acquired, was considered by many to be a leader in internet technology and brainpower. With the acquisition of MCI, Ebbers got his hands on a large, well-established marketing network for telecom services. In parallel to acquisition, the applications domain of the company expanded, as Ebbers wanted to do everything: long-distance services, wireless internet applications, hosting.

- As most telecoms domains were marked with the WorldCom stake, the bar got higher and higher.
- Along with this, Ebbers had to answer Wall Street demands for faster growth, bigger market share and better performance.

Like all of its competitors, WorldCom made mistakes. It made promises it could not keep, build networks faster than it could sell capacity, and overpaid for assets. Ebbers lost his way when he had to integrate all of his ambitious and expensive acquisitions into one cohesive business entity. Failure to do so was also Messier's downfall (see Chapter 7) and that of so many other rising stars of the late 1990s.

As in the case of Vivendi Universal, one of the errors that proved to be deadly to WorldCom was superleverage. Other new entrants to the telecoms market leveraged themselves in the late 1990s. WorldCom had done so in the mid- to late 1990s and as the old century was coming to a close it had reached a sort of saturation in debt. Figure 8.1 compares WorldCom's leverage to Vodafone's in 1998 to 2000.

On paper, the year 2000 debt of less than $30 billion for WorldCom and less than $20 billion for Vodafone compares favourably with the $70 billion of debt featured by AT&T and $50 billion by BT that same year. In real life, however, this is not at all the case. Both WorldCom and Vodafone were upstarts, and they did not have the fixed plant of AT&T, BT and the other incumbents – for what that plant might have been worth. Their collateral was a label-in-the-making wrapped around the name of their CEO.

*Leverage* is debt which has to be repaid and grows steadily because of due interest. A company foolish enough to take on loads of debt finds it difficult to service its loans, let alone repay the capital. Prices continue to be competitive on the market, while it tries to increase revenues at any cost. Eventually, its management loses control over services and margins, particularly in cases like WorldCom which, over the years, earned itself a reputation for provisioning services below cost. This reflected all the way to the carrier's

- sales structure,
- price schedules, and
- bottom-line efficiency.

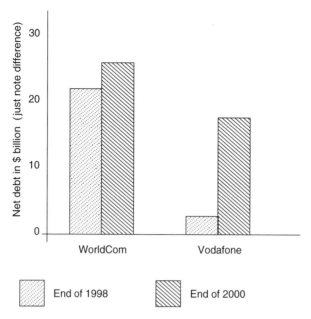

*Figure 8.1*   The leverage of Vodafone and WorldCom in the late 1990s*
\* Statistics Morgan Stanley Dean Witters.

Ebbers simply could not meet his target market share growth without an aggressive price strategy. On the one hand, he stated that there would be more discipline from the salespeople when it came to following pricing guidelines. On the other, he was talking about increasing the company's revenues by a massive 20 per cent to 30 per cent per year. These are two goals which are incompatible.

Both good profitability and a healthy cash flow are necessary because the nature of telecom business has always been to invest heavily in networks and potential new services – often with plenty of money *before* they are proven. The telecoms of the late 1990s, and WorldCom is the best example, have not been renowned for a measured capital policy.

Neither is aggressive pricing the only thing that spoils a market. The fierce competition of the late 1990s and early years of the twenty-first century in the telecoms market – between entrenched companies and upstarts – gave a number of user organizations the opportunity to develop their own contract clauses and demand that the vendor sign them. At the same time, as the financial weakness of vendors became known, telecoms users learned to ask about both:

- a provider's range of services and their price, and
- the providers' own financial spreadsheets and financial staying power.

Moreover, resale service providers got into the habit of asking not just about cost, but also what the top brass of their wholesaler receives in pay, perks and stock options.[2] All this changed the rules of the game quite radically, but most telecoms were very slow to adapt to the tougher environment of competition. While WorldCom's accounting fraud disgusted the market, the silver lining has been that it forced telecoms providers to rethink their financial models and their handouts.

Of handouts, WorldCom made a huge number – particularly to its CEO. For instance, on 10 September 2002 WorldCom's board of directors voted to ask the court overseeing its bankruptcy to rescind the former CEO's severance agreement, which awarded him $1.5 million a year for life, as well as the $408 million loan the company made to Ebbers at a bargain rate of 2.3 per cent. The vote was put on the recommendation of the company's bankruptcy lawyers at Weil, Gotshal & Manges, who argued that this agreement was void, and that Ebbers knew the company was insolvent when he reached for the severance package.

Investors, regulators and investigators also wanted to know if Ebbers sanctioned or encouraged double-counting of the company's revenue. If yes, then not only did he knowingly misinform the market, but he also led the company to make more handouts. The 1999 case of former government-securities trader Aubrey G. Langston provides an example of fraudulent booking of revenue.

Langston was a client company of WorldCom which negotiated a 50 per cent reduction for annual data services, to $15,000, as stated by one of its Manhattan branch managers. WorldCom responded by giving this price concession, but then allegedly upped the revenue to $45,000, in annual income from this firm, booking the old and renegotiated deals separately: one on MCI's system and the other on WorldCom's. As time went on and new creative accounting gimmicks came to light, investigators seemed to have little doubt that the company found nothing wrong in manipulating its financial results. Delinquent accounts seem to have been kept on the books for as long as seven years after customers stopped paying, and this meant such accounts were counted as revenue instead of as liability.

The more information became available on WorldCom's finances, the more a pattern emerged that besides double booking was a fountain of accounting tricks. For instance, an estimated $700 million collectible bills, some of them three years past due, were kept on to artificially inflate revenue. When the company's books are cooked to that degree, then they're not really worth the candle. But investors were not aware of the tricks when they bought the company's equity.

## 3.   MCI WorldCom and its creative accounting practices

As all other telecommunications companies, in 2002 WorldCom had no alternative but to face the hard facts of business life. Fast growth in the tele-coms industry was gone, while competition was driving down data service fees, and dropping revenue growth from 19 per cent in 2000 to practically zero in 2002. By contrast, debt skyrocketed and it had to be served.

Because of its huge leverage, WorldCom found itself with $30 billion in debt, and it had to pay $172 million in interest and maturities in 2002 alone. This was expected to rise to $1.7 billion in 2003 and $2.6 billion in 2004, well beyond the company's ability to face its financial obligations given the state of the telecoms market which was not foreseen to improve for at least another two years, if not more.

Apart from his own mistakes as an industry captain, and it seems that there were plenty, Bernard Ebbers was also undone by industrial and economic forces beyond his control. While consumers enjoyed the telephone company's long-distance price wars, entities engaging in it were under stress. Long-distance telephone service eventually became a commodity from which few carriers could squeeze a good profit – while email and cellphones siphoned off traffic from the more classical phone plant.

The glut of network capacity that was built by start-up companies (see Chapter 5), fuelled by easy financing during the stock market boom, further depressed pricing. Also, the bursting of the stock-market bubble in 2000, particularly the NASDAQ, made it more difficult to raise capital and finance takeovers, such as WorldCom's acquisition of MCI for $30 billion in 1998. The telephone industry's growth-by-acquisition engine finally ran out of steam.

In the aftermath of these events many experts have been asking themselves where the industry would go from there. Some suggested that in regard to competition there is a distinct possibility that regional Bell phone companies could step into the breach in global services, giving their customers a broader range of choices than other service providers featured so far, including:

- email,
- affordable long-distance calls,
- wireless communications, and
- cable TV-based calls.

Yet not everything in the telecoms boom of the late 1990s was in vain. By the early years of the new century, consumer communications options vastly exceeded the possibilities of the old AT&T system, where *choice* was a rare commodity. Industry and the consumers don't really care about the name of the service provider, as long as his product is:

- reliable,
- value-differentiated, and
- affordable in terms of costs.

Could WorldCom meet these targets? Could it find the money it needed to continue growing? Or was it so badly damaged that it could not keep in the race? Moreover, would the regulators bend over backwards to give its management the peace of mind to search for solutions? The answers were in the negative.

In March 2002 the Securities and Exchange Commission launched a broad probe into WorldCom's accounting in general, and more specifically goodwill accounting for 60 of its acquisitions, and its $408 millions in loans to Ebbers. In the aftermath, on 19 April 2002, the company sharply revised its financial projections for that same year. There was more bad news in store in the next couple of months.

- One statement admitted that revenues in its WorldCom Group unit, which serves business customers, would be flat in 2002 at $21 billion to $21.5 billion, down from previous expectations, and
- another statement said that, with the consumer long-distance business shrinking, the company's overall revenues would slip 5 per cent in 2002 to $33 billion, while net income was expected to drop 40 per cent, to $1.6 billion.

These revised forward statements prompted the analysts at brokers such as Merrill Lynch, Crédit Suisse First Boston and A. G. Edwards to downgrade WorldCom to *sell* – another pre-bankruptcy blow. For their part, Standard & Poor's and Moody's Investors Service cut the company's debt to two notches above junk status. With this, its stock plunged 43 per cent in two days.

As misfortunes never come singly, the SEC was also probing WorldCom's *take or pay* contracts, whereby customers get a discount if they agree to use a certain volume of service over a specific period of time. The hinge is that if they don't meet their quota, then these customers have to pay a penalty. With the aforementioned factors in the background, on Wall Street many analysts started to project a cash crunch which could become critical in the following months.

While in May 2000 WorldCom had $1.4 billion in cash and $8 billion available through its bank line, nearly two years down the line this situation had changed radically. For one thing, $3.8 billion of the bank loan was due to expire in June 2002, and WorldCom said it wouldn't try to extend it. But there was also the fact that in 2003 an additional $2.7 billion in bank credit was expected to expire, leaving just $1.5 billion in available credit while WorldCom was confronted with repayment of $1.7 billion in maturing debt.

With these pessimistic projections, by the end of April 2002 the company's debt traded as if it were junk bonds. The price dropped from 85 cents on the dollar in March 2002 to 67 cents, following the company's latest profit warning. The SEC inquiry also gave investors more reasons for concern because it revealed that in all likelihood Ebbers beautified WorldCom's financial results through aggressive bookkeeping. Among other negatives, the company took huge write-offs associated with acquisitions. This aroused the interest of regulators, and the SEC was looking into a $685 million write-off the company took in the third quarter of 2000 for the acquisitions of MFS Communications and MCI. In the boom years at the close of the twentieth Century, few companies truly appreciated that creative accounting may give a boost up to a point, but after that, it leads to downfall. This can be easily seen in WorldCom's case by comparing the events of April 2002 with those of September of that same year, post-Chapter 11. One of the major roadblocks to the survival of WorldCom after filing for bankruptcy protection was the difficulties associated with measuring the value of its assets. A dependable calculation of fair value would have enabled an agreement with creditors, who by September 2002 were $41 billion in debt.

Some analysts noted that though huge, such debt was about $30 billion less than the debt of France Télécom (see Chapter 6). The difference, however, is that the French carrier was still by majority government owned, and therefore lenders counted on the French taxpayers' involuntary but expected contributions.

A major problem in untangling WorldCom's finances post-bankruptcy was that Bernard J. Ebbers, the former CEO who ran the company almost single-handedly, rarely disclosed even to top company executives the full financial picture. He kept quiet at staff meetings regarding financial issues, and most strategy sessions with former chief financial officer Scott D. Sullivan were behind closed doors.[3]

This proved highly counterproductive when, in the post-bankruptcy months, pressure was mounting to discover true value of WorldCom's accounts. Creditors were dismayed by the lack of substance which the company tried to cover through accounting cosmetics. Creditors were not interested in guestimates and in bookkeeping tricks, but in net present value. And this was far from evident.

## 4.  Restatements, proforma earnings and mounting uncertainty

As with many areas of accounting, the line between operating expenses and capital expenditure can sometimes be fuzzy. In a number of cases, what is capitalized and what is written in the year's expenses depends on the nature of the business and what regulators admit as proper practice. In others, it is the nature and scale of accounting transfers that arouses suspicion. In still others, restatements become the focal point of an investigation. In World-Com's case, for example, the *restatement* was equivalent to 33 per cent of 2001 EBITDA and it increased to 37 per cent in the first quarter of 2002. Such a large discrepancy in financial reporting lent weight to the likelihood of outright fraud. Notice, however, that within limits, booking some operating expenses, such as part of employee costs, as capital expenditure is deemed 'legitimate practice' for telecoms operators. The reason is that they are investing heavily in new infrastructure, such as the rollout of broadband services or third-generation networks. Therefore, they add labour costs associated with infrastructural expenses to their capital budget.

True enough, the practice of manipulating expenses is even older than the inflation of revenues that time and again has proved so attractive to fast-growing technology and energy companies. This practice is well known to accountants, which made the exculpatory statement by Arthur Andersen, WorldCom's auditor, all the more surprising. So what were the auditors doing?

- Andersen said that its work for the company complied with all accounting standards. (!!)
- The probe which brought to light the scam was conducted by WorldCom's new auditor, KPMG, and WorldCom employees.

At the completion of the probe, WorldCom announced the restatement and fired its chief financial officer, Scott D. Sullivan. Subsequently, Sullivan was arrested by the FBI and accused of seven counts of securities fraud, as well as making false filings with the Securities and Exchange Commission. The charges carry a combined potential penalty of 65 years in prison. Also arrested was David Myers, WorldCom's chief controller. Both were released on bail.

But is the permeability between operating budget and capital budget rare, or unheard of? 'Everyone does it,' said one analyst. 'The question is, to what extent and is it credible?' Accounting experts said that this practice is questionable to start with, and as the WorldCom scam demonstrates it is wide open to abuse – all the way to a major accounting scandal.

In fact, it was the size of the financial misappropriating revealed by WorldCom's announcement on 26 June 2002 that took bankers, investors and regulators by surprise. Like all telecoms, the company was known to have problems and to try to cover them, but not *that* type of problems.

- During 2001 and the first quarter of 2002, $3.8 billion costs that should have been recorded as expenses were treated as capital spending (more on this in section 4).
- Without the transfers, WorldCom would not have made a profit; it would have had net losses of $1.4 billion in 2001 and another $130 million of debt in the first quarter of 2002.

When this news about financial restatements hit the market, few people remembered that WorldCom and its top financial officers were pioneers of a controversial method of reporting financial results. When first introduced, proforma accounting was hailed as a wonder, and it assisted in cooking the books during the takeover boom of the 1990s.[4] This practice basically involved stripping all post-merger charges and other one-time expenses out of a company's financial results.

Theoretically, the goal of such creative accounting inventions was to show what was claimed to be a 'clearer picture' of the firm's underlying performance. Practically, as a financial accounting gimmick, proforma's mission was that of showing a steady improvement in WorldCom's earnings. But by depriving investors and analysts of financial detail, it left them dependent on the company's rosy interpretation of its own results.

Post mortem, the irony connected to this fraudulent approach is that nobody truly objected to it as long as WorldCom's stock continued to rise. The same is true of other companies which enjoyed a strong following among the analysts. The proforma users shaped financial market opinion, but only up to a point:

• after the easier tricks became widespread, holding the higher ground meant bolder swindles, and
• these led to the $3.8 billion fraud, revealed in July 2002 after the company filed for bankruptcy, grew and grew.

August 2003 brought to light another big creative accounting practice: a $3.3 billion scam by WorldCom done to inflate its earnings. This was of a different kind than the previous one of $3.8 billion – but nobody failed to notice that the two together brought the company's fraudulent financial reporting to over $7 billion – and many experts expected that more revelations would come.

Indeed, the analysts were right in that bleak projection. On 5 November 2002, the $7 billion accounting scam by WorldCom rose to $9 billion, and it kept growing in 2003 as new revelations at the high-risk end of cooking the books came to the fore, and the dry hole in WorldCom's finances went past the $10 billion mark.[5]

Investigators continued poring over the WorldCom books and practically everyone expected new audits would reveal additional examples of expense hiding and profit massaging. Experts said that in their book it is quite obvious that a $3.8 million scam (the original one) could not happen without higher-up approval. They suggested that other members of the company's top brass had known the firm filed false financial statements with the SEC.

On Wall Street, some analysts suggested that Sullivan had surely informed his CEO about the figures in the filings. There was a close relationship between the boss and his financial wizard. According to published reports,

Bernard J. Ebbers never made a move without the approval of Scott D. Sullivan, WorldCom's CFO, and he always deferred to Sullivan to see if 'the numbers work'.

One of the funny sides in this case was that after Ebbers was ousted by the board, in late April 2001, and while the company's financial problems mounted, Sullivan was given promotion by John W. Sidgmore, WorldCom's new and ephemeral CEO. He was also put in charge of persuading bankers to refinance the entity's ballooning debt burden.

During the 8 July Congressional hearing, Ebbers and Sullivan pleaded the Fifth Amendment, but another player in the drama – the former Andersen partner in charge of auditing WorldCom's accounts – did talk, and blamed Sullivan's aggressive financial statements for WorldCom's downfall. This testimony included reference to the company's disclosure, in late June 2002, that it had uncovered the more than $3.8 billion in accounting irregularities – which put WorldCom in violation of its debt covenants and basic accounting principles.

Part of the evidence that the multi-billion scam was planned, not just a random happening or oversight, lies in the fact that at WorldCom Scott Sullivan quickly rankled division managers by sending junior accountants to double-check their books. This was viewed by the different managers as unnecessary and demeaning – as *BusinessWeek* reported.[6]

*BusinessWeek* also suggested that, over time, some of WorldCom's division managers began to suspect that, with Ebbers's support, Sullivan was increasingly pushing the envelope with his hyperaggressive accounting. 'We'd send in one set of numbers and then see different numbers in the final financial reports,' one executive in WorldCom's MCI division reportedly said.

John Ashcroft, the US attorney-general, stated that the arrests of Sullivan and Myers were part of a stepped-up effort by the Justice Department to move decisively against corporate wrongdoers. These arrests came amid a controversy over the billions of dollars in salary and share sales pocketed by executives of US companies before they collapsed into bankruptcy.

Scott Sullivan, for example, was among the 25 most highly paid executives of the larger US bankrupt corporations, receiving a total of $49.4 million in salary, options and share sales. Figure 8.2 shows other cash-outs he allegedly made over a period of seven years. Experts were to comment that WorldCom's financial wrongdoings were so complex that they would take a long time to untangle.

## 5.   Differences between operating expenses and capital expenditures

The Securities and Exchange Commission filed fraud charges against WorldCom a day after the $3.8 billion revelation, while on Wall Street there

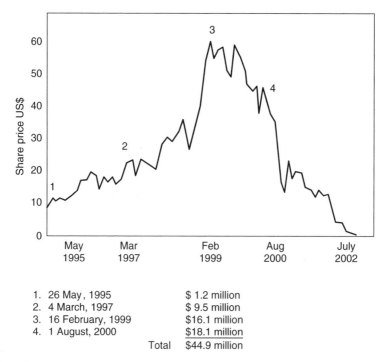

| | | |
|---|---|---|
| 1. 26 May, 1995 | $ 1.2 million | |
| 2. 4 March, 1997 | $ 9.5 million | |
| 3. 16 February, 1999 | $16.1 million | |
| 4. 1 August, 2000 | $18.1 million | |
| | Total | $44.9 million |

*Figure 8.2*  Cash-outs at the peaks of WorldCom's stock price*
*Statistics from *Usa Today*, 1 August 2002.

was talk that there might still be more skeletons in the closet. Rumour had it that WorldCom's internal auditors were uncovering further troubles such as:

- debt that may not have been previously disclosed, but which continued to weigh heavily on the firm.
- booking of revenues that were not yet received from long-term contracts, but were reported in the income statement, and
- double-counting of revenue as far back as 1999, making investors wonder if the 1999 huge profits were just accounting fiction.

According to some estimates, these and other issues could push WorldCom's ultimate restatement to an unprecedented level of discrepancy with originally released numbers. Even the company's (then) new CEO was not spared criticism. John Sidgmore was WorldCom's vice-chairman during 2001. Therefore, it is not possible that he did not know what was going on.

'What was going on' was so twisted and so perverse that more than five months after WorldCom went bankrupt, several analysts expressed the opinion that the company would not survive independently in the long term. 'We are just waiting for it to complete the archaeological digs into its financial records,' said Scott C. Cleland, of an investment firm. 'It will probably be spring or summer before it has its books in order, but it'll be acquired sometime after that. They've got to merge to lower costs. Both WorldCom and AT&T are likely to get merged into a Bell.'[7]

This projection did not materialize – at least not up to now. What took place is some cosmetics (a change of the company's name from WorldCom to MCI) and an agreement, on 19 May 2003, with the Securities and Exchange Commission to settle for $1.51 billion an investigation into the company's books. That was the price tag attached to the biggest fraud in accounting history thus far.

Since on 19 May 2003, when the settlement took place, MCI/WorldCom was in the bankruptcy court, the SEC had to enter its claim along with WorldCom's other creditors. Some experts said that it would get, in all likelihood, only 30 cents or so on the dollar. Still, the $500 million that seems to be earmarked for a new SEC investor restitution fund has been by far the biggest fine ever levied on a non-financial firm.

This fine also draws attention to new rules, passed with the Sarbanes–Oxley Act in 2002, which make it easier for shareholders to recover money from bankrupt firms. The new policy disturbs the ranging of creditors, which usually has shareholders at the bottom of the heap as the residual-risk takers. Therefore, the aftermath of such a development is not yet completely understood, and its existence makes bank lenders and bond investors nervous.

Readers will note that a result of the Sarbanes–Oxley Act is to make it much harder for firms to get private securities fraud claims thrown out by the bankruptcy courts, as used to happen routinely. Other bankrupt companies, like Enron and Adelphia, face a similar case, and it is most advisable to watch carefully the developing new jurisprudence.

There is no doubt that fraud cases unearthed in the 2000 to 2003 timeframe would have a significant after-effect not only on the market, but also on economic and financial theory. Both academics and market experts expressed widespread condemnation regarding the morality of the different creative accounting frauds – like WorldCom's case, which reclassified operating costs as capital expenditures. But opinions about the fraud's P&L aftermath are divided.

In WorldCom's specific case, some people said that it should not affect the company's cash flow after expenses have been deducted, but they did recognize that the firm's creditworthiness was severely damaged. For obvious reasons it is unlikely that bankers will be willing to lend to WorldCom rebaptized MCI until the extent of the fraud has been established and documented. Furthermore:

- securing a loan on WorldCom's assets may be difficult even if the company has extensive long-distance and local networks in the US and around the world; and
- in a business sense, the value of these assets is largely dependent on customers signed up, but because of the glut of telecom capacity constructed the value of physical networks is at best uncertain.

Also, big customers hate to be exposed to a company with an uncertain future. WorldCom was already known for manipulations in acquisition accounting and company loans to senior executives. One of the ironies about the $3.8 billion fraud was that, as contrasted to the rather sophisticated manipulation through EBITDA, this was a sort of old-fashioned dirty accounting trick played on a huge scale.

Since the Industrial Revolution, experts in financial reporting have concerned themselves with one of the most fundamental accounting issues: whether to capitalize or expense an outlay. WorldCom's huge fraud made use of the fact that there are grey areas in accounting standards on how to capitalize or expense the different financial outlays.

The WorldCom case is neither the first nor the last case of that nature. The accounting literature lists numerous cases of aggressive and improper capitalization of expenses. Among experts, the majority opinion is that, on two counts, there was no doubt WorldCom broke both the spirit and the letter of the law on accounting principles. The company opened its 2001 annual report with the statements:

- The principal components of line costs are access charges and transport charges.
- These are essentially payments for the use of other companies' telecoms networks.

For all practical purposes, the expenditure to which reference is made is paying for a service during a particular period. As a result, it is in no way a physical asset that's going to have a seven-, ten- or twenty-year life.

The other breach in accounting principles was that according to WorldCom's brief report on what happened, the expenses were not wrongly classified as capital assets; they were *transferred* to capital accounts. This suggests that such costs were formally recorded as expenses, then simply switched to the capital line when the accounts were drawn up to mask financial losses.

- Transfer implies an active change in accounting treatment, and
- one of the characteristics of an accounting transfer is its visibility to every person studying such a statement.

The conflict of interest was evidenced by the fact that the unwarranted and illegal transfer of $3.8 billion from line cost expenses to capital in 2001 and the first quarter of 2002 had several flattering effects on key measures of the company's performance. Besides, this took place at a time when WorldCom was under intense pressure from the market to show good financial results.

The massage of the company's manipulation of its balance sheet did not end there. Line costs were said to be higher than reported. In 2001, WorldCom suggested that such costs had edged up from 40 per cent to 42 per cent of revenues. But in reality they had shot up to 50 per cent of revenues. Some experts added that two things were inconceivable regarding this transfer of costs into capital investment:

- it was not picked up by Andersen, WorldCom's auditors, and
- it was 'too simplistic' to escape everybody's attention for so long.

While it is not possible for auditors to investigate that every single transaction has been properly treated, such large sums of money should not have escaped attention. The principle of materiality requires extra vigilance in those areas of financial statements which are felt to be most susceptible to mis-statement or error that is material to the company – and, therefore, of concern to the auditing firm.

As for the 'too simplistic' argument, its underlying hypothesis was proved by the fact that it took a routine internal audit to uncover this corporate fraud. One of the internal auditors employed by WorldCom discovered something strange: the amount WorldCom had spent on capital investment since the beginning of 2001 appeared to have been boosted by substantial amounts that did not look like capital spending at all. Basically, this is what rang the alarm bells.

## 6.   On 21 July 2002, WorldCom filed for bankruptcy

On 'Sunday, 21 July WorldCom, with over $107 billion in assets, filed for Chapter 11 protection. This was the largest bankruptcy in history, somewhat less than twice Enron's, the former 'largest' bankruptcy (at $63.4 billion); three times as big as that of the Financial Corporation of America ($33.9 billion); and over four times that of Global Crossing ($25.5 billion); see Chapter 9.

World'Coms bankruptcy took place in an environment where other telecoms companies also reported bad news. At about the same time, AT&T had announced a $12.7 billion quarterly loss; BellSouth had said that its earnings would fall far short of expectations; and Lucent Technologies had come up with a $7.9 billion loss and 7,000 new job cuts. Also, in July 2002, Verizon, the largest US telephone operator, reported a $2 billion second-quarter loss as it suffered from the fall-out of business failures in telecoms and the internet.

In the aftermath of the Global Crossing, Adelphia Communications and WorldCom bankruptcies, and the heavy, unbearable debt of other telecoms, corporate network managers said that even providers who are not on the bankruptcy or near-bankruptcy lists are suffering in many countries and many geographic regions.

For WorldCom, there was a silver lining. The torrent of bankruptcies and near-bankruptcies, as well as user perception of reduced service levels, have helped to explain why corporate managers were not switching away from its services in big numbers:

- there was a distinct likelihood that, service-wise, alternatives might turn out to be worse;
- there was also a legal tangle in connection to customer defection.

Defection is difficult as nobody has the legal right to terminate a contract just because a company files for Chapter 11. A reason for change, however, may be found in the fact that some network providers have been rolling back international operations in the aftermath of a policy by domestic parents to withdraw financing.

In the specific case of WorldCom, its massive ongoing financial problems had resulted in significant layoffs that some analysts, and customers, maintained affected customer service in a perverse way. Even well-funded companies like Equant have been making savings and reducing headcount in operations, with the result that the concept of service quality was put in abeyance.

While clients were concerned about WorldCom's survivability, both analysts and investors tried to guess what remained of WorldCom's asset value. However, as we have seen in section 5, this was by no means an easy task. Neither could other telecoms assets be taken as a reference. As far as asset valuation is concerned, there are enormous differences among operators.

- Asset value and revenue potential vary by network type and infrastructure combination, and
- a case-by-case, very thorough analysis is required to properly contrast supposed enterprise value versus liquidation recovery.

Analysts, investors and the supervisors also tried to guess how was it possible that a small group of people at WorldCom's top were able to fool so many other people for so long. Was it because the company's internal control was abysmal, or because financial fraud was so deeply masterminded that the company's top management was able to present a semblance of prosperity? Besides:

- why did the external auditors not alert public authorities,
- where was the company's audit committee? and
- why did some of the managers not face up to their responsibilities?

The fact that external auditors and the board's audit committee seem to have had no inkling of this huge manipulation of financial accounts posed troublesome questions. Arthur Andersen had a close involvement across a wide range of advisory roles. Indeed, this close proximity prompted questions about the independence of auditors in relation to some of the biggest corporations they work with. Of the $16.8 million in fees WorldCom paid Andersen in 2001, only $4.4 was in connection with the annual audit.

As for the chairman of the audit committee, Max E. Bobbitt, he was said to be an old friend of Ebbers, the CEO. Bobbitt has been a consultant involved in numerous telecoms start-ups. He joined WorldCom's board in 1992 after the company took over Advanced Telecommunications, where he was a director.[8] The audit committee did not do its homework. Yet it is supposed to be the watchdog of possible malfeasance, not an old boys' club.

Long-running inconsistencies in financial reporting, cover-ups and misrepresentation of facts, as well as the aforementioned difficulties in present value appreciation, saw to it that any guessing game was senseless – while at the same time prices of telecoms under Chapter 11, and those of their assets, continued to drop. Their breakeven scenarios were suspect when relying on services not successfully sold or in existence before or during restructuring, or when they try to emphasize their supremacy in 'this' or 'that' *killer technology* rather than:

- carefully analysing their portfolio of service offers, and
- estimating on a sound basis the market value of each of these services.

Difficult as this guessing game has been in practically every case, with WorldCom it got even more twisted because creative accounting called the tune. As will be recalled, WorldCom had revealed in June 2002 that it fiddled its accounts by $3.8 billion in the 15 months to the end of March of that year – a sum that rose to beyond $10 billion as time passed by. Employees have since alleged that the practice had been going on for much longer than originally thought. Moreover,

- malpractice was not confined to the accounts department, and
- WorldCom's sales staff were also fiddling the figures.

In February 2002 three WorldCom salesmen at the company's Arlington, Virginia office were suspended in a case involving millions of dollars of overpaid commissions. The company's Chicago and Baltimore offices were investigated at the same time. According to former WorldCom employees, a practice known as *rolling revenue* was endemic in the sales hierarchy of the company. This involved registering a single sale many times over, even if it meant paying salesmen several commissions in the process.[9]

There was also the case of fake profits engineered through telecoms capacity swaps – a widespread practice. Ironically, this was not an illegal practice in the deregulated telecommunications industry. Only in August 2002 did the Securities and Exchange Commission say it would not allow capacity swaps to be treated as revenue. Analysts expected the new guidance would force many operators to re-file revenue statements with the SEC. A bankrupt WorldCom needed downwards restatement of revenues as much as it needed a bullet in the head.

In retrospect, there is still another way of looking at WorldCom's bankruptcy. The company serves some of America's biggest corporations. With 20 million customers, its MCI unit has been the No. 2 long-distance carrier in the US. While the risk of a sudden interruption in service was not necessarily at the top of its clients' worries, that of a gradual degrading of the quality of service has been a worrying possibility.

One of the least appreciated concomitants of inflated balance sheets and other creative accounting gimmicks is the growing amount of operational risk.[10] Such risk increases for two reasons: to cut costs and improve their P&L statements, companies sharply reduce the headcount and allow their quality of service to deteriorate. At the same time, management is so preoccupied with the cosmetic surgery of financial data that it devotes precious little time, or no time at all, to the control of operational risk.

Matters concerning quality of service and operational risk generally get worse when a company files for bankruptcy, as everyone around – including the service personnel – becomes depressed. Even if a new management starts a rebuilding effort, this takes time to establish. Moreover, to get the company moving again everybody has to sacrifice something. Unwillingly, the customers contribute the all-important service quality as their part of the contribution.

## 7.   Investors and bankers most exposed to WorldCom

The bankruptcy filing was the final straw in WorldCom's investors' drama. Their equity was first inline to be wiped out by any reorganization plan. At the same time, from bondholders to banks, creditors were asked to forgive debt in return for ownership in the company. WorldCom's investors watched retirement savings and nest eggs shrink to almost nothing as the company's shares tumbled from a high of $64.50 in 1999 to a few cents (first 6 cents, then 9 cents) at bankruptcy time. Among the largest institutional investors were:

- Wellington Management
- Barclays Global Investors
- Alliance Capital Management
- Oppenheimer Capital
- State Street Global Advisors.

There were also, of course, other smaller equity holders, among them the company's own employees. Still other investors lost part of their wealth through mutual funds holdings. Mutual funds with the biggest stakes at WorldCom were:

- Oppenheimer Quest Balanced Value A1
- Vanguard 500 Index2
- Pimco Renaissance C Shares
- Hartford Capital Appreciation
- Templeton Growth A.

A couple of statistics are worth noting. WorldCom's 2001 revenue of $35 billion, at its time of glory, was about the same size as the gross domestic product of Ecuador. This $35 billion was reached in a quick succession of run-ups, which have been a major factor in inflating the company's equity price. Then, WorldCom's bankruptcy filing wiped out a market capitalization that, at its peak, hit about $180 billion. That's like erasing the assets of 1,450,000 American families.

Roller-coaster rides have been part of a pattern bound to haunt investors and creditors in the years to come. In the wake of the high dishonesty in financial reporting, in 2001 and 2002, which saw huge amounts of money in investments and loans evaporate, not only private investors but also institutional – banks, insurers, pension funds, and other financial entities – kept on bleeding as a result of their WorldCom holdings. This had an effect on their own equity.

Banks with heavy exposure to WorldCom were hit especially hard. Shares of ABN Amro, for example, fell 11 per cent to $13.22, while Citigroup dropped 11 per cent to $32.04. Deutsche Bank shares slid 8 per cent to $58.99. The bankruptcy news was hurting because analysts suggested that WorldCom might be able to pay back only about 17 per cent of its debt. Figures which were made public have shown that American banks with the largest exposure as unsecured creditors were:

| | |
|---|---|
| JP Morgan | $17.2 billion |
| Mellon Bank | $6.6 billion |
| Citibank | $3.3 billion |
| Bear Stearns | $2.7 billion |
| Bank of New York | $2.6 billion |
| State Street Bank | $2.0 billion |
| Morgan Stanley | $1.9 billion |
| Goldman Sachs | $1.5 billion |
| SunTrust Banks | $1.2 billion |

*The Washington Post* reported that WorldCom had secretly raised billions from Citigroup, JP Morgan Chase and other banks in the year before its bankruptcy filing. This says a great deal about on how unwise lenders can be. They could not see the danger, even though the control of credit risk is supposed to be their forte. Altogether, WorldCom was crippled with $41 billion in debts.

But then there were also some surprises, at least to the untrained eye. According to WorldCom's bankruptcy filing, the telecom operator owed JP Morgan more than $17 billion. But a big chunk of that debt seems to have been resold to other banks or securitized, limiting JP Morgan's exposure to less than $20 million. This meant that nearly $17 billion has been taken off the books and sold to other credit institutions and institutional investors. These are the ones most affected.

In a way, what has happened with the bankruptcy of companies considered to be 'too big to fail' is a replay of past experiences which led to the Great Depression. We are back to the 1920s with the unsecured second leniens on skyscrapers, eagerly bought by foolish investors. And while a good part of loan exposure was passed to third parties, bondholders did not have much reason to celebrate. WorldCom's biggest bondholders were:

- Prudential Investment Management
- Alliance Capital
- Vanguard Group
- Deutsche Investment Management Americas
- Wellington Management.

Readers should also note that the aftermath of WorldCom's bankruptcy is not necessarily confined to the banks, bondholders, shareholders and other aforementioned parties. Its suppliers and insourcers, too, were badly hurt. Electronic Data Systems (EDS), the computer services company which runs multi-million-dollar projects, not only failed to receive timely payment of its invoices, but could also be sucked into the scandal surrounding WorldCom.

A former employee of WorldCom's UK subsidiary has produced a number of invoices from EDS to WorldCom which she alleges helped to inflate the telecom firm's profits.[11] In 1999 EDS had signed a $6.4 billion contract to provide technology services to WorldCom, and a related deal to take $6 billion worth of the telecom firm's services. The claim came at a bad time for EDS, which had been suffering from:

- sluggish global demand for information technology services, and
- self-inflicted wounds such as the $255 million losses, revealed in September 2002, in connection with unwise bets with derivative financial instruments.

Other WorldCom suppliers were also casualties of the bankruptcy. Phone companies that charged the fallen giant $750 million per month to connect calls have been worrying that they won't get paid. WorldCom said it owes Verizon Communications $121 million, but insiders suggested it could be $100 million higher. SBC Communications said it was owed $250 million. BellSouth was tallying the total, but generally it was billing WorldCom about $80 million a month.

Also hit were the telecoms equipment sellers. WorldCom could no longer afford to buy equipment for its network. A case in point is Juniper Networks, which got 10 per cent of its sales from WorldCom in the last three quarters in 2001, though WorldCom accounted for less than 6 per cent of its second-quarter 2002 revenue.

In conclusion, shareholders, bondholders, bankers giving loans and lines of credit, bankers securitizing highly risky loans and their clients, suppliers of services and equipment to leveraged companies, and many other actors have a great deal to lose from the bursting of the bubbles they helped to create. This is the process of creative destruction which from time to time brings the financial markets into deep trouble.

## 8.   Players in a process of creative destruction

Optimists may look at WorldCom's case as being one of creative destruction. The fall has been hard on many players, but the pieces will be picked up by someone else. While it is spoiling resources, creative destruction brings with it renewal. This process, however, requires transparency, if not fair notice to investors and workers about a company's mounting problems. This is something WorldCom, Global Crossing, Enron and far too many other firms have tried to hide.

In their own way, the financial markets gave the sign of forthcoming disaster. As shown in Figure 8.3, unlike other company failure where the equity suddenly drops into the abyss, the WorldCom share price slid over a period of three years. But the financial markets are generally inefficient, and as far as the bubble of the 1990s is concerned, such inefficiency was augmented because of the wrong signals given by:

- investment bankers, in terms of equity analysis, and
- the company itself, by means of fraudulent financial reporting.

Both reasons meant that investors were deceived in a big way. On Wall Street and in the City of London, analysts were to suggest that investors and companies who bled from the WorldCom débâcle learned a lesson. I am not sure that this is true. It is more accurate to suggest that not one but several lessons *could* be learnt, but were *not* necessarily learnt, from the unwise

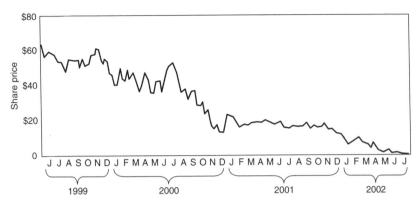

*Figure 8.3* The WorldCom story. Mismanagement can be seen through the steady loss of capitalization

investments made in the past. Here are some examples with particular focus on financial companies.

Beyond the list of banks we have seen in section 7, other companies too had exposure levels which became known shortly before and after the bankruptcy of WorldCom. For example insurer Aegon had an exposure of $200 million, and its shares fell with the telecom's bankruptcy. Another insurer was Prudential in the UK – which said it had $150 million of World-Com bonds, and dismissed concerns that they might have to sell equities because of potential pressure on their solvency. Other exposed entities were: Deutsche Bank, Abbey National, BNP Paribas, Crédit Lyonnais, Allied Irish Banks, Banca di Roma and Tokyo Mitsubishi.

Among banks, Deutsche Bank and Abbey National moved to reassure investors by saying that their exposure to WorldCom was 'limited'. Munich Re, the world's biggest reinsurer, said it was exposed to about $80 million from shares or bonds with WorldCom, and this only represented 0.05 per cent of its €160 billion portfolio of shareholdings. Allianz, Germany's largest insurer, was estimated to have an exposure of between $100 million and $200 million, but the company declined to comment.

While initially US bank lenders to WorldCom, such as Bank of America, Citigroup, JP Morgan Chase, Mellon and Bank One, all declined to discuss their exposures, citing client confidentiality, the figures eventually became known, as we saw in section 7. At the beginning banks would only say that their WorldCom exposure would have no material effect on earnings per share. But, after the bankruptcy, analysts calculated that earnings would most probably be reduced by:

- 3.6 per cent at Mellon,
- 1.8 per cent at JP Morgan,

- 1.7 per cent at FleetBoston,
- 1.2 per cent at Bank One,
- 1 per cent at Bank of America,
- 0.7 per cent at Wells Fargo, and
- 0.3 per cent at Citigroup.

Among Dutch institutions, ABN Amro stated that its likely maximum provisioning would be about $100 million. The bank left its total provisioning for 2002 unchanged at $1.5 billion. ING would not give details of its exposure to WorldCom but stated that loan-loss provisions and impairments on fixed income securities in its insurance business would be $230 million of an institution.

While direct financial losses were severe, whichever way one looked at them, some experts suggested that perhaps the more important effect of the WorldCom bankruptcy and revelation of fraud in the aftermath of the collapse of Enron was that it further dented public confidence in company accounts and forecasts. Many investors said they would now put a premium on reliable and credible management, and take more time and greater care to scrutinize accounts. Fund managers should have always done so, as a matter of policy. They did not and, as a result, they had some nasty surprises. One of the worst exposed was Alliance Capital, a heavy buyer of depressed WorldCom equity in 2002. Alliance Capital had built a 7 per cent position to become WorldCom's late-day shareholder, even as the shares slumped. Alliance Capital was also the largest holder of Enron as it hurtled towards bankruptcy in December 2001. Investments in falling companies can become the nail in the coffin of an institution.

Abraham Lincoln once said that you can fool some of the people all the time or all of the people some of the time. WorldCom had managed to lie to all of its bankers and investors all of the time. As a result, despite huge losses in their loans, bonds and equity investments, and amidst the revelations of fraud and the fact the company was drifting towards bankruptcy, credit institutions had to decide whether to agree on a new $5 billion credit facility to help WorldCom survive, or force the company into liquidation.

Bank of America, JP Morgan Chase, Citigroup, ABN Amro, Deutsche Bank, Bank of Tokyo Mitsubishi, Industrial Bank of Japan and others were faced with this tough choice. Also participating in the syndicate were Allfirst (an Allied Irish Banks subsidiary in the US, with its own problems),[12] Arab Bank, Bank One, BNP Paribas, Banca di Roma, Banco Bilbao Vizcaya Argentaria (BBVA), Bank of Nova Scotia, Bayerische Landesbank Girozentrale, Crédit Lyonnais, Dai-Ichi Kangyo, FleetBoston, Fuji, IntesaBCI, Lloyds, Mellon, Norddeutsche Landesbank, Royal Bank of Scotland, Wells Fargo, Westdeutsche Landesbank and Australia's Westpac.

This meant that WorldCom was technically in default. 'It's good that WorldCom risk has been very dispersed, but bad to the extent everybody has some,' said Mary Rooney, head of credit strategy at Merrill Lynch four weeks before WorldCom's bankruptcy. 'The banks have really dodged the bullet.'[13] The bankers' decision was that much more complex as, by admitting that its accounts were false, WorldCom had violated the representations and warranties that are part of its credit facility.

What about personal accountability connected to the scam? In June 2003, two reports about the huge scandal that bankrupted WorldCom blamed Bernie Ebbers, the company's former CEO, and a small group of top executives, for 'financial gimmickry, deception and outright fraud' that brought about the demise of the ephemeral telecoms giant. Released by an examiner for the bankruptcy court, this report described WorldCom as having committed a smorgasbord of fraudulent activities – suggesting that Ebbers directly put the company at risk when he took more than $1 billion in personal and business loans, using the company's stock as collateral.[14]

A critical question has been whether new revelations will lead to criminal charges being filed against Ebbers. A centrepiece to this issue was the memo sent on 10 July 2001 by Ebbers to Ron Beaumont, the chief operating officer. In this, the former CEO asked whether the COO had found 'one-time revenue items' – a practice used to raise WorldCom's revenue growth.

'I would ask that you ... see where we stand on those one-time events that had to happen in order for us to have a chance to make our numbers – we should know those by now,' Ebbers's memo said.[15] What's important about this evidence is that it is one of the written pieces against Ebbers, who refused to use email and seldom penned messages to other executives. 'Such revelations are likely to increase the size of shareholder lawsuits against the company,' suggested Richard Tilton, a bankruptcy attorney and CEO of Greenacre Asset Advisors.[16]

Last but not least, a lesson to be learnt from the fall of WorldCom is the risk associated with high leveraging which, as we have already seen, was one of WorldCom's strategies, with more than $41 billion of bonds and bank debt outstanding. The crucial question facing bankers and investors alike, when confronted with an entity that has leveraged itself so much, is whether they can trust any of its financial numbers any more. Enron, WorldCom and a horde of other companies suggest that this is unwise. But do shareholders, bondholders and bankers ever learn?

## 9. The year after WorldCom's bankruptcy

There is an interesting postscript to the WorldCom crisis, concerning its new management which rebaptized it MCI. The bankrupt company promised incoming CEO Michael Capellas upwards of $30 million in stock if he pulls it out of bankruptcy in 2003.[17] As of 31 December 2003, this has not yet taken place. But as we have seen in Chapter 5, Figure 5.1, MCI has held to most of its market share, in international minutes of use, ranging No. 1 among bug carriers.

The year 2003 has, however, seen other events worth recording. On 23 August, the New York Stock Exchange fined Salomon Smith Barney – now operating as Citigroup Global Markets, a unit of Citigroup – the trivial penalty of $1 million and temporarily stripped one of the brokerage firm's regional managers of his duties, for failing to supervise brokers dealing with employees of WorldCom.[18] The action is sensitive for the brokerage, which on 28 April 2003 paid $400 million as part of an industry-wide pact to settle charges it issued, misleading stock research to win investment banking business.

At issue in this case are lending practices to WorldCom employees, who on the advice of Salomon Smith Barney brokers often borrowed large amounts of money to cover taxes on their stockholdings, which are now almost worthless. In the late 1990s, Salomon Smith Barney and other investment banks courted employees from big companies with high share prices. In WorldCom's case, Salomon Smith Barney was the exclusive administrator of its stock-option plan, which gave it the advantages of a lucrative account and instant access to a significant client base of WorldCom employees.

There was also a twist to the aforementioned deal. Stock options give holders the right to buy a stock at a set price for a set period. When clients seek to exercise their options, an investment bank's brokers can suggest that rather than buy the stock, the investor sells the shares and walk away with the profits – minus taxes and the initial value of the options. According to this formula, employees should:

- exercise the options,
- hold the shares, and
- take a loan from the brokerage firm to pay for the options and the taxes.

This sort of flawed advice, which seems to be quite common, is based on the idea that equity always continues to rise. If the price of shares rose, clients could pay off the loan, using profits from the share increase. But if the value of WorldCom's shares declined, the gamblers would potentially lose their shares, but pay taxes on profit they never realized. Indeed, for WorldCom employees the decision to borrow money eventually proved costly. That scheme, which in the late 1990s became classic, joined the other bad advice to borrow money or mortgage one's house to play the stock market.

A retiree said that he lost his $2 million life savings when his stock in WorldCom plummeted during the company's collapse in 2002, and sued Citigroup for pain and suffering. The suit would be the first to compel depositions from Bernie Ebbers, Jack Grubman and Sanford Weill, Citigroup's chairman.[19]

Then, on 25 August 2003, MCI was ordered to make its corporate governance most rigorous after its more than $10 billion fraud under former CEO Bernie Ebbers's reign. A 150-page report by MCI's corporate monitor, Richard Breeden, a former SEC chairman, detailed 78 reforms aimed at shifting more power to shareholders while keeping MCI's board and executives, both of whom failed shareholders, in check. Breeden was appointed to oversee MCI's reform as part of the SEC's fraud lawsuit against WorldCom. MCI must adopt these recommendations as part of a record SEC settlement that will pay $750 million in cash and stock to victims. Breeden's report applauded several changes MCI has already made. Many of them are followed by other companies, but some go beyond existing standards and at least one – the process of selecting new directors – will be unique to MCI.

Still, past deeds of the WorldCom era continued to haunt MCI. On 27 August 2003, the State of Oklahoma filed the first criminal charges against MCI and former CEO Bernie Ebbers – but they might not be the last, said state attorney-general Drew Edmondson, who pointed out that Oklahoma pensions lost $64 million from the collapse of WorldCom because of its huge accounting fraud – the largest ever. Edmondson stated that federal penalties, including a $750 million fine, are 'inadequate'.[20]

On 3 September 2003, WorldCom's former CEO Bernie Ebbers was arraigned by Oklahoma prosecutors on criminal charges associated with the company's over $10 billion accounting fraud. In fact, not only Ebbers but also five former subordinates were charged with 15 counts of securities fraud. These charges might hurt MCI's relationships with their customers; they could also create friction with federal officials, much as New York attorney-general Eliot Spitzer rankled some with his probe of Wall Street firms.

On that same day, nine other states in the US announced that they wanted more time to look into tax-avoidance schemes by MCI that could result in big payments. The states, which represent a broad spectrum from Massachusetts to New Mexico, asked a bankruptcy judge overseeing MCI's Chapter 11 case for permission to extend the deadline to file claims against MCI, to audit the company.

The timeframe of WorldCom's tax avoidance is 1999 to 2001, while former CEO Bernie Ebbers was at the helm. At issue is a complex scheme in which MCI allegedly set up a Delaware company that levied as much as $19 billion in royalty charges against subsidiaries in various states for use of the company's brand. As a result, the subsidiaries could deduct those payments as an expense and lower their state tax liability.

On 11 December 2003, Judge Cots of the Southern District of New York issued a deadline for current and former MCI WorldCom shareholders (pink sheets: WCDEQ, MCWEQ, MCIAV) to opt out of the WorldCom shareholder class action by 20 February 2004 if they wanted to pursue individual claims against the defendants, including Salomon Smith Barney. Those who did not specifically opt out are automatically included in that lawsuit.

The complaints already filed by Parker & Waichman, the class action's counsel, charge Salomon Smith Barney with violations of Section 15(c) of the Securities Exchange Act of 1934, as well as various state statutes. These have to do with issuing fraudulent research reports, and violating NYSE Rules 401, 472 and 476(a), and NASD Rules 2110 and 2210. According to the complaints, such research reports:

- were not based on principles of fair dealing and good faith,
- contained opinions for which there was no reasonable basis,
- did not provide a sound basis for evaluating facts, and
- contained exaggerated or unwarranted claims about the covered company.

Also in December 2003, the United States Bankruptcy Court approved MCI's Plan of Reorganization, which paves the way for the company to emerge from Chapter 11 bankruptcy. As a result of MCI's eventual emergence from Chapter 11, it is likely that its equity shares will be cancelled, leaving existing shareholders with a mere fraction of their initial investment, if any.

Class actions and the fact that states might audit MCI's books could result in more dark clouds descending on a company that is trying to leave behind its past and its creative accounting frauds. Legal experts said that states could use possible findings in any tax audit to launch civil or criminal actions against MCI, which means that the renamed telecommunications operator is far from being out of the tunnel. The time is past when WorldCom could create money, real or fake, from anything it could lay hands on – and get away with.

Finally, the US law enforcement industry got a break in its efforts to bring WorldCom's ex-CEO Bernie Ebbers to justice, even if the man who steered his company into the bankruptcy and through a $12 million accounting fraud, had done his utmost to leave no paper trail behind him. For instance in his refusal to use email, Ebbers was not unlikely Enron's ex-CEO Jeffrey Skilling and other chief executives who built their defenses way ahead of trouble.

The lack of evidence electronically tracing the fraud to the chief executive's door had handicapped the work of government prosecutors who, to find a smoking gun, had tried to secure guilty pleas from the CEO's underlings. In Ebber's case, this happened the first week of March 2004 with the capitilation of WorldCom's former finance chief, Scott Sullivan, who pleaded guilty to his role in the fraud.

With Sullivan now co-operating, the US Justice Department swiftly indicted Ebbers. In the aftermath, developments at WorldCom mirrored those which took place one month earlier at Enron, when Justice indicted Jeffrey Skilling, the company's former CEO, following a guilty plea and a co-operation agreement from Enron's ex-CFO, Andrew Fastow.

There are also differences on how these two fraudulent companies cooked the books and took investors and regulators for a ride. In WorldCom's case, when in September 2000 performance begun to deteriorate, to the extent that the company was going to miss its profit targets with disastrous effects on its market capitalization, Sullivan and David Myers, the financial controller, allegedly directed accounting staff to *close the cap*. In company jargon this meant using creative accounting to meet market expectations – mainly done by booking billions of dollars – worth of costs as capital expenditure.

The March 2004 indictment filed by the Department of Justice alleges many connections between Ebbers, the chief executive, and Sullivan, his finance chief, in accounting and reporting improprieties. As the government prosecutors have it, both men instructed staff to make the accounting twists, and Ebbers participated 'extensively' in these exercises – while Sullivan is said to have acted with the 'knowledge and approval' of World-Com's CEO.

Moreover, despite his aversion to email, Ebbers seems to have carelessly left behind some hard evidence, including a memo to executives concerning 'those one-time events that had to happen in order for us to have a chance to make *our numbers*'. There is also a June 2001 voice-mail left by Sullivan for Ebbers about the books 'getting worse and worse' thanks to 'accounting stuff' and about the 'one-time stuff or junk that's already in the numbers'. Lies, a Chinese proverb says, have short legs and eventually truth catches up with them. See also at the end of Chapter 11 the reference to a settlement by Citigroup as the WorldCom shareholders – at $2.65 billion, on 10 May, 2004.

## Notes

1. *BusinessWeek*, 6 May 2002.
2. Chorafas, *Management Risk*.
3. *BusinessWeek*, 23 September 2002.
4. Chorafas, *Management Risk*.
5. A swindle to be exceeded by the bankruptcy of Parmalat, in December 2003, which passed the €13 billion mark in fraudulent financial reporting (see Chapter 3).
6. *BusinessWeek*, 8 July 2002.
7. Ibid., 30 December 2002.
8. *Financial Times*, 27 June 2002.
9. *The Economist*, 27 July 2002.
10. Chorafas, *Operational Risk Control with Basle II*.
11. *The Observer*, 21 July 2002.
12. Chorafas, *Corporate Accountability, with Case Studies in Finance*.
13. *Financial Times*, 27 June 2002.
14. *CommunicationsWeekInternational*, 27 January 2003.
15. *Financial Times*, 11 June 2003.
16. Ibid.
17. *BusinessWeek*, 2 December 2002.
18. *Sunday Times*, 24 August 2003.
19. *International Herald Tribune*, 23/24 August 2003.
20. *USA Today*, 28 August 2003.

# 9
# Lessons from the Fall of Global Crossing, Qwest, Exodus, Adelphia Communications and More

## 1. Introduction

This is a chapter on lessons learned from basket cases: those of telecommunications companies that have misrepresented facts and figures, have taken investors to the cleaners, or nearly so, and finally run for cover under Chapter 11. They were all highly leveraged companies of the late 1990s which crashed when hot air, their most important asset, escaped to the environment. Investors finally understood the Ponzi game behind the supposedly 'huge cost savings' connected to the ever-increasing capacity for broadband transmission offered by the *law of the photon*.

The law of the photon is a technical, not a business, proposition; it does not guarantee that highly increased capacity at equal cost can be sold to the market. In the early 1980s the telecoms, particularly AT&T, had made a similar mistake when they said that all the costs of laying fibre would be recovered by selling recovered copper, the pulled-out twisted pair, to the copper market.

With a couple of exceptions, the case studies in this chapter concern highly indebted *alternative carriers*. This means companies which have, or had, set their sights on challenging the incumbents. For this reason, section 2 addresses leverage and (poor) financial management by alternative carriers in a generic sense – setting the stage for the case studies that follow.

Most of these companies came into the market after the Telecommunications Act of 1996. Some, like Global Crossing, Williams Communications of Tulsa, Oklahoma, and ICG of Englewood, Colorado, have emerged from bankruptcy. Others have a long way to go before they are allowed back to market respectability – and then they will have to compete on more than just price. For all of them, or at least those that wish to survive, at the top of their priorities should be to determine:

- which applications will appeal to customers, and
- for which applications customers will be willing to pay.

This definition must be made without the trickery used in the late 1990s, from creative accounting to the total confusion between business references and scientific facts. WorldCom (see Chapter 8) was part of the group to which I refer, but no other company so well illustrates the modern alchemy using the law of the photon than Global Crossing, a carrier based in Hamilton, Bermuda. As readers will see in sections 3 and 4, its case illustrates one of the major weaknesses of protection under Chapter 11.

Companies emerge from Chapter 11 by discharging their obligations, but the degree to which this is done varies from one entity to the next. The company 360 Networks emerged from bankruptcy 17 months after it filed for protection in Canada and the United States. Greg Maffei remained chief executive of the company, which started life again with $100 million in cash, $215 million in debt, and the intention to concentrate its operations in North America.

However, the parent company of 360 Networks has yet to sell all of 360's old assets. At the time this text was written, these included transatlantic cable that cost around $800 million to construct, but will probably fetch only around $16 million on the market today – just 2 per cent of invested capital.

Chapter 11 companies are a worry for the industry at large. Experts think that if the doors of Chapter 11 continue to swing, they could fundamentally change the telecommunications market and its ranking, as firms which have been very heavy on liabilities use the bankruptcy protection it provides to clean up their balance sheet. This is no level playing field for those companies that try to survive the honest way, without going bankrupt.

The target of Global Crossing's business plan with the bankruptcy court was to emerge from Chapter 11 with just $200 million in debt. This is a small fraction of its original liabilities of $12.4 billion. Since it represents no more than 1.61 per cent of the money which it had borrowed, it leaves its creditors with 98.39 per cent of losses. Rivals complained that the firm would enjoy an advantage as debts of more than $12 billion have been written off.

Notice that Global Crossing's 1.61 per cent figure is very interesting for another reason. A recent study in Germany – where there is nothing like Chapter 11 – suggests that when a company goes into bankruptcy all that its creditors can hope to get back for their assets is no more than 1 per cent to 2 per cent, after the government has taken due taxes and the lawyers collected their fees. If this 1 to 2 per cent trend persists, it is going to kill trust – and therefore the basis for credit.

## 2. Handling the debt of alternative carriers

A study by Kodak in the early 1980s gave evidence that six consecutive years of mismanagement bring a great company to its knees. This was the case of

Compagnie Générale des Eaux (renamed Vivendi Universal), as well as of France Télécom, Deutsche Telekom and British Telecom, among so many others. The difference between the four examples I have given is that Vivendi was a company which tried to become a sort of state monopoly in several business lines – while the other three were mammoth ex-state monopolies in telecommunications turned into publicly quoted enterprises, but run in the most ineffective, bureaucratic way. Practically all ex-state monopoly telephone companies rushed out of a highly protected environment with just one thought in mind: expand in all directions and get bigger and bigger. This is the philosophy of the cancer cell – which Vivendi Universal had also chosen.

The story is different for the start-ups, the so-called *alternative carriers*. They, too, got overleveraged and they overbuilt channel capacity, but in the majority of these cases rather than plain mismanagement the crucial factor behind their failure was a lack of risk management in two domains:

- the rising amount of *credit risk*, because of their rapidly mounting liabilities, and
- *market risk*, since even a novice should have been able to see that channel overcapacity meant price wars, therefore dropping revenues non-compensated by 'more capacity'.

One of the ironies with Vivendi Universal and its foray into the telecoms area, is that it somehow succeeded to find itself in both camps: the very poorly run mammoth telephony and/or media conglomerates, as well as the start-ups through its holding in Cegetel, the mobile communications company. The problems were compounded by the creative accounting practices of which we spoke in Chapter 6 in connection to Deutsche Telekom.

Post mortem, many experts have been suggesting that unreliable statements and the debt of alternative carriers are correlated, because alternative carriers are struggling to deal with crippling debt. To justify such a statement, analysts are looking back to the end of January 2002, when the mounting debt of alternative carriers became a critical issue. There were Global Crossing (see sections 3 and 4), Level 3, Williams Communications (see section 6) and Qwest (see section 7) in the United States, as well as Energis and NTL (see Chapter 6), in the United Kingdom, which either filed for bankruptcy or joined the sick list. In all these cases the company's management came under scrutiny, and the company's equity lost a big chunk of its value.

Vivendi's Cegetel escaped this misfortune, but as far as the telecoms market is concerned, Cegetel is small fry, even if what remains of Vivendi pins on it most of its hopes for the future (more on this in section 7). Another example of a small mobile telephony company with problems is Level 3 Communications, which followed up Energis with bad news, by warning that it may breach its bank covenants around the second quarter of 2002, because of sluggish revenue growth.

With this, and other tricks of creative accounting, there did not seem to be problems in financing. The company had come a long way from late 1997, when CIBC had led the syndication of a $482 million loan to Global Crossing, as well as an $850 million round of financing for the telco's first undersea cable four months later.

Other companies looking for an alternative network provider contributed to the leverage. As Winnick found out, signing up customers for Global Crossing's network even before it was built was as easy as raising money. Investors did not challenge statements which made no business sense, for example, that, as traffic volume grew, Global Crossing would be able to quadruple the capacity of the network simply by changing out the electronic gear at either of its ends.

- As with the case of the twisted pair, mentioned in the introduction, this may be technically feasible,
- but were business, cash flow and profitability also going to quadruple? This is what should have interested analysts and investors.

Because of its huge leverage, its mountain of liabilities and its questionable assets, when on 28 January 2002 Global Crossing filed for Chapter 11 bankruptcy protection, it became the largest telecom bankruptcy filing ever – and fourth largest of any kind in American history. The company's failure had further significance, in that telecoms have been a large part of the 'new economy'.[2]

- The crash of telecoms made a much bigger wave than that of the dot-coms, even in their heyday, and
- telecoms also represented much more physical plant and equipment than all internet companies taken together.

Like Enron, and many other entities whose management ran wild during the late 1990s, Global Crossing had no system of checks and balances which should characterize any prudently governed enterprise. This could be seen throughout, from fat executive-pay packages, particularly when these went to poor performers, to the use of telecommunications capacity swaps as proxies for real revenues. 'The parade of executives who left Global Crossing with multimillion-dollar payoffs is just obscene,' said James E. Heard, chief executive of Institutional Shareholder Services (ISS).[3]

For instance, *after* its bankruptcy Global Crossing lent $15 million to John Legere, its then CEO, and agreed to let him keep the money if he stayed on until February 2003. While a company spokeswoman said that executive compensation would be addressed in the bankruptcy court,[4] huge handouts are gone forever because that sort of money is not hidden under the mattress.

With these different events it came as no surprise that the Securities and Exchange Commission, the FBI and various congressional committees started investigating Global Crossing's practices. The media, too, focused on the illicit swaps, as well as on the fact that this strategy was used, above all, to make it appear that a company had huge revenue and profits – both an illusion. Remember that Global Crossing's certified public accountant is Arthur Andersen, and it was again Arthur Andersen that advised on how to structure the capacity swaps.

## 4.  Undercutting incumbent carriers' pricing. A Chapter 11 aftermath

One of the ironies connected to the aftermath of bankruptcy protection is that many of the surviving telecommunication companies have been afraid of Global Crossing emerging from Chapter 11 with a cleaned-up balance sheet. These competitors are particularly concerned about the company's new business plan which depends on building a retail marketing capability which, if successful, will provide it with steady cash flow and take that business out of the established telecoms balance sheet.

The telecommunications retail market will also be an organizational twist for Global Crossing because the company used to be structured around vertical sales channels addressing other telecoms and big business. Each of these channels had its own sales, technical support and product development. With the new organization there are just two channels: wholesale and retail. In fact, if information known by the market is accurate, Global Crossing targets a retail–wholesale revenue, with more favour to retail sales. Analysts, however, think that the company will need a big workforce if it is to attract retail customers and shift the balance away from its traditional wholesale business.

In January 2003, well before emerging from bankruptcy protection, Global Crossing had 5,000 staff worldwide with the headcount for Europe being 1,300. This was judged by experts as totally inadequate for retail sales. The company said it would use indirect sales partnerships to boost its retail business – but analysts were not convinced this formula would work.

Experts were to suggest that even if such partnerships will help, the company's business partners themselves, as well as systems integrators, will remain wary of the company for some time. 'I don't think the likes of IBM will jump on board quickly,' said Frank Dzubeck, president of Communications Network Architects, of Washington, DC.[5]

Competitors did not fail to notice that Global Crossing's restructuring plan, approved in both Bermuda's Supreme Court and the US Bankruptcy Court in Manhattan, gave the company a very important advantage in a depressed telecommunications market: very little debt, achieved to the detriment of its creditors and investors. The pricing made possible by the company's low level of debt could add a new pressure to pricing in the telecoms market and give Global Crossing the potential to be a real disruptive force by under-cutting incumbent carriers who are suffering huge debt.

While the negotiations for refinancing went on, optimists said that Global Crossing was set to benefit from the injection of fresh capital as Hutchison Whampoa and Singapore Technologies Telemedia wanted to take a 61.5 per cent stake in the company, enriching it with new capital and the right products. Global Crossing, these optimists advised, might become one of the better smaller but dynamic players in the telecommunications market, particularly if it is able to maintain its key clients. In early 2003, a year after the bankruptcy, the company's management said that it was able to keep nearly 95 per cent of the customers on roster when the firm went into bankruptcy.

Subsequent events indicated that the optimists and the company's own management had definitely got it wrong. From emergence from bankruptcy until mid-August 2003, the only thing Global Crossing was able to accumulate was another $89 million in debt. No wonder its equity was worthless trading (on 11 August 2003) at 0.018 cents, and fluctuating between a 52-week high of 0.30 cents and a 52-week low of 0.00013 cents.[6]

One of the things that Global Crossing's management did not say publicly is that after bankruptcy it had to renegotiate terms with customers. Also, some big customers left. For instance, in April 2003, Swift, the global financial messaging network operator, ended an exclusive network services deal with Global Crossing, returning the X.25 and IP-VPN network operations in-house and transferring its global IP-VPN service to Colt, Equant, Infonet and AT&T.

According to some industry watchers, Global Crossing was gambling its survival on network upgrades, such as integrating its existing IP and MPLS network platforms into a single one with MPLS at the kernel. But this and some similar feats were insufficient to lift the company out of the abyss, and also required investments the cash-strapped carrier could not afford.

Still, with the planned network upgrades and retail client focus, supposed to start in 2003, the company has been projecting 20 per cent revenue growth per year, with revenues 'expected' to reach $5.5 billion by 2006. Several analysts, however, questioned whether a streamlined Global Crossing could attract large corporate customers which are vital to its longer-term survival. An entity's cash flow is very sensitive to the existence of:

- big-name clients, and
- systems integrators.

It takes a great many upgrades to be able to serve both populations, particu-larly the latter of these two markets, which may also turn out to be the more lucrative since big-name clients negotiate their contracts to make sure they are low cost. Moreover, network upgrades must be steady and should reflect the requirements posed by the changing role of systems integrators.

Like a person who degrades by not using his resources, so does a technological infrastructure which remains idle. Coming out of Chapter 11 is no sort of business panacea. As Iridium, another fallen alternative carrier, and many other cases show, the company may never again be able to stand on its feet as a significant player in its line of business.

Global Crossing must have been aware of these challenges when, in early August 2003, it filed an 8-K report, which speaks volumes about its total lack of financial health. The report contained Global Crossing's monthly operating data for June of that same year, to the US Bankruptcy Court. It included:

- monthly disbursements of $184 million,
- monthly operating *loss* of $99 million,[7] and
- total revenues of $252 million.

The company had total assets of $10.63 billion and total liabilities of $10.94 billion, of which $8.04 billion were subject to compromise in provisional liquidation in the Supreme Court of Bermuda. This was the August 2003 estimate by Global Crossing and its debtor subsidiaries of total claims that will or may be restructured in their Chapter 11 cases. With liabilities more than assets, the financial results were dismal.

What about refinancing by the Asian telecoms? A curious lobby of companies – curious in terms of its composition, which included Nestlé of Switzerland and Nokia of Finland – said that Singapore Technologies Telemedia should be allowed to buy 61.5 per cent of Global Crossing for $250 million, or about 2 per cent of its debts. That's a bargain basement price, and the lobby tried to overcome objections by the US Defense Department to the buyout because of concerns about foreign ownership of a network used by US government entities.

Finally, in October 2003, government-controlled Singapore Technologies Telemedia (STT) was given the go-ahead to purchase a 61.5 per cent, $250 million stake in Global Crossing. Hutchison Whampoa was not included in the deal. US government security watchdogs, which reviewed whether the sale would violate foreign ownership restrictions, seem to have lifted their objections.

In December 2003 Global Crossing emerged from Chapter 11 bankruptcy, after nearly two years. The company, however, announced that it lost $25 billion between 2000 and 2002 and that it would not be able to generate enough money to meet its near-term expenses. Singapore Technologies Telemedia, the carrier's controlling shareholder, said it would inject up to $100 million more to fund operations through to the end of 2004.

## 5.   A pattern of abuse, with deals made on the back of investors

As far as Global Crossing is concerned, it all began in March 1997 when Gary Winnick and the Canadian Imperial Bank of Commerce (CIBC) were brought together by Bruce Raben, a dealmaker for the Canadian bank in Los Angeles, who was also a Drexel alumni. CIBC paid $41 million for a 25 per cent stake in Global Crossing. Less than a year and a half later, in August 1998, Global Crossing sold stock to the public, valuing CIBC's stake at $926 million – a hefty profit of 2,246 per cent.

In principle, there is nothing wrong with capital appreciation and extraordinary gains. But then it later came to the public eye that this was like a revival of the defunct's Drexel, Burnham Lambert line of business, rather than a telecommunication services outfit. CIBC's seats on the board of Global Crossing were filled by some of the Who's Who in Drexel. Dean C. Kehler, Andrew R. Heyer and Jay Bloom, who ran CIBC's high-yield bond department, had all worked under Drexel dealmaker Leon D. Black. Heyer had also bank-rolled takeover artists like Saul P. Steinberg.

CIBC might say that all of this talent was needed since the bank served as an underwriter for Global Crossing's initial offering. According to Thomson Financial, the bank earned $20 million in fees for that and other related work. Also, it received $12 million in stock from a consulting contract with Global Crossing. The two together represented a hefty 78 per cent of CIBC's initial capital investment in Global Crossing – making subsequent profits practically free of risk.

*BusinessWeek* has written that according to sources familiar with CIBC's investment in Global Crossing, the trio of Kehler, Heyer and Bloom invested the bank's money through a partnership that allowed them to keep 18 per cent of the profits from the deal. In a March 2000 filing with the Securities and Exchange Commission, Kehler and Bloom claimed voting control of 11.4 million Global Crossing shares worth $680 million.

As Global Crossing stock climbed in 1999 and 2000, CIBC was a steady seller. By October 2000 it had locked in $800 million in profits. Its chosen directors on the board of Global Crossing also sold equity. At that time (October 2000) the bank announced that it had pledged the bulk of its remaining holdings with other parties, ensuring that CIBC would get no less than $20 per share. Even after Global's bankruptcy, the bank still had unrealized gains of $300 million on that position – though it announced that it might have to write off $242 million in Global Crossing loans and preferred stock that it had not hedged.[8]

Selective share selling to make a huge profit before the equity crashes is a deal made on the back of investors. It is also a sort of insider dealing, which has become common throughout the telecoms industry. Such practice has been particularly encouraged by executive pay packages that were heavily weighted toward stock compensation.[9] Neither was this behaviour at Global Crossing a one-off.

At Exodus Communications (see section 9), whose remains have been sold to Cable & Wireless, 19 officers and directors sold 10.6 million shares, split-adjusted, valued at $232.4 million, from February 2000 to January 2002. There was also heavy selling in February 2000, as the stock approached its all-time split-adjusted peak, and again in August 2000 as the stock recovered before falling once again.

At Qwest Communications, 18 officers and directors sold 11.6 million shares valued at $530.4 million from January 2000 to July 2001 (see section 7). Much of the selling was by Qwest's chairman and chief executive Joseph Nacchio, who cashed in $200.9 million of stock. By early March 2002 Qwest's shares slid below $9 from a high of $64 in early 2000.

At McLeod USA, a competitive local carrier (see section 6), insiders were big sellers at the most opportune moment: as the stocks peaked. Among those whose timing was particularly beneficial to the seller was McLeod USA chief executive Stephen Gray.[10] Insider information is always handy (though illegal) in deciding when to get in and out of an investment – and stock options are a good way to do it.

Executives overcompensating themselves for their services is by no means only found in the US. In Europe, in late February 2002, as Asea Brown Boveri (ABB) was fighting for its life after having lost $691 million, came the news that former top executives had walked away with pension and retirement benefits worth a combined CHF 233 million ($183 million) by taking advantage of the company's slack structure of corporate governance.[11]

One of the people involved in ABB's exorbitant pension scandal was Percy Barnevik. In the 1990s, he was the man often revered as the exemplary high-skills manager and architect of the merger that formed ABB by bringing together Asea and Brown Boveri. Barnevik was chief executive from 1988 to 1996, and then chairman until 2001.

- Barnevik's overcompensation has focused attention on plush rewards enjoyed by top executives.
- In the aftermath, several big companies have been moved to explain in detail the pension arrangements for their bosses.

What shocked most people about Barnevik's overgenerous pension deal is that it was not approved by the company's board. ABB had no proper remuneration committee, and Percy Barnevik used executive fiat to push through the payments – though he subsequently came under heavy scrutiny when such self-gratification became publicly known.

After being overpaid for their services, some CEOs, albeit very few, have the decency to return the money. This was the case with Pierre Bilger, retired president and CEO of the nearly bankrupt French–British company Alstom,[12] who restituted to the firm €4.1 million ($4.1 million) of the €5.1 million he had received. Bilger said that he did so because 'he did not want to be an object of scandal for the one hundred thousand Alsthom employees'.[13] Bravo Bilger!

The moral of all of these stories is that this new sort of insider trading by using information about an oncoming crash, bypassing the board's authority to get greedy overcompensation for past services, as well as handing out all types of 'executive loans', do much more than pose conflicts of interest issues and complicate disclosure. They are also one of the forms of operational risk to which a great deal of attention should be paid during the coming years.[14]

Well-managed companies do not grant loans to executives as a matter of course. Even if this ever takes place under rare and special circumstances, it should never reach even 1 per cent of the level it did at WorldCom, Global Crossing and ImClone. Neither should senior executives of companies rip off their investors by creating a bubble, then punching it by unloading the stock while the equity kite still flies high. Let's face it. The moral fabric of our society has weakened. Ethics aside, this is not what is needed to restart the economy.

Neither was Global Crossing irreproachable in its dealings, which means that it had plenty of business in court. In the US, it has been fighting Level 3 Communications after this carrier demanded a $21.2 million payment from Global Crossing's UK subsidiary for amounts allegedly owed under a co-build contract from 2000. Level 3 has been disputing Global Crossing's right to put a UK registered subsidiary into Chapter 11.

And as we saw in section 3, following its bankruptcy protection filing in early February 2002, Global Crossing has been under investigation by the Securities and Exchange Commission and the Federal Bureau of Investigation for its accounting practices, specifically in relation to revenue reporting. Part of this examination concerned the fact that the company's executives sold off more than $1.3 billion in Global Crossing shares in the years before the crash. In this way they surpassed the equally greedy executives at Enron who had sold 'only' $1 billion in shares over the same period.[15]

Lust and greed may be well-known human traits, but at the same time they are anathema to a market economy. The excesses which we saw in this section, and the resulting pattern of abuse of the many by the very few, kill business confidence. A long-standing industry maxim holds that honesty is the best policy. But honesty in the late 1990s and early years of the twenty-first century has departed, and with it has gone shame and personal accountability.

## 6.  McLeodUSA, Williams Communications, Marconi and Viatel

Within days of Global Crossing, McLeodUSA Communications filed the fourth-largest telecom bankruptcy in American history, then swiftly re-emerged from bankruptcy protection – in April 2002. This was another example of the abuse of protection offered under Chapter 11. Williams Communications, too, filed for bankruptcy protection and redistributed its equity between bondholders and its parent energy outfit: Williams Companies.

At the end of 2001, Williams Communications was nearly $6 billion in debt. Its parent, Williams Companies, was owed around $2.4 billion. These heavy debts for a relatively small telecom were incurred in constructing a fibre-optic network which was part of the telecom industry's problem – because it added to massive overcapacity rather than to income.

While management at Williams Communications was filing for Chapter 11 protection as part of a restructuring plan, experts said that it was difficult to see how it could survive given its very heavy liability. Analysts added that while with bankruptcy filing the stockholders would be the first to be wiped out, bondholders would probably end up with no more than 5 cents in recapitalized stock for every dollar.

In other words, equity investors and bond investors were relieved of their money, and banks which had given loans to the company had to make special provisions. Yet at the same time that it was getting ready to ask for protection from creditors, Williams Communications paid five of its top executives a total of $13 million in retention bonuses. It did so just three months before it filed for Chapter 11.

There is another disturbing issue related to this pattern. Like McLeodUSA and Williams Communications, too many companies have gone over the cliff even if a few years earlier they seemed to be invulnerable. Many of these were not fly-by-night dot-coms, but relatively large and well-established entities, such as Lucent Technologies, Nortel and the British Marconi (the former General Electric of the UK), which defaulted on its financial obligations on 22 March 2002.

Marconi was a 116-year-old British electrical engineering company, when it was known under the General Electric brand. It specialized in defence contracts and time-honoured electric engineering manufacturing. These products were not fancy, but they were cash cows. However, a new management changed all that and put the company in peril.

In the late 1990s, Marconi abandoned its defence equipment production, sold its defence division to British Aerospace, and then spent more than $8 billion to become one of Europe's largest producers of internet equipment. With the dot-coms bust, Marconi's sales collapsed, and the firm had to fire 13,000 workers. On 22 March 2002, Marconi announced that its main creditor banks had refused to grant any new loans. The company had reached the end of the road.

Fourteen months later, in May 2003, Marconi made its relisting debut on the London Stock Exchange, closing its first day of trading with a value of £590 million ($1 billion). Notice, however, that Marconi had a paper value of £35 billion ($60 billion) at the peak of the market but had been on a financial downward spiral after releasing a profit warning in the summer of 2001.

Another basket case is carrier Viatel. In May 2002 bondholders of the bankrupt entity approved a reorganization plan that would allow it to emerge from Chapter 11 protection debt-free. This agreement assigns a value of $80 million to the company, which was believed to be in debt to the tune of some $2.1 billion when it filed for bankruptcy a year earlier, in May 2001. When Viatel Global Communications was launched in 1996, it said that it needed 'only' $107 million for network expansion. That did not seem so much, especially considering that analysts were projecting revenues of more than $1 billion by 2004. Viatel, however, continued to ask investors for money, and by the end of 2000 had raised more than $2 billion from people and companies who thought that with Viatel they had hit the jackpot. Then came the bust, followed by filing for protection from creditors.

Still another interesting case of boom and bust is UPC, the second-largest cable operator in Europe. By mid-April 2002 it had asked for bankruptcy protection after failing to reach a debt restructuring agreement with its bondholders. The company reported losses of over €4.4 billion ($4.4 billion) in 2001 and debts of €7.5 billion ($7.5 billion).

Yet, just a year earlier, in 2001, Europe's three main cable operators – UPC, Telewest and NTL (see Chapter 6) – had publicly expressed their confidence that they could ward off any threat from digital terrestrial TV (DTT), even if privately there was some anxiety that DTT's plug-and-play concept would tempt existing cable subscribers as well as potential viewers. The market's scepticism (and warnings) had gone unheeded.

Reader will remember that, in May 2002, still another of the former European top-fliers, KPNQwest, said that without additional financial support from shareholders, strategic buyers or third-party investors, it would not be able to meet funding requirements for the rest of 2002. In light of its deteriorating position, 'there is substantial risk that there may be no underlying value to either [KPNQwest's] debt or equity securities,' said a company statement.

The operator retained Bear Stearns and Bank of America Securities to advise it on alternative means of recapitalizing its balance sheet, but the real saviour was the Dutch taxpayer. As is so often the case, the taxpayer's deep pockets have been a source of new life in all cases where the government still has a substantial stake – and in several others. Employees and workers also gave a helping hand as they voluntarily kept on running KPNQwest's internet infrastructure even if they were not paid their wages.

## 7.   Conflicts of interest at Qwest Communications International

Qwest was one of those companies that were a mare's nest in terms of conflicts of interest. Its founder and chairman, Philip Anschutz, had extensive dealings with the company. He was also a member of its compensation and nominating committees. Described as 'comatose' by one expert, the compensation committee awarded ex-CEO Joseph Nacchio an $88 million pay package in 2001, one of the worst years in the company's history.

Neither was 2002 a good year for Qwest. In the first quarter, the company had a rough time. On 11 March 2002, the telecoms operator said that the Securities and Exchange Commission had launched an inquiry into certain accounting practices. On 1 April of that same year, Qwest stated that it would have to take a charge of $20 billion to $30 billion to write off goodwill, while the SEC had launched a second inquiry into its accounting.

Following this, in a 9 April 2002 statement, the Denver-based company informed publicly of the need to make a material restatement to its earnings. With the accumulating effects of this statement and some others, it is no surprise that the price of Qwest's stock dropped 55 per cent, in 2002 alone. To increase its liquidity, Qwest had to make an emergency $1.5 billion bond issue.

Then, in September 2002, congressional investigators in the US accused Global Crossing and Qwest of engaging in capacity swaps with each other that had no purpose other than illicitly to boost revenues (see section 3). Qwest had announced that it would restate $960 million in revenue that was improperly recognized from the capacity swaps from June 2000 to June 2001. In so doing it implicitly recognized that at least some capacity swaps were done to:

- meet Wall Street expectations, and
- help in fulfilling sales quotas.

By November 2002, the market widely expected not only bad news related to Qwest Communications' restatement of revenues, but also an additional write-down of $40.8 billion. Of this, some $30 billion was in goodwill and other intangible assets, while the rest was accounted for by the decreasing value of:

- the fibre-optic network,
- customer-related assets, and
- product technology.

This increase in liabilities meant that shareholder equity dipped into the negative side. It stood at $34.9 billion in June 2000, but then it continued to slide in tandem with the company's disappearing business fortunes. The SEC has also been looking into whether Qwest should have provided investors with more financial details regarding its merger with US West.

For any practical purpose the former upstarts, Qwest Communications, Global Crossing and WorldCom, found themselves swimming in the same sort of self-made troubles – and all have been asked by the Securities and

Exchange Commission to produce documents for separate, informal investigations into:

- their accounting practices, and
- the swaps of optical capacity it made with competing operators.

Analysts on Wall Street suggested that there was also conflict of interest involved. For instance, the chairman of Qwest's audit committee, responsible for overseeing its accounting practices, had a potential conflict that has never been disclosed in the company's financial documents. W. Thomas Stephens was the former chairman and then a director of a Mail-Well, a printing company that got a multi-million-dollar contract from Qwest in December 2001 – raising concerns that Stephens may not have been as critical of Qwest's accounting as a truly independent director would be.[16]

Neither was W. Thomas Stephens the only audit committee member with a possible conflict. Linda G. Alvarado, another member, was president of Alvarado Construction, which received $1.3 million from Qwest for construction services in 2000, according to Qwest's proxy statement. That particular contract was awarded by US West before being acquired by Qwest in June 2000. According to experts' opinion, conflict of interest issues do not end when the directors of companies stop getting cash.

Then, on 25 February 2003, four former Qwest executives were indicted by a grand jury in Denver on criminal charges stemming from an alleged accounting fraud that investigators said improperly boosted the US telecom group's revenues by $33 million. The indictment claimed that the executives registered prematurely results from a sales contract with an Arizona school district in order to meet aggressive quarterly earnings targets.

Qwest's four indicted executives were Grant Graham and Thomas Hall, chief financial officer and vice-president in Qwest's Global Business Unit; John Walker, a vice-president in the government and education group; and Bryan Treadway, an assistant controller. Warrants were issued for their arrests.

Apart from the grand jury investigation, the Securities and Exchange Commission filed a civil complaint against those executives and four others at Qwest, claiming that they manipulated another contract to inflate revenues by $100 million. John Ashcroft, the US attorney-general, characterized the investigation of the telecoms group as 'active and ongoing', suggesting that additional action may follow.

The four indicted Qwest Communications International executives could face up to 40 years in prison for securities fraud, wire fraud and conspiracy, as well as $1 million (a triviality) in fines. The indictment alleged that behind the alleged swindle was the fact that Qwest's Global Business Unit was struggling to achieve growth targets for the quarters ending in September 2000.

Also close to home was the case of Qwest Digital Media (QDM), a joint venture that specialized in converting video footage into computer files that could be transmitted over the internet. Qwest took charges of $33 million to write down the value of QDM, in 2001, and closed the business in February 2002. But to some Qwest shareholders, QDM represents more than just another bad investment because it raised questions about whether Philip F. Anschutz, Qwest's founder and chairman, put his personal interests ahead of Qwest's.[17]

QDM was created in 1999 as a 50-50 joint venture between Qwest and Anschutz, who was acting on his own behalf. The telecoms company contributed $85 million to the venture, payable over nine years, while Anschutz chipped in TV production assets whose value was not disclosed in public documents. Then, in 2000, Anschutz received $48 million from Qwest for selling the telecoms company an additional 25 per cent of the equity in QDM. In the end, Qwest lost its entire investment while paying Anschutz big money, thereby reducing his losses in the joint venture. The pattern of these different conflicts, characterizing a publicly quoted enterprise, is disquieting.

## 8.   Using a public company as family fief: Adelphia Communications

In early June 2002, Adelphia Communications, a publicly owned cable TV operator with a stock worth very little nowadays, fired its certified public account, Deloitte & Touche, after having to restate cash flow and revenues for the past two years. Adelphia had made off-balance-sheet loans to its founders, the Rigas family. The board of Adelphia put the company's name in $2.3 billion worth of bank loans to the founding family, which owned about 20 per cent of the shares.

Adelphia was the No. 6 cable TV company; and it was run like a family outfit. Until May 2002, its board accommodated no fewer than four members of the Rigas family: the company founder, John Rigas, and his three sons. The father and two of the sons, along with two other company executives, were arrested by the FBI in late July 2002, then released on bail (more on this later).

John Rigas, the former chairman of bankrupt Adelphia, had started the; cable company in 1952 with $300. By the time it filed for Chapter 11 bankruptcy protection in June 2002, the firm had accumulated nearly $20 billion of debt. Investigated by the Securities and Exchange Commission, the company bowed to the inevitable, listing 234 subsidiaries. This was the fifth largest bankruptcy in US corporate history up to that time, as shown in Table 9.2. In its Chapter 11 filing, Adelphia Communications indicated:

- assets of $24.1 billion, and
- debits of $18.6 billion.

As usually, not only creditors and shareholders but also Adelphia's suppliers got burnt. In 2000, Scientific-Atlanta sold set-top boxes to the communications

*Table 9.2* The ten biggest US bankruptcies in the 1990 to 2002 timeframe[18]

| Company | Date | Assets ($ billion) |
|---|---|---|
| Enron | 2001 | 63.4 |
| Texaco | 1987 | 35.9 |
| Financial Corp of America | 1988 | 33.9 |
| Global Crossing | 2002 | 25.5 |
| Pacific Gas & Electric | 2001 | 24.5 |
| Adelphia Communications | 2002 | 24.1 |
| Mcorp | 1989 | 20.2 |
| Kmart | 2002 | 16.3 |
| First Executive | 1991 | 15.2 |
| Gibraltar Financial | 1990 | 15.0 |

company, and offered to advance $26 per box to help market a new digital service. Two years down the line, on 10 June 2002, the cable TV operator acknowledged that it never spent the marketing money – using it instead to reduce reported expenses. With Adelphia in bankruptcy reorganization, Scientific-Atlanta had to write off the $83.8 million.

Suppliers of programming and technology have also been bracing themselves for big losses from Adelphia contracts. Walt Disney, which sold Adelphia its ESPN sports programming, saw its cash flow cut by $50 billion as a result of the bankruptcy. News Corporation said it was owed as much as $20 million for Fox News and FX. Other channels, too, were licking their wounds. Neither could they expect to recover much out of some $3 billion in off-balance-sheet loans to the company's founders, the Rigas family.[19]

The spirits of creditors were not lifted by the fact that Adelphia has gone from one creative accounting revelation to another; and the founding family also had its own legal woes. On Wednesday, 24 July 2002, Manhattan US Attorney James Comey accused 77-year-old John Rigas and two sons, Timothy and Michael, of 'one of the largest and most egregious frauds ever perpetrated on investors and creditors'. With TV cameras capturing the humiliating moment, the founder of Adelphia Communications was led away in handcuffs.

There were 24 separate counts against John Rigas in connection with hiding $2.3 billion in debt, misstating profits, and using the company as his own 'personal piggy bank'. Charges range from mail and bank fraud to securities law violations. Bank fraud alone carries up to 30 years in prison. Apart from John Rigas and his sons Timothy and Michael, James Brown, former vice-president finance, and Michael Mulcahey, former director internal reporting, have also been facing charges.

In his way, Rigas became a celebrity as the first CEO arrested and handcuffed in the 2000/2002 wave of corporate accounting scandals. He also gained the dubious honour of becoming the most vivid symbol of white-collar crime since Michael Milken and Ivan Boesky in the 1980s. In a filing in Federal Bankruptcy Court in New York, the remnants of Adelphia, the company, charged Rigas and his family with violating the Racketeer Influenced and Corrupt Organizations (RICO) Act. Charges leading to the Rigases' arrest include various facts and figures:

- the family began using Adelphia as collateral for private loans in 1996, even though the firm was one of the largest junk bond issuers in the United States;
- the Rigases secretly inflated Adelphia's cable TV subscription numbers to make investors think it was still growing at a healthy pace;
- Adelphia began adding customers who just ordered high-speed internet services from the Rigases, not-Adelphia systems;
- the Rigases used creative accounting to disguise Adelphia's actual expenses for digital decoder boxes; and
- in 1999, they told analysts that Adelphia could provide two-way communications to 50 per cent of its customers. The real figure was 35 per cent.

Also, starting in 2000, Adelphia spent $13 million to build a golf club on land mostly owned by John Rigas. To cap all that, the Rigases took more than $252 million from Adelphia to pay for margin calls on their equity purchases, while the company's stock price continued falling, as shown in Figure 9.1. This and the other case studies we have seen in this book show that ripping off investors through creative accounting, manipulated

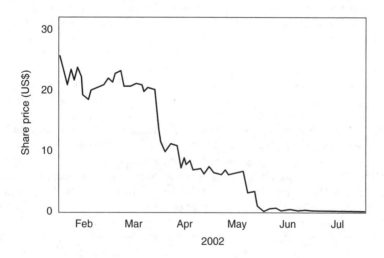

*Figure 9.1*   In four months Adelphia became a penny stock

financial statements and self-gratification are not isolated accidents. They are embodiments of a mindset.

As a port-mortem, on 25 February, 2004, Adelphia Communications secured $8.8 billion in new financing, the largest amount ever for a bankrupt company. This came after it submitted its reorganization plan to the US Bankruptcy Court for the Southern District of New York, which valued Adelphia at $17 billion. The financing was led by JP Morgan Chase, Citigroup, Credit Suisse First Boston, and Deutsche Bank. Sometimes red ink is so thick that certain bankers believe it is black.

## 9.  Exodus Communications

Exodus Communications was a storage company for internet traffic, whose capitalization rose sharply, and then came crashing back to earth. The company has some distinction: it was launched on a shoestring budget of $5,000 with the help of credit card debt assumed by its founders. In March 1998, it made it to the stock market through an IPO, and its shares immediately rose 85 per cent. Two years later it reached a valuation of $30 billion.

Before Exodus Communications went bankrupt, K. B. Chandrasekhar, one of its co-founders, was to reap some $130 million from share sales. After the Exodus bankruptcy, Chandrasekhar bounced back with a new venture known as Jamcracker.

- Chandrasekhar defended his inordinate gains while investors lost hundreds of millions of dollars.
- So did Ellen Hancock, former chief executive of Exodus and a former senior IBMer, who featured $15.5 million of share sales connected to one of the biggest technology collapses in 2001.[20]

In a way that proves the low moral standing of our society, none of the people involved in Exodus seems to have regretted what they did. They simply cashed in their equity in the company in time, leaving the misled investors to hold the bag.

May 2001 was the month when Ellen Hancock and other insiders sold shares. This was followed by a 20 June profit warning, with shares falling 30 per cent in a day. In early September 2001 Hancock quit and L. William Krause became the CEO. He was offered a $600,000 initial bonus and another $1 million if he could turn Exodus around or sell it. Some weeks later, unable to meet interest payments on its more than $3 billion of debt, the company filed for bankruptcy. It was sold to Cable & Wireless for a fraction of its value in its heyday.[21]

Investors lost in a big way, but Chandrasekhar and Hancock profited heavily, and so did several Exodus directors and other executives. Some walked away with double Hancock's amount. Records show that Exodus insiders made more than $350 million from share sales in the 1999 to 2001 timeframe, including $41 million of gains on options exercised one day before to the high-water mark of the company's equity.

- The top day for insider share trading seems to have been 31 August 2000.
- A month later, in September 2000, Exodus announced a $6.5 billion deal to buy Global Crossing's Global Center – all that on an initial capital of $5,000.

This sort of irrational euphoria did not last long. In mid-January 2001 Exodus warned of slowing demand from internet companies, and ten days later it announced a plan to raise $800 million from bonds and secondary offerings. It also tried to slim down when on 9 May it announced 675 job cuts and associated restructuring charges.

What was it, after all, that Exodus was selling under the vague and general name of 'communications'? An equally vague answer was 'internet infrastructure'. Indeed, as far as internet infrastructure went, Exodus Communications was the investors' darling. This was the company to watch as long as the web's server-hosting business boomed. The company ran server farms that provided internet site services for businesses. Major brokerage houses recommended it as 'strong buy', and investors obliged with their cash, without any critical analysis of risk and return.

The rise and fall of Exodus Communications equity has been historic. In March 2000, at the peak of the internet bubble, Exodus stock hit $85 and though in the next months it lost some of its glamour, by October 2000 it held still at 75 per cent of its peak. Then started the rapid descent, as shown in Figure 9.2.

Broker promotion was the trick. In its early days, when it sold for $5, Exodus equity was promoted as worth at least $15. Then, when it hit $15, brokers advised clients to buy it because its intrinsic value was at least $50. But it did not take long until investors saw their nest-egg shrink to $1 per share. This happened in August 2001. Subsequently, Exodus went bankrupt.

- From $89.81 in March 2000, two years later, in March 2002, Exodus equity could be bought for three cents ($0.03).
- Enron, another now bankrupt high-flier, did better than that: after its bankruptcy its stock fell to 'only' $0.17.

Neither were the shareholders the only ones to be taken to the cleaners. Bondholders, too, paid a high price. Exodus had eight different junk bond offerings totalling about $3.4 billion, and it had run up more debt than it could ever handle. 'Management over-leveraged the company and it's their fault,' said Cary Robinson, an analyst at US Bancorp Piper Jaffray.[22]

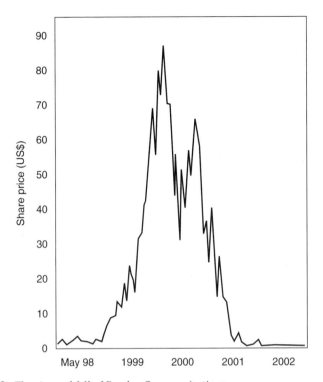

*Figure 9.2*   The rise and fall of Exodus Communications

While the rapid rise in capitalization was absurd, the fall from grace was not surprising because Exodus never made a profit since it went public in March 1998. The company claimed to run 44 internet data centres on four continents. When it filed Chapter 11 papers on 26 September 2001, in the US Bankruptcy Court in Delaware, it listed $5.98 billion in assets and $4.44 billion in debts. Sounds familiar? Mismanagement seems to have been rampant, with running the company regardless of huge debt the rule.

Exodus losses increased more than tenfold in the second quarter of 2001, and it fired workers as it failed to win new contracts fast enough to replace those it lost. The bankruptcy filing allowed Exodus to escape some $75 million to $80 million in quarterly interest payments on its bonds. HSBC Bank USA, representing six different groups of bondholders, was listed in court papers as Exodus's largest unsecured creditor.

According to a Securities and Exchange Commission filing, Global Crossing, which, as we have seen in sections 3 and 4, itself went bankrupt, was the biggest Exodus shareholder as of 30 June 2001, with a 19 per cent stake. There were cross-holdings. Exodus had acquired Global Crossing's Global

Center unit in January 2001 for $1.91 billion in stock, providing itself with new centres in New York and Amsterdam.

Following its filing under Chapter 11, Exodus closed ten data centres that were under construction, fired more employees, and tried to pull itself up by its shoestrings by focusing on existing customers in its bid to turn a profit. It also arranged a $200 million bankruptcy credit line from General Electric Capital to fund operations – which can be interpreted as meaning that GE Capital was betting on an eventual Exodus revival, or a sale to another telecoms firm. It was sold to Cable & Wireless for a small fraction of its value in its heyday.

## 10.   Metromedia and MobilCom

There are two case studies on management in this section: one American, the other European. Metromedia bet on optical fibres for metropolitan area networks (MAN) and lost in a big way. MobilCom, a German company, sought its future in mobile communications but it was governed in the worst possible way, and also hurt by scandals.

At the height of the telecoms bubble, Metromedia Fiber Network was considered one of the stars in America's new communications infrastructure. When, on 28 October 1997, its shares went public, the market pushed them up by 34 per cent in one day – and it continued propelling them. From a few dollars the shares rose to $48. This high valuation happened over 17 to 19 November 1990, precisely when several of its key executives sold more than $200 million worth of shares.

Put together by Stephen Garofalo to address demand for metropolitan area networks, through broadband at low price, Metromedia was one of the alternative carriers of the late 1990s with an original idea. As the growth of the internet began to create demand for new communications capacity, the company attracted several sponsors, but the profits investors expected were not just around the corner. As the market was flooded with network oversupply,

- Metromedia turned in only *one* profitable year, making less than $1 million in 1998;
- by contrast, in 1995–97 and in 1999–2001 it produced combined losses of more than $1.35 billion.

Even with this doom and gloom, management profited, as Metromedia's soaring share price helped to make many of its executives and directors rich. Garofalo himself cashed in more than $50 million worth of stock two years after Metromedia's 1997 IPO. Nick Tanzi, the president and COO, raised some $30 million when Metromedia's share price peaked, and more cash later on. Howard Finkelstein, who spent three years as No. 2 to Garofalo, collected $104.5 million from his stock sales.[23] So did others.

Investors careless enough to go by rumour rather than through analysis of financial statements got themselves burnt. On 18 June 2001 Metromedia cut its 2001 revenue guidance. A few months later, on 21 November, Tanzi resigned as CEO after just six weeks on the job. Then on 22 April 2002, Metromedia announced that it would restate previously reported results. A month later, on 20 May 2002, it filed for Chapter 11 bankruptcy protection. The end came swiftly.

The case of MobilCom, the German mobile telephone operator, is not too different. While the company was never a star performer, it had attracted investors. Negative publicity hit when Gerhard Schmidt, its CEO, took €68 million ($68 million) from his publicly quoted company without the board's approval. Post mortem he said 'he loaned that money so that his wife buys MobilCom shares to launch a stock option scheme', adding that 'I did not know this was a violation of the law'.[24] (!!)

Not only was Schmidt's self-made 'loan' illegal, but also his wrongdoings created a huge liability for France Télécom (see Chapter 6), which experts said at that time might have to shell out an additional $4 billion to protect its investment in MobilCom. France Télécom came into the picture because, without much thought it acquired a big chunk of MobilCom, to be a player in the German market. Eventually the heavily indebted France Télécom could not afford the debt and decided to opt out – but not for long.

France Télécom was right when it came to the conclusion that damage control and self-preservation required letting MobilCom go down the drain, but this happened in September 2002 amidst federal elections in Germany, and it created a political storm. Running hard for re-election, German chancellor Gerhard Schröder crafted a $392 million rescue package to save 5,500 jobs at MobilCom (later raised to $600 million), and also pressed the French government to reverse France Télécom's decision.

Schröder was irked that Paris allowed state-controlled France Télécom, which owned 28.5 per cent in MobilCom, to decide to stop investing in the company before Germany's national elections. Determined to fight back, Schröder's ministers said they would provide MobilCom legal help in its bid to obtain the $17.5 billion it said France Télécom promised to invest but changed its mind.

For its part, the French government was busy working out its own rescue package for France Télécom, after pushing out CEO and chairman Michel Bon. The French government's hope was that a $14.5 billion rights offering would bail out France Télécom but the state's 55 per cent stake saw to it that the majority of this money will come out of the French taxpayer's pocket. Basically, both governments, German and French, were hugely embarrassed by MobilCom's sinking boat.

The way out seems to have been to push the banks in a rescue mission. In November 2002, MobilCom received another deadline extension from banks on the repayment of a €4.7 billion ($4.7 billion) loan, the fifth since it fell due in July of that same year. In continental Europe, companies in trouble are more skilful in milking the taxpayer than their counterparts in the US and the UK.

Finally, former shareholder France Télécom, itself deeply in debt (see Chapter 6), helped refinance around €7 billion for the company. France Télécom's cooperation hinged on founder Gerhard Schmidt finally signing over a 40 per cent stake in MobilCom held by him and his wife, which he did in early November 2002. Even with that condition, MobilCom's case proves that political favours are not averse to filling the gaps left by company governance that is dismal.

## Notes

1. *CommunicationsWeekInternational*, 1 April 2002.
2. D. N. Chorafas. *Managing Risk in the New Economy*, New York: New York Institute of Finance, 2001.
3. *BusinessWeek*, 20 May 2002.
4. *Bloomberg Markets*, March 2002.
5. *CommunicationsWeekInternational*, 26 January 2003.
6. *Bloomberg*, 8 August 2003.
7. Ibid.
8. *BusinessWeek*, 11 March 2002.
9. Chorafas, *Management Risk*.
10. *Wall Street Journal*, 4 March 2002.
11. *The Economist*, 2 March 2002.
12. See also in Chapter 11 the fate of Alsthom, formed from the merger of one of British General Electric's divisions with French interests.
13. *Le Canard Enchaîné*, 20 August 2003.
14. Chorafas, *Operational Risk Control with Basle II*.
15. *CommunicationsWeekInternational*, 18 February 2002.
16. *BusinessWeek*, 22 April 2002.
17. Ibid., 27 May 2002.
18. Note that five out of ten took place in 2001/2002.
19. *BusinessWeek*, 8 July 2002.
20. *Financial Times*, 1 August 2002.
21. For how badly Cable & Wireless has performed, see Chapter 3.
22. *Bloomberg Professional*, 27 September 2001.
23. *Financial Times*, 1 August 2002.
24. *Libération*, Paris, 27 June 2002.

# 10
## Third-generation Mobile and the UMTS Licences

### 1. Introduction

In the 1980s, the first-generation (1G) wireless systems were analog. In the 1990s, with the second generation (2G), digital approaches became available, but baseband. The first years of the twenty-first century saw third-generation (3G) broadband digital solutions – at least on paper and by means of extremely expensive radio wave licences. Basically,

- 2G systems were designed and used primarily for voice;
- 3G solutions are projected for convergent technologies, and big-volume wireless transmission if there is a use for it.

This transition from older to newer mobile generations could be significant because one of the important changes in technology today is the contemplated move towards mobile internet. In rapid succession we have gone from analog cellular to digital cellular and mobile internet, which is third generation.

Between 2G and 3G, as we shall see, there are some interim developments involving new technologies to be integrated into existing networks. 2G and 3G are also divided by a credibility gap connected to business opportunity analysis, and the existence of a market for 3G – or lack of it.

In his book on *Business Blunders*, Geoff Tibballs makes reference to an event in mid-nineteenth-century Ireland which matches perfectly the current 3G craze. In 1840, a canal designer planned to link lakes Corrib and Mask in western Ireland. The construction was undertaken by a local company but since the men built the canal entirely on porous limestone, no sooner had the water been poured in than it drained away again.

Not surprisingly, this set the project back several months, but a solution appeared to have been found by the laying of a clay bed at its base. This meant that, for a while, everything progressed smoothly. But with the canal almost completed, it was discovered that one of the lakes was several feet lower than the other.[1] With that, the entire project was abandoned. We are not yet there with 3G, but with good money running after bad, neither is abandonment impossible – at least in this decade. Telefonica and Sonera have given an example by writing off the 3G investment they had made in Germany.

On 19 February 2004, in Madrid, Telefonica Moviles said that it had recorded a net profit of €1.608 billion in 2003 as it achieved strong growth in its client base. With this, the company closed the chapter on its ill-fated third-generation UMTS venture abroad, which forced it to book huge writedowns and provisions in 2002, resulting in a record loss in that year of €3.724 billion ($4.730 billion).[2]

There is also another precedent to feed the thoughts of those who question the business opportunity of 3G. The same rush to judgement that happened with ISDN (see Chapter 5) characterized the universal mobile telecommunications system (UMTS), only on a much larger scale. Moreover, by the time internet came around and ISDN capacity was needed, ISDN was forgotten. The telecoms that bought UMTS licences failed to properly account for the facts that:

- they were spending billions on UMTS;
- they were taking on loans they could not afford; and
- they were giving proof of management ineffectiveness.

Few people would argue, today, that such heavy spending was foolish, and represented very poor business judgement. Critics would openly say that the incumbents and other telcos rush in, throwing away billions of euros in an effort to recreate monopolies by overexpanding, overleveraging and overdoing old solutions.

To better appreciate the 3G blunder, we should take a closer look at wireless telecommunications. Readers should, however, be aware that any discussion on wireless communications brings with it a great many acronyms. Examples are: global system for mobile communications (GSM); personal communications services (PCS); cellular digital packet data (CDPD), also known as wireless IP; wireless personal access network (PAN or WPAN); mobile telephone switching office (MTSO). Notice that MTSO is one of the three components of a commercial mobile system, the other two being cellular phones and base stations.

Another group of acronyms found with mobile communications solutions addresses different types of entities: multiple virtual network operators (MVNO); internet service providers (ISP); application service providers (ASP); and the ubiquitous universal mobile telecommunications system, which is central theme of this chapter. The objective of all of these services, entities, or systems is that of creating and capturing value from the provision of:

- commerce-related content, and
- applications served over mobile networks.

There are also a great deal of protocols around, the most important being: frequency division multiple access (FDMA); time division multiple access (TDMA); code division multiple access (CDMA). The last is the most modern, addresses 3G solutions, and will concern us in this text. To underline lack of standardization, there is wideband CDMA (WCDMA), a protocol adopted in Europe and Japan.

## 2. Mobile technology and the telecoms dilemma

Invented by Bell Labs, when this former unit of AT&T (now of Lucent Technologies) was the largest and most famous laboratory in the world, the analogue cellular telephone used FDMA. This system is based on an FDMA 800 MHz to 900 MHz spectrum subdividing it into 25 kHz channels, and it is also known as advanced mobile phone service (AMPS).

As far as technology is concerned, over the years cellular phone designers have examined different access methods to find a protocol more efficient than FDMA, and able to serve the growing base of users. An advance has been TDMA, also known as digital-AMPS (D-AMPS), which divides radio channels into time slots at subsecond level.[3] Slotting increases cell capacity, as these time slots are divided between subscribers.

- PCS solutions typically refer to TDMA-based cellular systems.
- TDMA coexists with analogue channels on the same network (more on technical characteristics later).

While companies manufacturing telecoms equipment wanted to design and build a better mousetrap (and this is precisely what they should be doing), the telcos thought that the public's adoption of mobile devices would become a highly profitable income stream. During 2000 and 2001 imagination ran wild, from fiddling with 3G broadband to using:

- jackets with integrated bendable displays offering receiving and sending capability,
- smart cards that can be worn on the body like a tattoo and used as authorization codes for mobile services and payments, and
- exotics like so-called *not badges*, or love getties, that blink when they recognize others bearing a similar profile.

This craze for the mobile wonders of the future was interpreted, through wishful thinking, as meaning that there is an unstoppable interest in mobile data communications. Some experts said mobile communications will not be limited to the development and use of short message services (SMS; see section 4); others were predicting the miraculous emergence of a *supranet*.

Companies whose directors, CEOs and business planners proved to be chicken-brained were officially announcing that the physical and digital worlds were being definitely linked and broadband internet access could be guaranteed at all times, regardless of location – and evidently, also regardless of cost, since no one seems to have bothered to establish:

- whether there was *really* a market, and
- what kind of pricing, as well as content, would make that market tick.

Instead, vague types of services were projected out of Cloud 9, to assist in opening up new sources of income, like tele-medicine and payments by mobile phone: pay as you walk. The old, established telecoms with their bureaucrats and inefficient structure were dreaming of becoming super service providers, hoping that imaginary developments would bring with them vastly increased sales per customer, the so-called average revenue per user (ARPU).

Not to be left behind in this twenty-first century gold rush, investors pushed the price of old telecoms to unheard-of levels, in spite of those entities' mismanagement and arteriosclerosis. These are the case studies on former state monopolies we have seen from Chapter 6. No wonder that day-dreaming and ineffectiveness led to a huge business misjudgement connected to third-generation mobile and UMTS.

There have been, of course, exceptions to this craze, but exceptions don't prove the rule. Experts I talked to in my research thought that European telecoms operators were unrealistic in pinning their hopes on a successful rollout of services which provide fast online access on mobile phones for voice and data, including video.

This has not been a case of conflict of interest, but one of plain misjudgement. Theoretically, the fast roll out of 3G might have helped the telcos recoup the huge fees paid for licences during UMTS auctions in 2000/2001. Practically it remained unclear:

- what the 'must-have' services will be, and
- whether customers will be prepared to pay for them.

Such ambiguities and uncertainties don't seem to discourage some telecoms from continuing 'to hope'. For instance, although Sonera pulled out of the German 3G, and has been licking its wounds, it is helping Finland Inc. in its hopes to be the first European country to launch third-generation telecoms services.

The former Finnish monopoly, which went almost bankrupt since its 3G foray and subsequently merged with the Swedish telco, is planning to launch a commercial UMTS service in four of Finland's biggest cities – Helsinki, Tampere, Turku and Oulu – with Nokia the principal supplier. And then there is the 3G Hutchinson gamble in the UK (see section 7).

The good news for UMTS fans is that while Sonera pulled out of the German UMTS (see section 1), Telia Sonera Mobile (a subsidiary of the merged company) would benefit from its parent's decision to go completely mobile internally. This means that over 2005, or so, roughly 20,000 employees in sites across Scandinavia will lose the phones on their desk.[4]

In Greece, on 27 January 2004, mobile operator Stet Hellas launched UMTS services, available in the greater Athens and Thessaloniki areas with possible extensions to Patra and Irakleion, depending on the Athens/ Thessaloniki results. This is a controlled experiment whose results are, at best, uncertain. We should know more about its deliverables in a couple of years.

With no evidence to support the hypothesis that 3G has a reasonable future, for the time being it is better to be prudent with UMTS, in regard to both its technical problems and its financial advisability. In August 2003, in a research project on the real-time enterprise,[5] I asked Stanton J. Taylor, partner in Accenture Laboratories in Chicago, whether 3G solutions would be manna from heaven for the global system of intelligent sensors on which he was working. That might have been a good market for UMTS, Taylor said:

• 3G networks will not serve reality online, and they cannot support the system of real-time sensors.
• Intelligent sensors will communicate through radio waves only in short distances of about 200 yards. Then transmission will be by broadband wire.

The irony embedded in this reply is that a global system of intelligent sensors can consume lots of bandwidth, much more than UMTS offers. That makes 3G bandwidth too small for intelligent sensors – while for other better-known and existing applications it is too large and very difficult to fill. Given these, and other references in this chapter, we shall see that 3G projects have condemned themselves to failure because:

• companies promoting them have failed to take the system view, and
• there is no long-term evolutionary perspective in terms of product and market developments.

In short, the 'business opportunity' is based on arguments which are lightweight or, at best, totally unproven. Projected 3G 'solutions' have not convinced anybody that they can contribute to the growth of the economy, or that they can help their users to cut their costs and improve their profits. The sex appeal is not there. But before coming to this subject, and in order to make this discussion meaningful, we should first look into the bolts and nuts of certain protocols.

## 3.   CDMA, WCDMA and the lack of good sense

The introduction made reference to a palette of protocols: FDMA, TDMA, CDMA and WDMA, pressing the point that technological evolution does not end with any one of them. Code division multiple access is a protocol which became popular in the early 1980s in connection with local area networks (LANs). Today it is employed by cellular operators. In North America, CDMA is based on the IS-95 standard.

Instead of creating time slots or dividing the radio frequency spectrum into separate channels by frequency, CDMA uses spread spectrum transmission. This has certain advantages because spread spectrum transmission helps to obtain radio channels about six times wider than TDMA. By assigning digital codes to active subscribers, CDMA enables pieces of a conversation to be spread out within a channel by frequency and time, with each small voice sample repeated several times.

Some carriers are fully converted to CDMA. Sprint PCS, for instance, today has the largest all-digital CDMA network in the US with an equivalent megahertz of spectrum. This was a deliberate strategy to avoid being burdened by a mix of analogue and digital wireless technology, or hampered by spectrum differences requiring:

* duplicate operating systems, and
* inefficient capital deployment.

Sprint says that it avoids the need to acquire expensive additional spectrum by capitalizing on CDMA's ability to extend system capacity by providing 10 to 20 times the capacity of analog AMPS, and four to six times the channel capacity of TDMA. CDMA-based systems also enable a subscriber to monitor and communicate with multiple cells, as well as make feasible a cost-effective expansion of wireless web services. A major downside is lack of global standards.

Cellular operators and product manufacturers in Europe and Japan selected as a technology wideband code division multiple access. WCDMA is substantially different from North American CDMA. Also used in Latin America, the western hemisphere version is supported by Lucent Technologies, Motorola, Nortel Networks and Qualcomm, who together with other manufacturers formed the CDMA Development Group (CDG) and called their solution CDMAOne.

In June 1999 there was an International Telecommunications Union (ITU) meeting in Beijing which came up with an approach to harmonization for CDMA. Theoretically, the proposed parameters for CDMA are structured to develop inexpensive multimode phones, which will enable WCDMA and CDMA2000 phones to interoperate. In practice, this is still to be seen. There are also plenty of other questions to be answered:

- what will be the industrial implications of WCDMA and CDMA2000 interoperability?
- what lessons can be learnt from their initial deployments in Japan and Korea?
- what will be the result of technology-type and market splits between TDMA, CDMA, and WCDMA?
- what will be the impact of 3G spectrum auctions on the shape of the global wireless industry?

Another major query with longer-term consequences is the industrial effect of moving from 2G to 2.5G and 3G. Here come in some more acronyms associated with the interim phase between second and third generation, widely known as 2.5G. Two protocols dominate the 2.5G perspective: wireless access protocol (WAP) which, as stated in Chapter 5, has been a flop, and general packet radio service (GPRS), which is packet switching, but so far has not fared much better.

WAP was rated as a success in the making after Ericsson, Motorola and Nokia followed up their creation of the wireless access protocol with the WAP Forum. With a membership of over 100, WAP and its microbrowser targeted *lite* devices such as handheld mobile phones, rather than heavy-duty PDAs. But as we have already seen, WAP has been no outstanding success, let alone an industry standard. Some start-ups which bet their future on WAP have folded for lack of clients.

To begin with, the general packet radio service is also an intermediate technology, like WAP, designed to allow operators to provide higher-speed data transmission, being 'always-on connection' over their existing second-generation networks. Typically, 2G uses the global system for mobiles (GSM) standard[6] – and GPRS was conceived as something higher level.

The market, however, voted with few dollars and GPRS adoption is way below expectations. There is a continued shortage of GPRS handsets; and people don't go for this protocol. Some outfits which launched GPRS business back in 2000, and have been offering services at about 30 kilobits per second (KBPS) got a meagre number of users, particularly among corporate clients. Experts say that it's a money loser.

Yet, in spite of the fact that WAP and GPRS did not deliver on their promises, egg-headed planners at telecoms continued hoping that, for mobile data technology based on GSM, GPRS will bridge the gap to 3G, providing experience on data services and a good income stream. The fact that some people never learn has another after-effect. It raises questions over who will eventually have the brains to gain from the UMTS – if and when it takes off.

Both WAP and GPRS are 2.5G, and a basic notion behind 2.5G is that of extending the life of current plant which has not yet been depreciated. This, too, is an illusion, because even a half-way technology calls for investments.

For instance, BT says its GPRS offering will feature about three times the speed of GSM. This will not come all by itself:

- third-generation technology requires entirely new infrastructure,
- but 2.5G solutions, too, must work at a higher frequency than existing networks, and upgrades are costly.

Then there is the issue of applications and content. Optimists are quick to suggest that 3G mobile computing, or if you prefer the wireless internet, will bring with it a plethora of new applications and services for its users. But those who say so fail to spell them out, and there is shortage of ideas about what exactly these goodies will be, or whether consumers will pay for them.

What is certain is that 3G will present the existing players with a number of challenges. The lack of money to build the 3G infrastructure, after having paid unwisely some $130 billion to buy the airwave licences in the European governments' auctions, is one of these challenges. It is estimated the infrastructure alone will demand between $130 billion and $250 billion. Another key challenge is that the '3G solutions' currently surfacing on paper are incompatible, and this makes the breakeven day for the carriers even more remote. Let me underline once again these differences.

- The European landscape is dominated by the Universal Mobile Telecommunications System.
- In Japan, DoCoMo, an NTT subsidiary, has been working on the *i-mode*, its version of 3G technology.

Both UMTS and the i-mode are based on the WCDMA protocol which, as stated, is incompatible with the American CDMA. But there is also a major difference between UMTS and i-mode which is not often discussed. UMTS was originally designed as an evolutionary step from GSM in an effort to kill two birds with one well-placed stone. The reason was marketing. There are upwards of 500 million GSM subscribers worldwide, while the CDMA subscribers are many fewer.

As for the i-mode, DoCoMo has spent plenty of time and money with its suppliers for some years and its task seems to be inherently simpler than that facing the European operators. Its handsets need to operate only in WCDMA – while for the foreseeable future, European operators will have to provide dual-mode handsets combining today's 2G technology, GSM, with 2.5G protocols and UMTS. It looks as if good sense has departed.

Note that DoCoMo, too, is not out of the woods, as evidenced by the fact that it has several times delayed the launch of 3G wireless services from the original release date of 30 May 2001. DoCoMo's difficulties have to do with *hand-off*, the way in which the signal is passed between base stations as the subscriber moves between radio cells.

- WCDMA technology dictates that hand-off is controlled by the handset.
- By contrast, in the US version of CDMA, the base station has kept this responsibility.

In theory, putting at handset level the hand-off mission permits a more flexible design solution, which could evolve rather rapidly. In practice, this approach places substantial power demands on the handset, while also introducing the likelihood of an increased number of dropped or lost calls. DoCoMo says that while globalization has no doubt merits, it is not prepared to risk launching a full commercial service with too many unknowns because of uncontrolled variables. In short, even technically the versions of 3G are not yet out of the tunnel.

### 4.  3G: business plans built on quicksilver

There are plenty of challenges and opportunities in identifying and rolling out profitable new services. There are also plenty of players entering the mobile telephony market, such as incumbent telecoms hoping to sell bandwidth in a big way, media companies hoping to supply content, applications providers looking forward to lucrative contracts, and others. For each and every one of these parties, sound choices require criteria for sensible selection in the wireless world, as well as rethinking the role of mobile computing, both as a market on its own and in conjunction with wire-based services. Solutions will not come easily. There is plenty of homework to be done, including work at the drafting board, for which there is not much evidence that it has taken place. Serious studies can be of help, but daydreaming should not be welcomed in business plans, no matter who is making them.

A short while before going bankrupt, Arthur D. Little, the consultancy, assumed that, in the year 2005, mobile telephony customers will use their mobile phone for an average of ten minutes per day for data communications, with:

- 35 per cent of this time being used for downloading data, and
- 65 per cent for writing/reading the contents.

To say the last, this is an unprofessional assumption which has no relation to writing/reading/downloading in fixed lines, let alone the fact that 3G is supposed to be broadband. The Arthur D. Little distribution of applications shown in Figure 10.1 also makes amusing reading: email is king, in the image of email on fixed lines. To say the least, this is not serious business.

There is some email with 2G, but it does not approximate, even by long way, the amount suggested in the aforementioned study. Moreover, this issue has become controversial because – as has been recently revealed in France – for every euro billed to the user 15 cents is cost and 85 cents profit

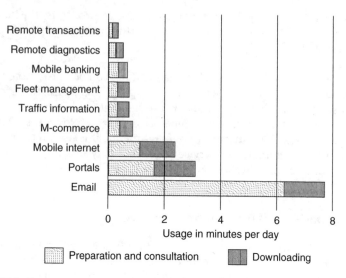

*Figure 10.1*   Projections on average daily usage of GPRS/UMTS data service by corporate users in Western Europe in 2005*

* *Sources*:   Arthur D. Little and Crédit Suisse Private Banking.

to the operator. Mobile telephony operators got very bad publicity for this reason.

Projections of market potential are nothing more than oracles unless they are grounded in costs of current methods versus the one that is proposed and well-documented advantages and disadvantages. This is not provided by the A. D. Little/Crédit Suisse assumptions. It is just as surprising that nobody among the different forecasters of 3G business has bothered to ask the critical questions:

- why companies would or should move from fixed lines to mobile for email, and
- what level of cost/benefit might make them willing to contemplate such a move.

While the costs of UMTS are not yet known, one can use the pricing of current voice circuits as proxy. Compared to fixed lines, minute-per-minute mobile telephony is 400 per cent more expensive. I have tested this pricing structure in Switzerland, France and Germany, both inland and cross-border – and it is a rip-off. Why would companies choose to pay four times more in telco costs for their email?

Another problem is that it is difficult to compose email on a phone. Usually what happens is that the one who is receiving emails finds something that is urgent and because it is urgent he wants to respond. Hence making email available to a wide proportion of the market could stimulate voice usage – but as far as 3G is concerned email does not look like a rich market.

All this goes way beyond the point Arthur D. Little made that email could be king in 3G – though the consultancy also noted that there is also the risk that the extra sales generated per customer could be offset by reduced sales in pure voice communications and by the gradual disappearance of short message service (SMS) sales – which are, ironically, a sort of email.

The killing of SMS not only contradicts the consultancy's email projections but could, in fact, prove to be something of a headache for mobile telephony providers. As I just mentioned, current SMS are far too expensive compared with what they cost to the operator; hence they are a source of good profits.

Neither should one forget that a white elephant like UMTS would be extremely hungry for euro, pounds and dollars to recover silly money paid for licences. In 2000 and 2001, telecoms hard pressed for cash overleveraged themselves with bank loans to buy the (air) ground on which to build a UMTS factory whose down-payment was, as we saw, $130 billion for airwaves alone, but which had no clear plans for products or their pricing.

Moreover, this rapid place in technological development creates imbalances which must be addressed through rigorous organizational studies and restructuring of the company's information system. This is a salient problem for the board of directors and the chief executive officer, and vital to the profession of information technologists. The problem is that very few people and companies appreciate these facts, let alone take advantage of them.

For the reasons I have just outlined I am not at all impressed when I hear or read that mobile operators are edging towards to the rollout of UMTS services. The fact is that they are just as far from good business models for 3G as they were when the licences were auctioned several years ago.[7] A good way to test if return on investment (ROI) is what is really meant is to ask: what has been and will be gained from:

- transistors shrinking by half, twice every 18 months?
- photonics doubling transmission speed every 9 months?
- wireless tripling its speed every year?

As the more serious professionals never fail to point out, any conversation about mobile services should start off with a question about the expected number of users, the type of users, and average revenue per user (ARPU) or, better, ARPU by class of users:

- where does this stand today?
- is it static, rising or falling?
- are data services having any impact, or are basic voice services still the main driver?

Working by proxy, in mid-2003 Vodafone and mmO2 announced their results and both have shown a year-on-year increase in ARPU as well as an increase in the share of data revenues over voice revenues. Neither, however, is dramatic. Also, experts say that Vodafone and mmO2 have done well because they have invested a great deal of their resources to roll out advanced data services and turn their marketing upside down. That's not the case of the average telecommunications company, particularly the big incumbents.

Furthermore, several experts argue that ARPU makes sense in a mature, commoditized industry, for instance, when talking about voice and SMS. But with third-generation services, it is better to focus on average *profit* per user, because the cost of rolling out these services and their support, including customer education, is a critical element in getting them up and running. Extra costs will be incurred to create content and social momentum that will carry into 3G networks, particularly given the current gaps between the:

- amount of content,
- channel usage, and
- capabilities of the network.

It is just as important to sort out the current big overlap between 2G and the projected 3G. At the bottom line, the customer does not care whether it is 2G or 3G. It needs no explaining that 3G cannot survive, let alone make money, just by addressing itself to an élite group of users attracted to it for reasons of prestige.

One of the earlier arguments in favour of 3G was that it was more cost-effective. But now mobile operators talk about sweating existing 2G/2.5G assets by growing services. Somehow, it looks as if the different telcos, their top managers and their experts experience a sort of frustration which leads to loss of direction.

Moreover, while they are faced with the 3G versus 2.5G versus 2G challenge, many mobile operators are trying to move on from a time when they were mostly or wholly in the consumer market towards becoming respectable players in the business market. This brings along a host of other problems: platform independence, manageability and longevity of contracts. We will return to these issues.

## 5.   Who was responsible for the white elephant?

In its origins, the financial precipice of UMTS started in Brussels, at the heart of euroland. The bureaucrats of the European Union had the brilliant idea that since Europeans were ahead in wireless communications (an unproved hypothesis), the new-generation gadgets and their airwaves were the ideal field to beat the American industry at its own game: internet and electronics.

Internet mobile was the bureaucrats' baby. Accordingly, in 1998 the European Commission decided that all the UMTS licences had to be given by 2001, and the first communications had to take place in 2002. This 'decision' was taken without examining if this was technically possible, and whether such moves were financially advantageous or disastrous. 'Brussels', says Elie Cohen, 'incited the governments to launch themselves in a process without visibility.'[8]

That's precisely a sign of bad management and a prescription for disaster. Neither did the different European governments bother to examine technical feasibility of strict deadlines and their economic soundness. Both the short and the long term fell in the sidelines, once the different governments discovered that they could make big money by selling UMTS licences.

- The British were the first to benefit from five auctions and their cash flow, with £25 billion ($40 billion).
- The Germans exceeded them with six auctions of airwaves and DM 100 billion ($50 billion).
- The Italians also had five auctions, but collected a meagre $12.2 billion.
- The French lost the race, because by the time they sold the licence the treasury of telecoms was dry. They collected 'only' FF 65 billion ($10 billion).

This is the big part of the massive $130 billion pocketed by the different European governments for selling fresh air. As for the empty-headed telecoms, they went into debt without examining if this UMTS operation could ever be profitable to them: how, when and by how much. 3G is an excellent case study on management ineffectiveness. Neither incumbents nor alternative carriers:

- study how much more money they had to put on the table to exploit the licences they bought, or
- did their homework on the services they would offer and the cash flow to be expected from these services.

The first soul-searching question should have been: What new services can we support with UMTS? How much money are these going to bring in? There was a vague idea that these consumer services would consist of meteorological bulletins; dictionaries; entertainment (including adult entertainment, read: porno); shopping on the run; paying bills without controlling them; recreation; traffic congestion information; stock market prices; different other banking services, and music.

Nobody had a clear idea if UMTS was really worth the trouble and whether there was any market for this vague description of disparate and incompatible 'personalized' services. Yet the telecoms, particularly the huge bureaucratic state monopolies, bought among themselves more than 300 airwave 'licences'.

Subsequently, when they discovered that to do anything with them they needed even more money, some of the 'buyers' dropped their licences, licked their wounds, and walked away. This was the case of Telefonica's and Sonera's joint project in Germany. Writing off very expensive licences was one way to stop good money running after bad.

Not all governments, however, took such pullouts kindly. For instance, the Swedes said 'No!' to 3G delays. Sweden's telecoms regulator told third-generation licence holders in the country that they could not have more time to complete the rollout of their UMTS networks. They had to move quickly. That taught the telcos a lesson in setting their priorities.

When the exhausted telecoms threw up their hands, the Swedish regulator reinterpreted his dictum by adding that if mobile operators demonstrate they are trying to meet the deadline, they might not be fined. This high-handed policy was based on the fact that licences stipulate that operators must provide UMTS coverage across 99 per cent of the country within a fixed timeframe.

Moreover, running out of one's assumed obligations can be very costly. France Télécom, for example, could face a bill of at least €109 million ($109 million) for pulling its mobile subsidiary Orange out of the Swedish 3G market. The operator had signed a contract to share the building of 3G network infrastructure with Hutchison and Vodafone.

- Orange said it would exit the Swedish market after the regulator refused to give it more time to build its network.
- But that deal included the clause that if any operator pulls out of the 3G deal, it faces a 1 billion Swedish kronor penalty.

France Télécom's travails in Sweden is one more proof that the whole UMTS business has been a torrent of blunders by the Brussels bureaucracy, the bureaucracy of supermarket telcos, and that of several of the governments. The failure came because of attacking without appropriate preparation:

- a problem with many unknowns,
- high costs without a visible return on investment,
- ill-defined potential market, and
- unspecified products to fill the broadband.[9]

All these miscalculations were made with in global and regional settings which definitely lack agreements on universal standards. They have also been deprived of ways and means to measure the response by business enterprises and consumers, since the content to fill the 3G broadband is still trivial – and totally unexciting for either of these two markets.

On paper, the Universal Mobile Telecommunications System protocol, delivering data transfer speeds of 2 MBPS, looked great, but the idea that real-time video streaming is good for mobile telephony usage led to the suspicion that those promoting it had lost contact with reality. Post mortem it was found out that most hypotheses about UMTS were wrong. No telecoms operator was worth his salt because none bothered to investigate risk and return with the UMTS licences.

• How many new clients were to be acquired?
• How much more would existing clients spend with UMTS?
• Why would people want to pay for services, when much of what entered into the UMTS content plans was already available free?

Again, post mortem, independent research outfits tested the market's response. The likely price structure coming with the finding was that, by 2005, on average, the money paid by wireless consumers would *drop* by 15 per cent rather than increase by 200 per cent as the telecom operators had thought. The whole UMTS enterprise was like spending $130 billion for licences and another $130 billion guestimated for infrastructure, to build a factory:

• which will manufacture an unspecified product,
• whose clients are not yet known, and
• whose products' market price might be half of what is currently guessed.

Indeed, anyone who witnessed the débâcle of the European phone industry's first internet push was bound to be sceptical that a new wireless fad could take off, let alone yield profits. UMTS was in no way the telcos' only white elephant. In 2000, in launching the wireless access protocol (WAP, see section 3), which worked on 2.5G, the telcos:

• hyped slow and nearly useless services, and
• scared customers and investors from the mobile internet.

While the telephone companies subsequently claimed to have learnt valuable lessons from the WAP failure, they have in reality learnt nothing. Nor are they forthcoming with 'killer applications' (see section 6). So far, the sexiest application is text messaging.

While money was being thrown down the drain through lack of preparation and professional consciousness, the telecommunications industry made the most job cuts of all industries in 2002. Even if in 2002 firing was lower than the cuts made in 2001, the year 2003 saw more downsizing and it's not necessarily over yet. According to outplacement consultancy Challenger, Gray and Christmas, in 2002 telecoms firms laid off 268,857 workers, compared to 317,777 the year before. Way down the line, people paid with their jobs for the mistakes made by the top brass of the industry.

## 6.   Killer applications are not the only challenge

Let's start with the principle that it is applications, not just technology, that will sell 3G, like any other telecommunications product, to companies and consumers. Particularly *killer applications*, which have not been possible so far and cannot be offered without broadband channels in mobile telephony. The challenge is to find them.

As an example of a killer application, analysts point to Napster. While the service was an infringement of rights and eventually failed, it did prove that if a company puts together a product that meets a need, people will use it. Napster, at one time, accounted for almost 10 per cent of total internet traffic – not at all bad for a start-up.

Nothing similar has so far come up with UMTS, i-mode, or CDMA2000. With the market's rejection of WAP, and other interim protocols, something similar can also be said of 2.5G. And there is always the challenge of both backward and forward compatibility between GSM, GPRS, UMTS and other protocols – implemented in a way that protects:

- the client's ease of use,
- the operator's existing investment, and
- the future-oriented core network system.

True enough, there are some applications at current state of the art that make sense. Coca-Cola uses telemetry services to fill up their vending machines when they are empty. Truck companies use GSM services to monitor their lorries. Location API is a good example of controlling valuable commodities when they are in transit. Other applications may come with reality online,[10] but as section 2 has explained, this is not the stuff for 3G.

In short, up to today there are simply no examples available to justify 3G, whose services present a wholly new set of challenges. Unlike traditional voice, mobile data connectivity involves diverse, demanding and probably short life-cycle application. On the other hand, operators wish to function as more than just channel providers, with goals such as:

- building the reputation of their services,
- enhancing customer loyalty,
- retaining or increasing market share, and
- driving revenues, profits, cash flows.

This they can do only when they establish an open value chain with their clients and with third-party content providers, attracting more subscribers and deploying killer applications. The last must be studied not just in terms of market attraction, but also in connection with their limits – including limits associated to personal privacy and safety.

For instance, several health club chains in Hong Kong now ban the use of new-generation cellphones that take and transmit video and still images over the internet. The gym facilities forbid use of these devices in locker rooms for obvious reasons of privacy. In nearby Macau, use of phone and camera devices is now forbidden in 11 of the territory's casinos.[11]

To be able to develop killer applications, both telcos and third parties such as content providers must be able to go back to basics: what can be done with digital broadband that digital baseband did not provide? With improved power management? With circuit-level efficiency? With wafer-level efficiency?

Digital baseband was thought to offer the possibility of more complex multimedia applications and a better answer to processing requirements, than analogue baseband. Although this has led to digital baseband solutions which are technologically interesting, no killer applications have so far come along.

Multimedia has been a progressive step, not a killer application. In fact, media convergence is a better term than multimedia support, because it identifies the process of merging bit streams belonging to different media. Convergence of voice, data, graphics and video necessitates faster traffic technology, involving solutions that:

- increase the bandwidth of existing networks, and
- allow sharing bit streams among mobile devices and local, metropolitan and wide area networks.

That can be also done with 2G; it is principally a matter of capacity. To better appreciate the trend towards media convergence we have to recall that even telephone calls are changing, with conversions converted into digital streams for transmission across fast networks, and marked with other digital streams. In this regard, digital data are evolving into the common language for all communications, while the solutions we are employing are growing increasingly complex.

To express the challenge posed by this process, R&D labs work to bring together technologies that, when aggregated, make media convergence possible. The markets addressed by such developments represent various facets of the bigger broadband picture, including datastreams ranging from optical networks to personal wireless connectivity and other types of two-way interactive communications devices – but still the content to justify broadband services is missing.

Beyond this, mobile operators courting universal wireless content face the dilemma of how far to go in opening up their networks to standard interfaces for developing and managing content. The answer must be given before killer applications are developed, not after, because a great deal of market acceptance will depend on interoperability.

'Many operators think content can make them unique and that they can retain customers and fight churn with it, but in the end consumer demand will come from opening up and accepting standards,' says Michelle de Lussanet, senior analyst at Forrester Research.[12] If they run away from industry standards, operators will lose control of how content is developed, delivered and paid for.

Moreover, when we talk of 3G applications, a distinction must be made between raw bandwidth and useful bandwidth. In terms of raw bandwidth, 3G is eventually promising $10^5$ more capacity than is available now, but many factors other than content help to decide how much of this will be useful.

Power management is an example. Power consumption is a major consideration at all levels of design in the migration from 2G to 3G. Many handset users now expect hundreds of hours of standby time and at least ten hours' talk time from one battery charge. 3G applications, however, will consume a greater amount of power owing to the use of higher-speed data processors needed to cope with the applications.

Circuit-level efficiency is yet another challenge. Special techniques help to reduce system power by operating circuits in a lower mode, moving to higher power mode to handle peak demands, which include dynamic voltage scaling (DVS) and dynamic frequency scaling (DFS).

Then there is wafer-level efficiency. Relatively low clock speeds used in 2G handsets (below 200 MHz) will not serve with 3G handsets which require high-speed wafer processing and at the same time significant reduction in power requirements through clever system and circuit design.

It may sound pessimistic, but on all available evidence, 2G will be around for a long time, either as mainstream implementation or the gap-filler providing 3G coverage. In such an environment where 'old' and 'new' must coexist, the important issue for telecom operators, and their customers, is to become flexible and provide a way of promoting hands-on experience in the transition from 2G to 3G, as well as ways and means to deliver a seamless service for the customers.

## 7.  Hutchison 3G: a test of third generation

Hutchison Whampoa, which has ties to China, was originally a partner in the Singapore Technologies Telemedia (STT) offer for the acquisition of Global Crossing in 2002/03. Eventually, however, it had to withdraw because of barriers posed to that acquisition, and STT proceeded all by itself in salvaging what remains of Global Crossing – as discussed in Chapter 8.

Hutchison also tried its hand at mobile telephony. First, and most successfully, with Orange. Then, with the third generation. In January 2003, Hutchison 3G (H3G, or '3') was all set to roll out its first UMTS services sometime in the first quarter of that year, starting in the United Kingdom. UMTS services were also due to start in Sweden. Chris Bannister, the chief executive of H3G, Hutchison's operation in Sweden, said that operator hoped to break even within four to five years of its launch.[13]

But a year later, in January 2004, Hutchison Whampoa said it would either need to delay its break-even date for its 3 service or boost funding by a further €1.5 billion to €2 billion. Blaming handset deliveries, in November 2003, Hutchison stated that it would not make its targets of signing up 1 million users in each market. Meanwhile, in Hong Kong, the company was preparing to launch its 3G service at the end of December 2004.[14]

To better appreciate the Hutchison Whampoa foray into 3G, it is advisable to turn back the clock a few years. The company is no newcomer to mobile telephony, having already made a very profitable investment with Orange in the UK. In 1999, Hutchison sold its stake in British cellular Orange for a rich premium, after it built Orange from scratch. The Hong Kong company was wise enough to cash out of Orange at the peak of the telecoms boom, with nearly $20 billion in profits when it sold to Mannesmann. Then (at the expense of the German taxpayer) it got $5.9 billion for its share in American cellular Voicestream, which it had bought for $1.3 billion.

In mid-September 2002, Hutchison Whampoa announced that it was staking $16 billion on a new 3G network in Europe. It also said that it had a fully funded business plan. Examined superficially, this came as a surprise at a time when 3G mobile telephony was in the doldrums and practically every incumbent telco found itself in debt because of the huge cost of airwave licences and associated expenses. But Li Ka-shing, the investor behind Hutchison, and Canning Fok, its managing director, have a first-class record in risky ventures.

- Key to Fok's strategy is low prices and simple, flat-rate tariffs.
- This strategy helped Hutchison win 3.1 million customers for Orange in the 1990s.

Hutchison had bid £4.38 billion ($7.45 billion) for its UK 3.5G licence. Estimates of what it will need to spend to build its third-generation network have varied between £2.3 billion and beyond £3.5 billion, making this the biggest and riskiest venture in the history of the European mobile industry.

As a 3G capitalist in the UK, Hutchison is not alone. The British third-generation experiment is a joint venture between Hutchison Whampoa, 65 per cent; NTT DoCoMo, 20 per cent; and KPN Mobile, 15 per cent (note that KPN had gone to the edge of bankruptcy and was rescued with Dutch taxpayers' money). But though this test has first-mover advantage, experts point out that Hutchison has stumbled even before its 3G services have arrived.

Some of the difficulties the Hong Kong company faces are technical glitches expected of a new venture, but according to different sources there have been several U-turns by management in the 3G project's short history, which should have been avoided. There are three crucial areas of difficulty faced by all 3G ventures:

- handset technology,
- content, and
- customer billing.

The handsets reportedly still have two problems: they are failing to hand over from 3G to 2G, despite their dual-mode design, and they need 10 to 15 minutes to search for mmO2's 2G networks as soon as they are out of 3's 3G coverage.

As for content, not only the subject is still fuzzy, but also, according to experts, management belatedly realized that content had to be bought, not created, through partnerships with media companies, banks, games developers and music outfits – aside from the fact that managing such complex relationships is a very difficult proposition.

Billing, too, poses a complex challenge, because companies, including Hutchison and its partners, still do not have the capability for pre-event billing for 3G services. Subscription models with free bundles avoid the need to bill per event, but pricing per event has not only proved very popular; it is also a 'good way of documenting the bill. Billing per megabyte might have been a better alternative if it were not for the fact that users find it confusing – and Hutchison's proposed pay-per-use pricing scheme *2ToGo* has still to prove itself.

As if these pains were not enough, some big investment banks advised their clients that the H3G network has holes in it. On 9 April 2003, analysts at Citigroup Smith Barney wrote, 'We believe that the 3G to 2G pass has been resolved in the clean room, but is still failing periodically in the field, particularly given the different vendor lines.'

A day later analysts at Crédit Suisse First Boston wrote, 'A week-long trial of phones on Hutchison's 3G network has left us still skeptical of the near-term potential for the services. Until considerable additional work is done on the network, terminals and services of 3 in the UK, we do not consider it to be a significant commercial threat to the incumbents.' CSFB's analysts were disappointed they could not get 3G service in Canary Wharf, 'an area where one would imagine a reasonable percentage of Hutchison's target customer market might be located during the day'.

Then, on 14 April 2003, analysts at Merrill Lynch wrote, 'Subscribers have suffered a number of problems, including delays on phone activation, poor signal quality and dropped calls when moving from the 3G to 2G environment.' This was followed by a comprehensive report by analysts at Goldman Sachs which reported black spots in Hutchison's 3G network. The analysts said the most persistent problem was that calls were being disconnected from the 3G network 'regardless of the availability of 2G coverage'.[15]

With technical problems refusing to go away, according to figures released in late August 2003, Hutchinson has booked $500 million of start-up losses on its 3G venture in the first half of 2003 alone. For this it managed to sign up a paltry 155,000 subscribers in the UK and some 300,000 in Italy. The length of subscriber lists and pricing are correlated. The great bulk of these subscribers were acquired in the two months after the company abandoned its attempt to sell the new network as a premium product, and instead started flogging its phones as a *heavily discounted* voice telephony service. Since then:

- the phones have been selling well off the shelves,
- but the cost associated to this exercise has been horrendous.

In voice telephony, Hutchison is up against hugely powerful incumbents, which would not allow a newcomer to eat their market. Still, Hutchison ordered 3 million more phones for winter 2003/2004 in its main markets in the UK, Italy, Australia, Sweden and Austria.

As of the end of 2003 Hutchison 3G, known as 3, is already up and running in Britain, Italy and Sweden, and is going ahead in Australia, Austria, Denmark, Hong Kong, Ireland and Israel. However, anecdotal evidence from 3 subscribers suggests that technological gremlins remain.[16] Still, Hutchison continues pushing ahead, though cost controls and budget cuts have been introduced. The move is part of the company's $16.7 billion gamble that consumers are willing to pay for new mobile handsets that will enable them to watch video clips and videostreams while walking. Nothing is less certain.

Neither were the suppliers' business news made for much comfort. On 25 February 2004, Jorma Ollila, Nokia's president and CEO, told the annual 3G mobile summit in Cannes, France, that the operators' networks had not been ready to test 3G handsets. A day prior to Ollila's lecture, Arun Sarin, Vodafone's CEO, said that the company's 3G networks and services were ready, but it was awaiting handsets that:

- Were not bulky,
- Were not prone to overheating, and
- Had good battery life.

Other operators voiced similar complaints, saying that the devices did not match existing 2G and 2.5G phones. These delays worked against the game plan of European operators, keen to get money out of investments in 3G networks that have cost billions in licence fees and capital investments with, so far, no return.

Who was to blame? To Ollila's opinion, Nokia, which has almost 40 per cent market share in mobile phones, had suffered from a chicken-and-egg situation in its development of 3G handsets. It had to have several stable networks available to test the devices, and the complexity of 3G meant this process had taken both time and money beyond original estimates – while hope for positive surprises did not materialize.

## 8.  NTT's DoCoMo: an uncertain 3G test

Most of the technical problems discussed in section 7 were to be expected, judging from the results of NTT DoCoMo's launch of 3G services in October 2001 in Japan. This launch had made the Asia–Pacific area home to the first commercial third-generation mobile network. NEC and Panasonic suppliers to NTT DoCoMo participated in the launch – as they intend to capitalize on the operator's head start in their home market.

Two years down the line, 'capitalizing' still looks like an empty word. It is also good to notice that, as far as mobile telephony experience is concerned, neither NEC nor Panasonic has so far been a major player in global mobile terminals' market share. In the histogram in Figure 10.2, both companies are among the 'others'. Neither is there evidence that their 3G partnership has yielded the expected results. Other handset vendors were relieved by the fact that in spite of money they spent on 3G handsets, NEC and Panasonic could pose no serious threat to them.

Experts have also pointed out that nearly three years have passed since NTT DoCoMo said on 26 July 2001 that it was on track to work out *most* of the many problems that have plagued its 3G mobile phone – though it did

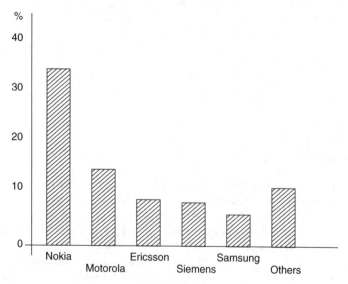

*Figure 10.2*  Market share estimates by mobile telephone handset manufacturers

warn that new problems were likely to emerge. In fact, as time goes by and results are still pending, some analysts have begun to believe that there is a growing possibility that DoCoMo will have to write down the valuations of 3G investments.

Since the start, results obtained in Japanese 3G applications have not been clear-cut. 'We have basically resolved the main hardware problems, like freezing,' said Shiro Tsuda, DoCoMo's executive vice-president. '[But] we believe that there will be new problems.'[17] This statement was made in July 2001. The bad news is that, on all evidence, it remains valid even today, making 3G implementation a sitting duck.

These are important references in connection with the future of Hutchison's UK and other 3G ventures, since NTT DoCoMo is partner to them. While commercial acceptance of 3G is still wrapped in uncertainty, unresolved technical problems cause the service to stumble, forcing carriers to delay commercial services.

Technical glitches can always happen, particularly with advanced products. They are part of the game. But when serious companies work on them and problems persist, *then* they are no glitches. They are the tip of the iceberg of much more serious challenges. This is no comfort to users and investors. Some analysts say that 3G is still mired in problems of the 2001 outcome when 4,500 triallists using DoCoMo's Foma were frustrated by:

- frequent cut-offs,
- screen freezing, and
- lack of new contents which could promote 3G services among consumers.

At the time, anecdotal evidence suggested that many of 3G's 4,500 users who tested DoCoMo's mobile service have been disappointed. One user pulled out the battery, as DoCoMo instructs users to do when the problem arises, only to discover that he lost all the personal data he had stored in the phone. Others said that they got cut off often, the screen freezes and the battery runs down very quickly.

A major disappointment in the 2001 DoCoMo Foma tests, which still does not seem to have found a satisfactory solution, was the promise that portable phones would be able to be linked to PCs for fast wireless connection. This proved unrealistic. Connectivity, and I mean very effective and dependable connectivity, would have done much to gain market confidence related to 3G propositions.

It is very difficult to connect PCs to 3G under current status, even for simpler services. Yet the growth potential of ARPU depends on such connectivity and, as we have seen, ARPU is of key importance in assessing the market value of mobile telephony and its companies. If content and technical connection problems are not solved, it is not unreasonable – in view of such considerations – to come to the conclusion that the whole sector of 3G applications could be designated as a 'loser'.

## 9.   Carriers who are prudent drop out of 3G, for the time being

On 26 March 2003, Vodafone announced it was prepared to postpone its launch of fast internet, third-generation mobile phone service until 2004 if the reliability of the technology does not improve.[18] Originally, Vodafone planned to start a 3G service in October 2003, but the company was concerned that handover problems between 2G and 3G coverage areas have not been resolved.

This measure of prudent governance contrasts with the early March 2003 Hutchinson Whampoa launching of 3G videophone service in the UK for which it had signed up 10,000 clients. A myriad of clients may look impressive, but it is tiny compared to Vodafone's 13 million-strong client base – and there is possible fullout from the fact that customers may react negatively. For instance, if a customer strays outside the limited third-generation areas, then any calls in progress will be cut off, even though the phone is supposed to be able to switch seamlessly to an existing 2G network.

In a way, in the background of the prudent decision of Vodafone to keep out of 3G for a while, and the opposite attitude of Hutchison, lies the difference between an incumbent and a newcomer. It is also quite likely that the change which took place in 2003 at Vodafone's executive suite also determined on this wait-and-see decision. It is a sound managerial practice to let the new CEO feel comfortable with taking charge of the steering wheel rather than presenting him with a *fait accompli*.

It should be remembered that in the past Vodafone was not shy of new ventures or acquisitions. The company has spent some $270 billion in acquisitions, mostly paid in stock, since Chris Gent became CEO in January 1997. That came to an abrupt halt in December 2002 when Gent lost his battle with Vivendi Universal to take control of French operator Cegetel from Vivendi (see Chapter 7).

Vodafone has not been the only company to have second thoughts about 3G. Back in the first week of February 2002, Sonera, the Finnish telecommunications group once seen at the forefront of mobile technologies, forecast that a mass market for 3G mobile services would not appear until 2004 or 2005. At the time, some people said such statement was pessimistic. In retrospect, it has been amazingly optimistic.

Sonera's statement was an after-effect of having written off, with Spain's Telefonica, in late July 2001, a €8.5 billion ($8.5 billion) bet on the future of wireless third-generation communications. After two years of unfulfilled promises, the two companies finally admitted what many in the industry have long argued:

- licences for third-generation mobile technology were not worth the paper they were printed on;
- telecoms could no longer carry those assets on their books at full value because they were simply not worth it.

Sonera's and Telefonica's decision to abandon Quam, their 3G joint venture in Germany, had the inevitable effect of triggering write-downs across the telecommunications industry. Indeed, some of Europe's big telecoms seemed to contemplate writing down up to 90 per cent of their 3G investments. Having spent billions in acquiring the 'fresh-air' licences, operators found themselves under pressure to justify that investment, or take the pain on their balance sheets.

Whether huge monopolies or start-ups, these telcoms had no choice but to push for third-generation mobile licences or risk going bankrupt. They openly blamed national governments for having became greedy with 3G auctions that nearly bankrupted the European telephone companies which had spent the often-mentioned $130 billion on 3G licences.

Telecoms have been under pressure to go ahead with write-downs because goodwill standards were becoming more stringent than they used to be. With the many scandals[19] came the switch to more careful accounting for non-performing assets. Some analysts estimated that Vodafone alone would have to drop $14.2 billion from both sides of its balance sheet just to revalue its 3G licences in three countries.[20]

Sonera's and Telefonica's announcement came as no surprise also because of the additional cost of developing networks enabling high-speed data transmission over mobile phones. Indeed, investors approved the drop-out decision by sending shares in both operators higher. This was a sharp contrast with the mood at the height of the telecoms boom, when investors rushed towards companies acquiring 3G licences, and the flow of hot money boosted their equity.

Will the mobile telecoms industry ever recuperate these 3G costs? Schroder Salomon Smith Barney had calculated that operators would need to generate additional revenues of at least €500 per year from every person living in Europe to justify their investment. European revenues are currently about €360 per user, and any new service such as 3G will eat up part of that pie. Therefore 3G launching might make sense for a newcomer to the European market, like Hutchison, but it could well be a cannibalization of current revenues for the European telecom incumbents.

For Telefonica and Sonera, who played in Germany more or less the role Hutchison plays with 3G in the UK and other countries, the decision to opt out of 3G, in spite of huge investments already made, was not easy. Sonera was from the start beenly interested in the 3G market – and it continues to be so, but this time limited to its native Finland. Through its joint ventures it held greenfield 3G licences not only in Germany, but also in Italy and Spain.

Quite significantly, with the same drop-out announcement Sonera also warned of slowing growth in its existing Finnish mobile operations, where the lack of handsets equipped to exploit the GPRS and 3G networks acted as a brake. This is an important point because while Finland is a small market, it is also one of the most mature mobile markets in the world, with a penetration rate of more than 75 per cent.

Other telecoms had looked at Sonera as a test case of whether new services and technologies can spur fresh growth in telecoms. Non-voice traffic, such as messaging and data, accounts for 12 per cent of mobile sales. The big question everyone asked was: will 3G change that statistic? To the dismay of mobile telephone investors, Sonera said that growth in its Finnish mobile operations is expected to slow down.

With this and other bleak news in the air, and some rumours surrounding them, it is not surprising that telecoms operators sought relief from the high cost of UMTS licences. Like Margaret Thatcher, they asked for their money back. But governments who overcharged for airwaves needed the money to plug *their* budgetary holes – and, therefore, they were not ready to oblige.

The telecoms kept on trying to recover whatever capital they could after the French UMTS licensees have been able to persuade their government to bend the high rates, and German UMTS licence holders have been pressing their agreements for a loophole that might allow them to recoup money to help their survival. At least three of the six German universal mobile telecommunications service licence holders have been actively pursuing deals to merge their operations, in a bid to stave off a spectacular failure to win market share once services are launched. But neither task – money refund or operator consolidation – is easy. The money paid to the government has already been spent to ease the budget deficit. As for consolidation, Germany's telecoms regulator is not convinced about changes in terms of conditions of the licences. Under current German licence regulations, the merging of licensed operations is forbidden, and refunds will not be made available for returned licences in the case of joint ventures. The wording of the licence agreement is clear enough, but faced with a huge debt the operators are looking into ways around these rules.

For more than three years, the telecoms operators' last line of defence has been the European Commission (EC), which started this whole unwise 3G rush. But the EC was powerless, even if it wanted to do something. In the end, Europe was standing by the lifeboats for the mobile telecoms industry; the message was that the lifeboat had nowhere to go.

## Notes

1. Géoff Tibballs, *Busines Blunders*, London: Robinson Publishing, 1999.
2. *El País*, 20 February 2004.

3. D. N. Chorafas, *Protocols, Servers and Projects for Multimedia Systems*, Basingstoke: Macmillan, 1996; D. N. Chorafas, *High Performance Networks, Personal Communications and Mobile Computing*, Basingstoke: Macmillan, 1996.

4. *Total Telecom Magazine*, February 2004.

5. Chorafas, *The Real-time Enterprise*.

6. GSM is pinned to 9.6 KBPS and this is increasingly seen as insufficient. Some potential users say the cost of GSM (at around €0.3/min) is far too high to encourage widespread mobile telephony usage.

7. *Total Telecom Magazine*, August 2003.

8. *Le Canard Enchaîné*, 28 March 2001.

9. D. N. Chorafas, *Enterprise Architecture and New Generation Information Systems*, Boca Raton, FL: St Lucie Press/CRC, 2002.

10. Chorafas, *The Real-time Enterprise*.

11. *Communications of the ACM*, Vol. 46, No. 3, March 2003.

12. *Total Telecom Magazine*, June 2003.

13. *CommunicationsWeekInternational*, 27 January 2003.

14. *Total Telecom Magazine*, January 2004.

15. *Ibid.*, June 2003.

16. *The Economist*, 11 October 2003.

17. *Financial Times*, 27 July 2001.

18. *The Times*, 27 March 2003.

19. Chorafas, *Economic Capital Allocation with Basle II*.

20. *BusinessWeek*, 25 February 2002.

# 11
# The Fate of Vendors who Leveraged their Clients

## 1. Introduction

The telecommunications industry's collapse was driven by two forces, both having their roots in mismanagement and in excesses: companies have been *overleveraged* and capacity has been *overbuilt*. During the late 1990s telecom companies borrowed enormous sums of money to finance an expansion of capacity based on radio waves and photonics, as well as a huge wave of mergers and acquisitions which made little if any sense. This was done without the benefit of rigorous strategic plans. The different companies, incumbents and newcomers, had set as their main goal to do 'more' than their competitors.

It therefore comes as no surprise that debt mounted to unprecedented levels. By mid-2002, before it more or less tapered off, the total outstanding debt by telecoms was estimated at over $700 billion. This means a debt service far larger than the portion of the industry's revenue stream available for payment of interest and repayment of borrowed capital.

Most of this money had been given to, and sent by, the giants of the telecoms industry, but smaller companies, too, took on inordinate amounts. As a result, telecommunications companies big and small were drowning in excess channel capacity, with the average transport network being used at just 6.6 per cent of capacity, according to Merrill Lynch.

Of course, averages regarding the wide spectrum of telecommunications don't mean much. They have to be supplemented with indicators of used capacity by type of channel. The trouble is that these statistics don't give a great deal of comfort either to telecoms or to manufacturers of telecoms equipment who sold the gear for that excess capacity to the phone companies and to their investors.

Even if, as some estimates suggest, US traffic at the core of the networks, particularly the fixed lines, is leaping ahead at 85 per cent per year, this is by no means enough to fill the empty telecoms channels – as the corresponding *land-based networks* in operation are running at 35 per cent of capacity (similar statistics prevail in Western Europe).

Even worse is the case of the level of utilization of long-distance channels, where during the late 1990s and early years of the twenty-first century decisions concerning new plant bet on the (wrong) hypothesis that internet traffic would double every three months. Today we know that internet traffic is growing at about a quarter of that pace. As a result:

- only 1 per cent to 2 per cent of potential *long-distance* capacity in North America and Europe is in use, and
- the vast majority of investments have gone to dormant cable in the ground, or under sea, with price wars being the result.

Price wars have seen to it that the cost of speedy business connection between New York and London has fallen 95 per cent in the 2000 to 2002 timeframe, squeezing the telecoms income. The telcos' and vendors' miscalculation started with the fact that with high-speed transmission technology out of the lab, and with management control having disappeared, capacity growth went wild. Nobody seems to have taken the proverbial long, hard look.

This is true both of optical technology and of radio waves, as we have seen in the preceding chapters. In North America, the $80 billion wireless market has been flat in 2002 and 2003. Experts suggest that before growth can resume, consolidation is necessary to reduce the field from six national carriers to two or three. European wireless, too, faces declining revenue from its voice business. It had been counting on high-speed data for growth. But for the time being what is clear is that those services have added billions to carriers' debt.

These facts about the carriers' distress are very important to the different telecommunications equipment vendors. The message is that with so much unused channel capacity around, so much debt by the telecoms, and demand which remains mediocre, the revival of telephone companies and their suppliers is not just around the corner. To a large extent, this is the vendors' own fault because in the good years they did whatever they could to over-leverage their clients.

Overleveraged with debt and overburdened with excess channel capacity, in 2002 the seven biggest telecoms in the world reduced their capital expenditures by an estimated 25 per cent, and their budgets for 2003 were no better. This has had evident effects on their hardware and software suppliers, all the way down the chain. And in software, tech-slump survivors said a recovery in the next couple of years is doubtful.

As a result, financial analysts don't expect any meaningful pickup until 2005 or later on, but they do believe that in the meantime there could be another wave of shakeouts among telecommunications equipment vendors.[1] The fate of manufacturers who overleveraged their clients is this chapter's theme.

## 2.   Overbuilding of telecoms capacity has hurt every firm

The overbuilding of telecoms capacity during the late 1990s was based on the wrong vision of the way the new economy works.[2] Not only the installed new optical fibre, and other gear, was overleveraged, but also – as we saw in Chapter 10 – a huge amount of money has been spent on buying fresh air, like the UMTS licences. This was done:

- without paying attention to market potential, and
- without accounting for the fact that blind competition led to a plant which is overdimensioned by a factor of at least 10.

Much of this capacity was built on the idea that the telecoms would expand *perpetually* by big leaps, but the economy can in no way sustain those 'expected' rates of growth. Overbuilding led to price wars, and price wars caused revenues to stagnate in many sections of the telephone company business. Telecoms equipment makers who suffered the most from disappearing markets have been in product lines such as:

- satellite equipment,
- cellular and fibre-optic systems,
- high-speed switches,
- messaging, alarm and data communications gear,
- providers to internet companies, such as service providers and dot-coms.

A clear sign of mismanagement was that the money for this huge expansion did not come from retained earnings but from bank loans and bonds; hence from leveraging. As shown in Figure 11.1, the US capital markets were put to the task, leading to an expansion in bond issuance from $30 billion to

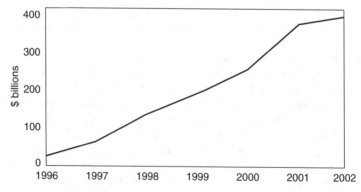

*Figure 11.1*   Cumulative bond issuance by American telecoms in the 1996 to 2002 timeframe

$400 billion in just four years (1996 to 2002). Bank borrowing followed a similar ogive curve, but with bigger numbers: from under $100 billion to nearly $800 billion, over the same timeframe. To better appreciate the nature and magnitude of the bubble, remember that during the 1990s economies which used to be based on manufacturing (and before this on agricultural production), became increasingly based on services – and on the use of novel speculative financial instruments which help in overleveraging. Investment banks and commercial banks:

- advanced the money to telecoms for their huge-capacity expansion, and
- underwrote the public offerings as well as sold the bonds to investors.

Nobody seems to have counted external rating risk factors (see Chapter 2). Since the telecoms did not have the required revenues to service their loans and bonds, it did not take long until their liabilities were downgraded – some to junk status. By 2001, the telecoms were borrowing principally to roll over their debts in an attempt to survive by avoiding default, a practice widely followed by Third World countries.

As in the Third World, this evidently made a bad situation worse. Readers will notice in Figure 11.1 that during 2002 telecoms debt increased only slightly in new bond offerings as compared with the rate of 2001 and preceding years, but it increased nevertheless. Bank lending also leaped forward, bringing bond issuance and bank borrowing to an estimated total of $1.20 trillion at the end of 2002. No other sector of the economy received such huge amounts of credit, or even remotely approached these numbers.

To appreciate the abyss between the telecommunications industry's outstanding liabilities and cash flow, it is useful to recall that, according to Wall Street analysts, the US telecoms raise approximately $300 billion in annual revenues. If so, about 45 per cent of the American telecommunications companies' annual revenues would be going to servicing their debt. This estimate is based on 'other things equal', because with overcapacity and fallen revenues the debt-servicing equation may be much worse – as is the case with France Télécom and Deutsche Telekom (see Chapter 6).

In the inevitable crash of some big companies, WorldCom, Global Crossing and Adelphia being examples, bondholders were not the only ones to feel the pain. The banks themselves had to lick their wounds. For instance, up until early 2002 JP Morgan Chase made $280 billion in bank loans to telecoms companies, and underwrote $48.1 billion in telecoms bonds, for a participation of $328.1 billion in credit extension to the sector.[3]

Other banks, too, have been on a fork. Citigroup/Salomon Smith Barney participated with $209.1 billion in the telecoms credit extension, which was mostly used for unwise acquisitions, as well as for building up channel over-capacity: some 39 million miles of cable laid underneath railway beds, natural gas lines and roads. Subsequently, the business problem all telecoms vendors faced is that only a small part of this cable has seen the light of day (as we saw in section 1). The rest remains dark, and earns no income. This, plus debt, cut the telecoms appetite for buying more equipment.

Neither were expenses in optical fibres and satellites the only outlays. For every $1 spent in laying cable, $10 to $20 needs to be spent on the so-called last mile connection. Much more money is needed for building switching stations and the equipment necessary to connect to the final customer than for the links themselves.

This sort of vicious cycle engulfed the whole telecoms industry, including several of its suppliers: Nortel, the former Northern Telecom of Bell Canada and Lucent Technologies in North America (see section 6); as well as Alcatel and Ericsson in Europe (see section 5). With profits continuing to shrink, the telcos' management does a large amount of cost cutting to turn the curve upwards. But overleveraging still ensures that some companies are heading for the wall. No cost measures can redress a huge drop in revenue combined with unbearable loans.

Throughout the telecommunications industry, at manufacturers and carriers alike, time and again frenzied cost-cutters come up short of turning the telcos around – while at the other end, that of equipment vendors, companies have been issuing dire revenue warnings, and announcing new layoffs.

The governments themselves, who made a bad situation worse with their UMTS licences, have run out of ideas and of initiatives. 'Things are totally out of hand at the moment,' said Kaisu Karvala, director, EU representation, at Sonera. 'There's no legal certainty, and instead we see politically-motivated bail-outs that will totally destroy the market.'[4] Citing the German government's €600 million lifeline in early September 2002 to bail out German mobile operator MobilCom (see Chapter 9), Karvala urged the EU to quickly establish interventionist policies – and there goes the free market.

Financial failures like KPNQwest and accounting scandals like World-Com's have called into question the future costs of running an international networking business. Both the telecoms and the equipment vendors are still trying to get to grips with the *total costs* picture, which time and again they miscalculated. Neither the carriers nor the equipment manufacturers have properly apportioned all their costs and operational expenses, let alone discounted their cash flows, and judged the ability of their cash flow to meet assumed obligations.

The experts opinion is that the survivors will be those companies able to clean their balance sheets faster and better than their competitors. However, as has been demonstrated in the case studies throughout this book, in all likelihood this will be largely done:

- at the expense of investors and creditors,
- through generous government handouts, or
- by using both strategies to refloat sinking telcos and stitch together equipment vendors that are falling apart.

Either 'solution' goes beyond just slashing costs and trying to come to grips with a massive debt by classical means. What is happening today in the telecoms industry is unprecedented. One of the ironies in this business is the helping hand given by bankruptcy protection under Chapter 11, which seems to penalize the non-bankrupt companies. Readers are already aware that Global Crossing is such a case, one which might be repeated several times over.

## 3.  Back to basics: the telecoms slide was a self-inflicted wound

The first big technology company to bend in the September–October 2000 market meltdown was Intel. Within three weeks from 22 September 2000, when it lost $100 billion of its capitalization in just 24 hours, to mid-October of that same year, when I was doing a research project on Wall Street, the NASDAQ dropped 18 per cent, with the result that paper values of nearly $500 billion evaporated.

The next milestone in the telecoms rout was a mid-sized US carrier, ICG Communications, with $1.9 billion in junk bonds outstanding. Morgan Stanley lost some $200 million on ICG bonds, but worse was to come as this and some other insolvencies signalled the collapse of the entire high-risk corporate bond market. In the aftermath, analysts started taking a closer look at credit institutions with large amounts of exposure in telecoms loans.

At the top of the list, at the end of 2000 when the telecoms industry started its dive, were Citigroup with $23 billion, HSBC with $19 billion, Chase Manhattan with $18 billion, Bank of America with $16 billion, Barclays with $13 billion, and Deutsche Bank with $11 billion. At that same time period, the largest telecom borrowers were VodafoneAirTouch with $46 billion of debt; British Telecom with $43 billion debt; AT&T with $39 billion; France Télécom with $28 billion debt (ballooned to $71 billion by September 2002, barely two years down the line); and Dutch KPN with $26 billion.

October to December 2000 saw just the opening shots of what soon became a rout. Nobody was thinking at that time about the big players such as WorldCom, Global Crossing and others going bankrupt. In fact, these and smaller companies like Metromedia and Exodus (see Chapter 9) kept on expanding their capacity and banks were happy to:

- issue them more loans, and
- underwrite their junk bonds.

Throwing good money after bad has a result of poor judgement as insiders knew well that many major Wall Street and European bond underwriters were sitting on billions of dollars of debt they could not sell, while prices were plunging daily.

The market gave a mixed signal. In two days in mid-October 2000, the stock price of Morgan Stanley lost 20 per cent. But Donaldson Lufkin Jenrette, the largest syndicator of junk bonds, was saved by an irrational takeover from Crédit Suisse First Boston to the tune of $11.8 billion, which wrecked the Swiss bank.[5]

One of the surprises of year 2000 events is that until October most of the telcos and the majority of designers, manufacturers and vendors of telecommunications equipment had escaped the meltdown which at the end of March 2000 hit the dot-coms and many other companies listed in the NASDAQ. When they were privatized, many of the former telco monopolies listed themselves on the big boards, and that is where also could be found the major telecoms equipment manufacturers.

In fact, as readers can see from Figure 11.2, from 1999 to 2003 the telecommunications industry did not crash because of sharply falling revenue. The reason why it went under was its superleveraging, requiring a cash flow the phone companies could not match. By contrast, readers will observe in the same figure that the equipment vendors' revenue slid by almost two-thirds. For any practical purpose by turning off their flow of cash the telecoms killed the vendors, who had overleveraged them, and the unwise sale of UMTS licences to the tune of $130 billion killed the telcos.

The brains of European socialist governments which initiated and carried out the UMTS auctions – in Britain, Germany, Italy and France (in that order) – left much to be desired. Much was also contributed by the telecoms' own mismanagement, which led to a deadly embrace between telcos and their vendors.

Indeed, in the first couple of years of the twenty-first century, the telecoms debt situation soon became so alarming that European government bank

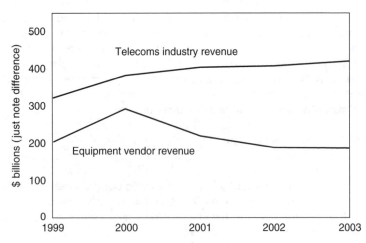

*Figure 11.2* Convergence and divergence of telecoms industry and equipment vendor revenue

regulators began to investigate the degree of bank lending to the big tele-communications firms. They wanted to determine if certain credit institutions had taken undue risk because of too great loan exposure in one sector of the economy.

On this issue of concentrated bank loans to telecoms, Sir Howard Davies, chairman of the UK Financial Services Authority (FSA), remarked that the level of lending by US and European banks to the giant telecoms firms was a matter of great concern to regulators. Their major worry was the extreme concentration of lending risks in defiance of the prudential rules set by supervisory authorities about diversification of exposure.

Davies was right in his remarks, which were made during a special meeting of international financial regulators. This concern was further fed by a report issued by the Bank for International Settlements (BIS), which suggested that:

- on average in the US and Europe, 30 per cent of year 2000 international syndicated loans were for telecom debt, and
- in Europe, in 2002, mergers of giant state-owned and private telecoms broke all records, with big money spent to buy UMTS licences.

In fact, as BIS statistics indicated, bank loans to telecoms were 40 per cent of total loans. This case of spending borrowed money in an unwise way was beautifully reflected in an editorial in the *Financial Times*: 'Just imagine, governments might be forced to use the receipts from their mobile phone licence auctions to bail out the banks that lent to the winning telecommunications companies.'[6]

We now know, post mortem, mid-2004, that this article in the *Financial Times* was prophetic. The sick list, which has been confirmed by the march of time, includes three major industry sectors which were in the past the motors of the economy:

- the banks, which leveraged the telecoms through their loans,
- the equipment vendors, which helped to overbuild to the tune of 1,500 per cent the capacity telcos needed, and
- the telephone companies, whose mismanagement build a tall skyscraper, then blew it up.

Years before this débâcle took place, the *Financial Times* editorial to which reference has just been made had gone a long way to explain the absurdly high sums demanded in various European government auctions for UMTS licences. It pointed out that UMTS technology on a mass scale:

- is at least several years ahead, and
- to get it would require an added telecoms investment in Europe alone of another €160 billion ($160 billion).

It is indeed surprising that highly paid people at the telecoms and their vendors could not understand that liabilities have to be managed, and loans have to be served. Along with this failure came the torrent of blunders by the Brussels bureaucracy, and the bureaucracy of national governments about the potential of UMTS, attacking without appropriate preparation problems with many unknowns associated with ill-defined products and potential markets. All these miscalculations were made in a global setting which definitely lacks agreement on universal standards and has no way to measure the business and consumer response. Chapter 10 explained the reasons.

## 4.   Alstom. A case study in leveraging through vendor financing

To push the equipment which they make and show the market more and more booked sales, the manufacturers of telecoms equipment financed the purchases by their clients. One of the disastrous aftermaths of such extensive vendor financing of client companies was the meltdown of big, mighty manufacturing firms in the telephone industry and in electrical – mechanical equipment at large, such as Lucent Technologies, Nortel, Alcatel, Ericsson and Alstom.

In order to show that this practice is not confined to the telecoms industry, I have taken shipbuilding as the first example in demonstrating the leveraging taking place against all logic. Vendor financing is in fact a three-party game:

- vendors are leveraging their clients, and
- they use for their own gearing loans from banks.

Take Alsthom, the Anglo-French group, as a case study. The company today bearing this name was created in 1989 by the merger of Alcatel's engineering business with that of GEC – Marconi's. Alstom was a big company, but not a financially healthy player. Its problems emerged soon after 11 September 2001, when Renaissance, the cruise-ship operator, went bust.

- Alsthom had built eight ships for Renaissance, winning the orders by offering vendor financing.
- The clauses included terms under which Alstom guaranteed the ships' residual value – by gearing its own balance sheet.

The tragic events of 11 September hit the cruise industry hard and, at the end of September 2001, Alstom made a €110 million ($110 million) provision. A short while later, it emerged that the ships' vendor financing contracts were supported through Alstom's off-balance-sheet deals, themselves being risky transactions. Financial analysts discovered that the level of such guarantees, which stood at €5.5 billion in 1999, had ballooned to €15 billion ($15 billion) by March 2001 – one period before adversity hit.

Nor was the Renaissance bankruptcy the only major credit risk for the vendor. As subsequently became known, Alstom also had seven contracts worth some €350 million ($350 million) with Enron, the bankrupt energy group. Alstom seems to have had a huge risk appetite, as it guarantees had jumped from 25 per cent of revenues in 1997 to 60 per cent of revenue in 2001.

A big part of that increase had taken place in 2001, and it related to guarantees that came with Alstom's acquisition of ABB's power production manufacturing. Besides this, Alstom faced three more tough financial issues:

- sliding sales,
- outstanding debt, and
- customer prepayments.

Sliding sales hit the future cash flow, at a time when outstanding debt was rising. In the first half of its 2001 financial year, Alstom's net debt rose by €400 million to €2 billion ($2 billion), despite a €700 million gain from the disposal of its contracting arm. And since misfortunes never come singly, another critical issue was the misallocation of customer prepayments.

How customer prepayments should, and should not, be allocated is a tricky issue which concerns many manufacturing firms, particularly those with big, expensive products. In electrical engineering, and in the telecoms business, . customer prepayments have always been a complex subject which is usually, though not always, mismanaged.

Understanding what happened in Alstom's case with shipbuilding helps in appreciating what has taken place with leveraging through vendor financing in the telecoms equipment business. In practice, every one of the big vendors whose case we examine in this chapter is himself caught in the same trap into which Alstom fell with Renaissance, Enron and some of its other clients – and everyone paid dearly for this mistake.

A high level of market competition sees to it that when a telecommunications equipment manufacturer signs a contract, he typically receives a relatively small up-front prepayment from the customer. That cash is used to finance the early stages of the project. This is no unusual practice. In cases of large-systems work, the downpayment may be supplemented by subsequent payments as work progresses, with the bulk of the money paid not necessarily on completion but over an agreed-upon time scale. Problems, however, lie in several areas:

- the vendor must have cash to finance his deals,
- the management accounting system being used should be fine grid – not coarse – and
- the relatively large size of each deal adds up to a quite significant budget, often financed by discounting the projected cash flow.

Here again, a glimpse of what happens with large-scale engineering projects is illuminating. On the positive side, the more money a company receives in advances, the less working capital it requires. In this sense, prepayments are positive. The downside comes from the fact that, for instance, at the end of 2001 Alstom had €6.27 billion ($6.27 billion) of net prepayments on its balance sheet – and this was a liability.

Liabilities must be managed carefully and prepayments should be husbanded so that the cash is not diverted to uses other than the project for which the money is taken. If this capital is simply absorbed into the vendor's general business, then there is a danger that the money has gone elsewhere, and ongoing projects will need large injections of cash that can be found only by borrowing. The rule is that:

- If a company manages its contracts poorly,
- Then it can soon resemble a Ponzi scheme, in which prepayments from new orders finance the completion of old ones.

In Alstom's case, analysts suggested that by late 2001, there were around €4 billion ($4 billion) of net prepayments on the liability side of Alstom's balance sheet. But, at the same time, these were not easy to identify liquid assets. Also, in November that same year Alstom announced a €421 million ($421 million) cash outflow and said that this related largely to four contracts for which it had received substantial prepayments, but which were reaching completion and so draining its cash reserves.

The dwindling cash position of telecoms suppliers works in a similar way. Their treasury is squeezed because they have run up big debts buying and installing the latest high-tech equipment at their clients through vendor financing – hence leveraging their clients rather than letting them use the more classical, but much slower, method of retained earnings.

Investors have every reason to be worried about these practices, because they have the nasty habit of ending very badly – for instance, as by the end of 2001 the global equipment manufacturing industry went into a tailspin. Companies in this sector were holding more than $15 billion worth of loans to carriers on their balance sheets – and this was up an impressive 25 per cent from a little over a year earlier.

Behind vendor financing hides a mountain of credit risk. In 2000, Cisco loaned Digital Broadband Communications $70 million to buy its networking gear. Digital Broadband was a start-up with a contract to provide high-speed internet service to schools. With that contract it appeared solid, but as investors soured on the entire telecoms sector, Digital Broadband ran out of cash. When it filed for bankruptcy protection in late December 2000, Cisco was left holding the bag.

Qualcomm was forced to write off $595 million out of a credit line of $1.18 billion to telcos and other clients, after the Globalstar satellite telecoms business defaulted on its debt in January 2001. Satellite carrier Globalstar also said it could not make a $45 million debt payment due to Loral Space & Communications and others. Ericsson provided vendor financing to Thai Telephone & Telecommunication (TT&T), a fixed-line carrier serving rural areas. But then TT&T went into bankruptcy and Ericsson lost its advances.

Questionable loans by vendors to carriers could be found all over the engineering companies in general, and the telecoms industry in particular. Motorola's, Lucent Technologies' and Nortel Networks' vendor-financed sales to risky start-ups have been legendary. Only after the débâcle, Lucent said it was shifting sales away from start-ups and towards established carriers. This came after September 2000, when it removed roughly $1 billion in debt from its balance sheet by peddling the loans to investors in much the same way that mortgage lenders package home loans and sell them as securities.

## 5.  Carrier failures led to earthquakes at equipment vendors: Ericsson and Alcatel

During the boom years of telecommunications and of the internet companies, in the 1997 to 2000 timeframe, communications equipment manufacturers got gradually into the bad practice of lending their clients all the money they needed to buy their equipment. After the telecoms market bust of 2000/2001, carriers and equipment vendors have been rethinking the deals which they made in the past to leverage themselves all the way to bankruptcy; but this new-found wisdom came a little too late.

* Part of the problem is that the credit arms of vendors have been acting very much as bank lenders.
* They also securitized and sold debt, so that it did not affect their balance sheets, but the day came when there were no more parties willing to buy these securities.

On Wall Street, many analysts think that the policy followed by vendors to provide much of the money new network operators have been using to purchase their equipment has backfired. Several business failures among major telecoms service providers have been blamed on badly arranged financial deals with equipment suppliers, and vendors found themselves obliged to work out which telcos they would be prepared to rescue.

This practice also opened the vendors' flanks to lawsuits. In April 2001, Winstar Communications, a US company, filed for bankruptcy protection, blaming Lucent Technologies for an alleged breach of a financing agreement. In May 2001, PSINet, a global service provider with more than 90,000 business customers, defaulted on a combined $36.7 million interest payment on notes and equipment lease.

Beyond those examples, many of the telecoms equipment vendors' customers have either gone bust, as in the case of the plethora of telecoms start-ups, or have been cutting back their network expenditures to reduce debt – as in the case of France Télécom and Deutsche Telekom. Also, in the longer term there is a synergy effect because of so many telecoms equipment companies facing the same problems. This leads to a glut of asset sales, pushing down recovery rates.

Faced with a torrent of problems on the financial side of their clients, some vendors have examined the wisdom of ownership of service providers – which would violate the so-called 'first law of holes' coined by Denis Healey, the former British Treasury secretary: 'When you are in one, stop digging.' Others kept up with financing the purchase of their equipment by telecoms, but on a very selective basis, and only for established customers.

Theoretically, the latter strategy makes sense. In practice, the trouble is that, because of bandwidth oversupply, even for the established telecoms companies the bandwidth market has become much tougher. Prices have been falling faster than business plans allow for. It is the kind of environment where to survive, a telecoms company and its vendors need plenty of money – and this is in short supply.

Financial staying power is the name of the game. With all the new broadband network offerings, there has been a major change in supply without an equivalent step-up in demand. In this perspective the rationale (or lack of it) for survival strategies by equipment vendors should be examined. Here are a couple of examples.

After laying off 20,000 employees in 2001, about one-fifth of its entire workforce, in a scramble to cut costs, Ericsson, the Swedish telecoms equipment manufacturer, decided to shed another 20,000 by the end of 2003. It also trimmed nearly $2 billion from overhead and from R&D, whose budget was reduced by 20 per cent.

Another move by the Swedish telecoms equipment vendor has been to divest itself from its mobile-handset business to a 50-50 venture with Sony. Analysts, however, said that the expected turnaround does not seem to come as fast as Ericsson has been hoping. By late 2003 the first signals were positive, but they were tentative and the light was still not visible at the end of the tunnel. The market did not fail to take notice:

- In March 2000, at the peak of Ericsson's market capitalization, its equity was worth more than $190 billion.

That represented 37 per cent of the value of the entire Stockholm stock market.

- By May 2002, a little over two years down the line, that figure was down to $20 billion – just the 11 per cent of peak value – and it continued falling.

As 2002 came to a close, battered Ericsson, which once claimed nearly 40 per cent of all 3G equipment deals under contract, raised concerns in the market about its liquidity position. Analysts suggested that, although reasonably successful, the company's cut-price rights issue in August/ September 2002 smacked of desperation. Added to this,

- Moody's downgraded the long-term debt rating of Ericsson to Ba2, which is a low junk status, and
- that downgrade cost the telecoms equipment company big money in interest payments.

Louis Landemann, a bond analyst at SEB Merchant Banking, in Stockholm, suggested that Ericsson had total gross customer financing exposure of SEK 27.7 billion (about $2.5 billion) as of the second quarter of 2002, and provision for customer financing risk of SEK 6.6 billion (more than half a billion dollars): 'As Ericsson has large amounts of committed but unutilized customer financing, the future development of the company's vendor financing exposure will need to be monitored,' said Landemann.[7]

Ericsson's receivables and vendor financing claims have been almost exclusively to wireless operators, according to Moody's. MobilCom was apparently only the first of a series of problem loans (see Chapter 9). With this in mind, it comes as no surprise that by the end of the third quarter of 2002 bond spreads of Ericsson (and of Alcatel which faced similar problems) widened. The two companies have been the largest European debt issuers in the sector, and spreads have gone to between 1,200 basis points (bp) and 1,400 bp, as shown in Figure 11.3.

In both cases, the widening of spreads reflected, among other things, that the market voted against the two companies' corporate governance. The spreads have blown out to that level from between 400 and 500 basis points. Going to 1,500 bp over government bonds in the space of three months is proof that the market votes down, with dollars, on the survivability of a firm. This, too, is an external rating risk.

Neither were Alcatel's profit figures that exciting. Even in 2000, at the height of the technology boom, Alcatel's margins never rose beyond 7.8 per cent. Yet the company's stock was approaching €100 versus the couple of euros it was worth in February 2003. The pattern of rise and fall is shown in Figure 11.4.

Alcatel's strategic plans to return to the level of 7 to 8 per cent margins on the back of demand for broadband networking equipment, of which it had a 40 per cent global market share, does not seem to add up. The big *if* has been the US broadband market, which nobody could really say when it would pick up.

Alcatel's survival plan also had other shortcomings. First, broadband business accounts for just 5 per cent of the company's revenues. Hence, Alcatel

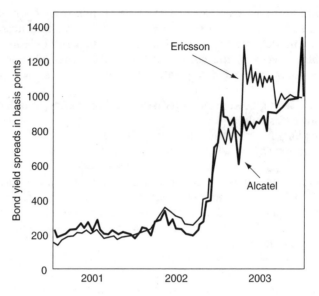

*Figure 11.3*   Ericsson and Alcatel bond yield spreads

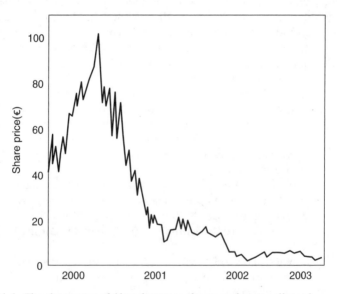

*Figure 11.4*   The share price of Alcatel went to the stars, then it collapsed

will have to look elsewhere in its product line to boost margins. Mobile tele-communications is unlikely to provide the impetus, given that the mobile phone operators' 3G plans are permanently receding into the distance (see Chapter 10).

Second, when the time does come to build out the networks, Alcatel will be competing with rivals so desperate to re-establish themselves that it will be lucky to grab any margin at all. Moreover, while Alcatel's mobile infrastructure business has seen strong growth in emerging markets, Nokia and Ericsson, too, have shifted their focus to new growth markets, while they wait for European and American investment to rise.

The third shortcoming of Alcatel's business plan has been that it bets on its clients to pay on time. To say the least, this is not realistic in the current business climate, because Alcatel's clients are the wounded telecoms. An ontime payment strategy would meet opposition from major customers such as cash-strapped France Télécom, which want to hold off paying their suppliers.

The fourth shortcoming of the new strategy is Alcatel's plan to move into the services business. Services account for 15 per cent of Alcatel's sales, but the company wants to double this. The downside of such a plan is that every equipment vendor has sought to move into the services area, and so far Ericsson and Nokia have grabbed the lion's share of the outsourcing deals in the mobile sector.

## 6. The downfall of Lucent Technologies and of Nortel

The downfall of two companies which sprang out of the Bell System – Lucent Technologies in the US (the former Western Electric) and Nortel in Canada (the former Northern Telecom) – has hit investors in a big way, because the equity of both companies was very popular. Although the plunge of their stock has been matched by that of many other communications and technology firms, investors were particularly hurt because Lucent and Nortel stock had an unusually large place in rather conservative portfolios.

The story of Lucent Technologies, the owner of the famed Bell Telephone Labs which after World War II were the largest in the world – and the birthplace of transistors and lasers – makes sad reading. Originally known as Western Electric, Lucent was one of the pillars of American Telephone & Telegraph, and this counted for a good deal of its appeal for family-type investing. Spun off from AT&T in 1996, Lucent has been damaged by:

- repeated hype,
- bloated costs, and
- management ineffectiveness.

The economic slowdown in the telecommunications sector also took a hand in its downturn, and hampered its recovery. For the quarter that ended 30 June 2001, Lucent's revenue was $5.82 billion, down 21 per cent from a year earlier. By mid-2001, with the global telecommunications industry in depression, Lucent Technologies had little choice but to cut costs in a bid to turn a profit but, as we have already seen, this has been the beaten path of all discredited telecoms equipment vendors – not an imaginative solution.

Because telecommunications companies are not buying enough new equipment to rescue their vendors, big and small telecoms equipment makers search for the easy way out by concentrating on job cuts and other half-measures, in the vain hope that these represent significant annual cost savings. They don't. If they did, Lucent, Nortel, Ericsson and Alcatel – who repeatedly tried this medicine – would not have been in a coma.

The real problem is mismanagement and this is not corrected through job cuts at rank and file level. What it needs is radical change at the two top levels of management to bring in new blood with bold ideas. At the end of 2002, Lucent's board got very low marks for governance because of a $679 million revenue restatement and a $200 billion loss in market cap since December 1999. Analysts also noted that:

- the company's performance is still very low, and
- forecasts for the future put its recovery way off, as with all other telecoms equipment manufacturers.

It therefore comes as no surprise that in mid- to late 2002 the equity price of both Nortel and Lucent Technologies has been hovering around $1. In Nortel's case, this meant about 1 per cent of its all-time high of $89. As so many other companies whose stock came under severe pressure, Lucent and Nortel have been trying – hard and unsuccessfully – to save themselves from sinking to oblivion. One of the dramas was the contemplated merger between Alcatel and Lucent. The merger of two sick bodies does not make a healthy one.

At the end of 2003 there was some good news. Lucent Technologies reported its first profit in three years. The telecoms equipment manufacturer showed a 2003 fourth-quarter net profit of $77 million, or 2 cents per share, compared with a loss of $2.88 billion, or 84 cents per share, in the same quarter a year earlier. As Lucent's 2003 Annual Report was to state:

> in the fourth quarter of fiscal 2002, we recognized approximately $200 million of charges related to capitalized software impairments and $50 million of charges related to property, plant and equipment impairments. These charges were primarily related to delays and increasing uncertainties in the development of the UMTS market.
>
> In the fourth quarter of fiscal 2003, we recognized a $50 million impairment charge related to capitalized software. This charge was required after reconsideration of the specific software that might be deployed due to continuing UMTS market delays.

Lucent's 2003 Annual Report informed the shareholders that the company's credit ratings were below investment grade. Correctly, it also underlined

*Table 11.1*   Lucent Technologies credit ratings by S&P's and Moody's

| Rating agency | Long-term debt | 8% subordinated debentures | Trust-preferred securities | Last change |
|---|---|---|---|---|
| Standard & Poor's | B– | CCC– | CCC– | 4 September 2003 |
| Moody's Investors Service | Caa1 | Caa3 | Caa3 | 2 December 2003 |

that any credit downgrade affects the company's ability to enter into and maintain certain contracts on favourable terms. It increases, as well, its cost of borrowing (see Chapter 2). Lucent's credit ratings as of 5 December 2003 are as shown in Table 11.1.

The bad news elected to lodge itself in the two electric and electronics equipment offsprings of the Bell system because, to their disgrace, neither Lucent nor Nortel were able to revamp their core strategy. Nortel's long-distance optical unit is a case in point. It made the company a star performer in the late 1990s, as free-spending customers, from WorldCom to Qwest Communications, bought its gear in large amounts. But that time is now past. By 2002, Nortel's long-haul optical sales dropped to an estimated $1.4 billion from $8 billion in 2000, and it is still not certain that the market has stabilized, while rivals like Cisco are eating up market share at Nortel's expense.

This is a dramatic change from the time investors had confidence in the company's management and its equity. It is precisely because of that confidence that Nortel grew to an outsized portion of the Toronto stock market, leading many investors to overweight the equity even when they thought they were diversifying by buying mutual funds. Also, ironically, US rules that limit how much in retirement plans can be invested abroad encouraged an overweighting in Canadian stocks, and most particularly in Nortel.

At its peak in 2000, Nortel alone represented more than 36 per cent of Toronto's TSE 300 index. Then, the equity fell off the cliff. In the short span of a year, the Nortel stock went from its peak of $89 in 2000 to below $8, after the company stunned the financial world by posting a second-quarter loss of $19.4 billion, one of the biggest ever. The pattern is shown in Figure 11.5. Eventually, Nortel equity slid down the financial precipice to become a penny stock.

Not only was the lavish market of the telecoms not longer to be seen, but also Nortel's competitive position was in disarray and new product introductions were not compensating for the loss of market share in the company's established lines. Swimming in debt, in early 2002 Nortel postponed indefinitely the launch of a large-scale optical switch that its management had once hailed as critical for enhancing communication via the internet. This has been the story of an acquisition which brought no benefit, only headache.

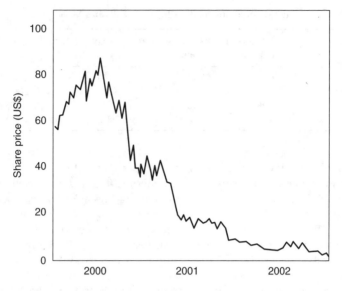

*Figure 11.5*   The crash of Nortel Networks

Nortel had acquired the optical internet switching technology when it bought the Xros start-up in June 2000, in a $ 3.2 billion allstock deal. Xros was one of a string of high-priced purchases made by Nortel in an aggressive pursuit of rapidly developing technology. The company apparently believed in an ever-growing demand for internet bandwidth and speed.

At the time of that takeover, the switch known as OPTera Connect PX was hailed by Nortel's top management as a revolutionary technology, which would give the company a great leap forward. This was an overstatement, and it was not the only blunder. Many of Nortel's technology purchases subsequently turned sour, while in June 2001 Nortel took a US$12.3 billion asset write-down amid weakening demand for its products.

In the meantime, not only did Nortel's long-distance optical business not produce the expected miracle, but also market share in other established product lines was lost to competitors. For instance, in ethernet switches Nortel's part of the pie has shrank to 5.4 per cent, below one-twelfth of the 68.5 per cent market share mastered by Cisco. The loss of market control in key product lines makes most difficult the management of debt unwisely piled up in the boom years. This state of affairs has been disastrous to:

- lenders,
- bondholders,
- shareholders, and
- other stakeholders

Equity investors in telecoms equipment manufacturers might take heart from the fact that bondholders, too, have not escaped unscathed. In early April 2002, Nortel Network's debt ratings were cut to junk status by Moody's, as the credit rating agency said it was concerned about the company's operating performance. The move came as a shock because Moody's had lowered Nortel's ratings only a month earlier – though it also warned it might do so again as the ongoing slump in telecommunications markets appeared to be deeper and more protracted than expected.

The April 2002 downgrade affected about $5 billion debt of Nortel, and Moody's said its outlook was negative. The Canadian company followed closely US rival Lucent Technologies in having been reduced to junk status. Moody's also cut Nortel's senior long-term debt to Ba3 from Baa3, which represents three notches in one go, on the basis that the company was unlikely to return to profitability soon. It also lowered Nortel's preferred stock to B3 from Ba2 and commercial paper to not prime from prime-2.

The crash of Nortel equity is dramatized in Figure 11.5. The flattened price of a major telecoms vendor equity had other perverse effects on the market. With major losses suffered in official stock exchanges while investing in big-name companies thought to be as solid as the rock of Gibraltar, both in the US and in Canada a long list of pension funds and individual investors tended to console themselves, and to ensure their future through alternative investments – which are a different, but potentially more deadly, gamble.[8]

Readers should note that companies sometimes make a bigger blunder to cover a smaller one, and that highly illiquid alternative investments are nothing more than a modernized Ponzi game by hedge funds and those banks peddling them. By shorting the market and investing in the obscure macromarkets and other alchemies, some people think they have found the elixir to diversify risk. The rude awakening comes when such gambles crash.

Neither were these travails the end of Nortel's problems. Mid-March 2004, a week after it revealed that it may have to restate results for 2003 and earlier for a second time, the company suspended two top finance executives. The whiff of an accounting scandal, once again, sent shares in the Canadian telecoms-equipment firm tumbling.[9]

## 7. Is there a 'sure strategy' to come up from under?

Corporate spending, in business and industry at large, and the price of technology stocks are correlated. Corporate customers account for 84 per cent of US technology purchases, and enterprise spending is not really picking up steam though there have been some minor improvements. This stagnation without inflation has been particularly visible in some industries and it is an important indicator affecting estimates of recovery.

Hardware and software for communications are mainstream products. According to the US Commerce Department, during 2000, telecoms accounted for 12 per cent of all business spending on equipment and software. For some companies, this market represented a share three times as big. Sun Microsystems, for example, derived 36 per cent of its revenue from telecoms in fiscal 2000. No wonder that, with the downfull of the telecoms, the equity of Sun Microsystems went down too.

In many cases, management made a cocktail of reality and hope. Like Sun Microsystems, Nortel did not spare the optimistic statements that recovery was not far away. Slowly, however, these projections became more conservative. In August 2001, John Roth, Nortel's chief executive, warned that business was unlikely to improve before the second half of 2002. This, too, proved to be overoptimistic.

The sinking of a formerly great company's equity came as a shock to Nortel's investors, including pension funds and tax-sheltered retirement saving plans. The Association of Canadian Pension Management estimates that group pension plans had total assets of 650 billion Canadian dollars ($422 billion) at the end of 2000 with about 300 billion Canadian dollars ($195 billion) more in individual plans – Nortel was one of their core investments, and that money is gone.

Experts say that Nortel's strategic plans were wrong well before the big stockmarket plunge, while afterwards its management failed to adapt to the new market realities. In 1997, John Roth had launched a strategy aiming to transform the company from one dependent on voice transmission, its traditional strength, into one focused on data networking. This led to an excess of mergers and acquisitions:

- between 1997 and early 2001, Nortel acquired 19 companies, and
- as it did so, its stock price soared to reach a capitalization value of $277 billion in July 2000; the high-water mark.

Eventually, this strategy of M&A in all directions backfired, but the firm was still under pressure to do deals to satisfy the analysts' growth expectations. Ultimately, it paid over $32 billion, mostly in stock, for the companies which it took over. Then, when management became aware of its strategic errors, and its huge leveraging, it tried to reduce the debts:

- it sold off most of those acquisitions for modest amounts, and
- what could not be sold was shut down, writing the money off entirely.

In retrospect, the quest to transform a company whose business reflected old solutions but was well established, like Nortel into a go-ahead outfit, immensely damaged the firm and its prospects. The same is true of Lucent Technologies in the US, of Alcatel in France and of British General Electric/ Marconi in the UK. Neither overpaying for acquisitions nor firesales helps a company's finances.

In Nortel's case, with year-end 2001 valuation of just $24 billion, the company's stock has fallen by more than 90 per cent from its peak in September of 2000, and year 2002 brought more bad news. Employment shrank from 72,900 people when Roth took over Nortel's reins, to less than 45,000 by the end of 2002. Ironically, that score was reflected in the company's stock price. Nortel's adjusted equity price was 44 per cent lower than its level of $13.16 on October 1997 when Roth became CEO.

- Nortel has been a talking example of how overexpansion ends in a significant destruction of value.
- The lesson every manager should learn from this tragedy is that growth for growth's sake is the philosophy of the cancer cell.

Whether we talk of Nortel, Lucent, Alcatel, Marconi, or a score of other fallen companies, the CEOs who brought them to ruin – and those executives assisting them in doing so – have supposedly studied the art management. If so, they should have learned that, as Aldous Huxley has aptly said, 'facts do not cease to exist because they are ignored'. Sometimes managers do not learn that unrealistic market expectations involve a long list of unexpected disastrous consequences which can be ignored only up to a point.

Neither can it be said that the only party responsible for the downfall of these firms was the 2000–2003 market downturn. In Nortel's case, for instance, the immediate post-1997 results were far from brilliant even though, at that time, the telecoms market was booming. In 1998, while the telecommunications industry was most prosperous, Nortel posted a 50 per cent decline in its earnings compared with the previous year – and this on 10 per cent higher sales. That set the stage for a cost discipline. The company closed plants and held research and development spending flat. Instead, it tried to solve the problems of the future through wild acquisitions. In cost-cutting, for instance, Nortel limited growth in travel and administrative expenses to half of its sales growth. To lead by example, the then CEO boarded a plane on a business trip and headed toward his seat in the economy section, passing a number of Nortel senior managers seated in first class. Few words were exchanged, but the incident sent a message.

This lesson-by-example was excellent. Companies overspend in travel expenses; cost-cutting is needed, but it is not enough to turn the company finances around. As Cisco's John T. Chambers said with hindsight in January 2004; 'CEOs are beginning to realize that cost-cutting can only do so much, and that they have to invest in new sources of revenues.'[10]

Another gimmick companies discovered in the post-2001 doldrums is that of large write-offs. Up to a point, these may be an asset for technology firms, but on their own they don't make a company a winner. In 2001, when everybody gambled on a quick turnaround, some analysts said that large inventory write-offs taken by technology companies could turn into major profits when the industry finally recovers. Accounting for write-offs can give an *artificial boost* to company profits *if*, and only if, they sell the massive amounts of inventory they have written off because any sales mean a 100 per cent profit. But is the market buying that stuff?

According to current regulations, companies are required to report when they write off the value of inventory, taking a charge against earnings, but not if they turn around and sell the goods later. Cisco Systems, for instance, hoped to profit from sales of any of the $2.2 billion in inventory it wrote off for the quarter ended 28 April 2001. It did not turn out that way. Nortel might have got a sizeable boost if it had sold the $650 million of inventory and other manufacturing items it wrote off, but the market was simply not there.

True enough, in the high-tech industries large inventories pose a dilemma: painful write-downs or slow rot. But they don't guarantee future profits, nor are they a strategy for turning a firm around. This is the answer to this section's heading. Coming up from under is part of the American dream; sometimes it works for people, and much less frequently so for companies, but it is not the 'sure thing'.

Every manager should appreciate that half-way measures and medieval solutions to twenty-first-century problems have short legs. There is also a major problem of personal accountability. The management which ruined once beautiful companies like Lucent, Nortel, Alcatel and Marconi cannot be trusted to act as change agent. Their only remaining asset, as for as their company is concerned, is to empty their chair – and fast.

## 8.  2004: the good news is not yet final

Readers knows from personal experience that neither the good news nor the bad news last for ever. Ancient Egyptians expressed that through the allegory of seven fat cows followed by seven meagre ones, and vice versa. Business can delay investments up to a point. After that, companies have to come to the market again, otherwise:

- competitive positions will be lost, and
- productivity will go down, with the result that costs will rise.

Upturns, however, are not characterized by a straight line. In fact, both upturns and downturns are non-linear and, as a result, it is too early to say that the telecoms industry's downturn is over – and with it the telecoms equipment manufacturers blues.

Optimistic reports indicate that in 2004 US telecommunication companies are expected to increase capital expenditures. This is a crucial measure of industry health, but the projected 5 per cent increase in 2004, to $58 billion, according to Lehman Brothers, is like the one swallow that does not make

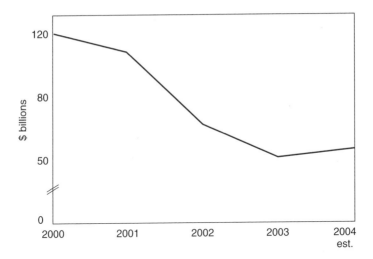

*Figure 11.6*  Capital expenditures by US telecoms seem to pick up slightly*
* Statistics from Lehman Brothers and *BusinessWeek*.

a summer. Still, 2004 estimates indicate a minor pick-up, as shown in Figure 11.6. This is the first increase since 2000 – and it is welcome.

The projected 5 per cent increase in capital spending by telecoms restores spending only to the 1996 level. This might have been all right, except for the fact that it is below 50 per cent the high-water mark in telecoms equipment spending, which came in 2000. In fact, that spending level is significantly less than 50 per cent if inflation is kept in perspective. In the eight elapsed years – 1966 to 2004 – inflation amounted to nearly 20 per cent, hence in steady dollars we are talking of $46.4 billion – or roughly 60 per cent off the peak.

Still, with these capital expenditures, and with consumer spending, revenues of telecoms equipment vendors are expected to grow some 8 per cent, to $190.5 billion, up from $177 billion in 2003. This is not big – but it is the first increase since 2000. Not every vendor will, however, benefit in the same way. Such a relatively modest increase will not be evenly distributed. According to some estimates, most of that growth will come from the $100 billion wireless services sector, which is expected to grow between 10 per cent and 12 per cent in 2004.

Faster networks, lower prices and new features are believed to drive cellular growth forward. Also to benefit from greater spending are a few niche markets, such as networking technology based on internet protocol. Sales of this type of equipment to big companies hit an estimated $2 billion in 2003 and might grow 50 per cent in 2004, according to some estimates (see Chapter 6 on VOIP).

Better news than the 5 per cent growth is how the lows of 2000–2003 transformed the telecoms industry. During this long downturn, many CEOs realized they had poor insight into several critical aspects of their operations – from customer demand to inventory and supply chain management. As a result, the more effective executives took steps to provide themselves with:

- better information on several fronts, and
- software tools and data links, allowing them to react more quickly and with improved analytics than in the past.

More relief for the more effectively managed telecoms equipment vendors comes from pricing. New models are about to be tested with telecommunications companies, getting away from the traditional way of charging by the minute to transport voice and data over the network. Some telecoms are now embracing flat-rate plans for everything from classical voice to wireless and broadband – and while those flat rates are falling, volume is expected to better than compensate for the fall. Some of the extra revenue will eventually go to new equipment orders.

This is good news for users of telecommunications networks. Broadband rates have already dropped as much as 50 per cent in some cases, to about $30 a month, and they are expected to continue downward in 2004 and beyond. If, however, the larger-volume hypothesis is not supported, then it is unavoidable that rising competition and falling prices will be felt throughout the chain, putting pressure on everyone, from telecoms to equipment makers and venture capitalists.

On the one hand, this means that raising money will remain difficult. But on the other, a broader market for communications at an affordable cost will create new business opportunities. To capture these developing opportunities, telecoms and their suppliers must set priorities, stick to them and move quickly. They must also realize how deep a hole they are in, and the challenge of getting out of it. This is what management effectiveness is all about.

Senior management should appreciate that its chances for getting out of a deep hole are compromised through legal risk.

Mid-May 2004 a grand jury in Texas subpoenaed documents from Nortel Networks as part of a criminal investigation into accounting irregularities. This has been the latest blow to Nortel, which is also being investigated by the US Securities and Exchange Commission, and the securities regulators in Ontario where the company has its headquarters. Both inquiries are related to the company's repeated restatements of earnings back to 2000.

In Texas are located some of Nortel's largest business groups; it is also the state where some of its finance executives are based. Nortel said that the 'materials sought are pertinent to an ongoing criminal investigation being conducted by the U.S. Attorney's Office for the Northern District of Texas, Dallas Division'. The subpoena compels Nortel to provide documents that include financial statements, as well as personnel and accounting records from the beginning of 1 January, 2000 to May 2004.[11]

This criminal investigation comes on the heels of Nortel's firing, in April 2004, of its top three executives 'for cause'; including Frank Dunn, the company's chief executive officer. An internal probe linked the three men to many accounting issues, while a further four employees were placed on indefinite paid leave.

Tina Warren, a Nortel spokeswoman, said the grand jury inquiry and the SEC inquiry are related to financial statements and corporate, personnel and accounting records – adding that she cannot speculate whether the inquiry was in any way linked to three top Nortel executives who were fired by the company. However, the three former executives have been named as defendants in two dozen class-action lawsuits by investors. The suits assert that the executives packed losses into earlier years to inflate the company's profits in 2003 and earn hefty bonuses for returning the company to profitability for the first time in six years.[12]

A good example on how costly these class actions by investors may be, is the 10 May, 2004, out-of-court settlement with WorldCom shareholders, reached by Citigroup. This cost the financial institution $2.56 billion – an enormous bill which might have been even higher if compensation was awarded by a jury.

These days, misleading investors for fraudulent purposes carries with it an oversized legal risk, and rightly so. Nortel would have had to declare bankruptcy if it were faced by a similar multi-billion dollars penalty. The ability to demonstrate that the company will not let itself be eaten from within, is a sign of management effectiveness.

## Notes

1. *BusinessWeek*, 22 April 2002.
2. Chorafas, *Managing Risk in the New Economy*.
3. *EIR*, 12 April 2002.
4. *CommunicationsWeekInternational*, 23 September 2002.
5. Chorafas, *Corporate Accountability, with Case Studies in Finance*.
6. *Financial Times*, 2 October 2000.
7. *CommunicationsWeekInternational*, 23 September 2002.
8. D. N. Chorafas, *Alternative Investments and the Mismanagement of Risk*, Basingstoke: Palgrave Macmillan, 2003.
9. *The Economist*, 20 March, 2004.
10. *BusinessWeek*, 12 January 2004.
11. *Financial Times*, May 15/16, 2004.
12. *International Herald Tribune*, 15/16 May, 2004.

# Appendix

## Management's Ineffectiveness has many Colours

Mid-2004 there have been several negatives developments concerning Vivendi Universal and its chosen product line, which worth bringing to the reader's attention as post-mortem. In March 2004 Vodafone blocked Vivendi from converting SFR, the French mobile network operator they jointly control, into a limited partnership. Such conversion would have been of interest to Vivendi, but senior management failed in the negotiations.

Another recent piece of news, relating to TA Orange Thailand, talks volumes of what some mobile telephony licences worth – and it also helps in documenting that not all mobile telephony stories have a happy ending. In March 2004 mobile phone operator Orange sold Thailand's number three mobile company TA Orange for one baht ($0.025). This has been the end of an investment that cost $550 million. TelecomAsia PCL will buy Orange's 39 per cent stake in TA Orange and take full control of the company after it completes a 32-billion-baht ($809 million) debt refinancing.[1]

As for Hutchison 3 financials (see Chapter 10), Li Ka-Shing, chairman of Hutchison Whampoa, and Canning Fok Kin Ning, his top lieutenant, have done what they could to persuade London's City that '3' can eventually be made to produce a return. Skepticism remains the order of the day, and to many investment banks the billions Hutchison invested in the 3G enterprise looks like money down the drain – or, more precisely, down the pockets of an enterprise which has yet to deliver anywhere near what it promises.

This, too, is a powerful message to Vivendi and its (ill-advised) choice of mobile telephony rather than water. Let's recall that with '3' Li Ka-Shing tried to replicate the success he had once achieved with Orange. In its early years, nobody thought Orange would work either, but by investing heavily in state-of-the-art technology and marketing, Orange eventually worthed billions. Li seems to believe he can repeat the trick with 3G, but it looks a lot tougher this time around.

- The glory years of mobile telephony are most probably over, and
- the valuations that ruled when Orange was sold, first to Mannesmann and then to France Telecom, were part of the go-go 1990s – and they are gone, too.

An even greater challenge is that 3G's lifespan might well be limited. The way a recent news item has it, Japan, China, and South Korea have jointly agreed to enhance communications services and other technologies for *fourth-generation* (4G) mobile phones, due to be available commercially around 2010. The 3G seems to be getting aged even before it has started to work. No wonder that the mobile operators' confidence in 3G seems more shaky by the day. Moreover, the mobile operators are getting further into trouble with their handset suppliers – while, at the same time, from a potential cash flow perspective, the 3G network rollout is agonizingly slow. This, too, is bad news to Vivendi given the amount of money it paid to buy the airwave licences.

And as one piece of bad news never comes alone, there is another event much more damaging to the reputation of the battered French company and that of its new CEO. On 5 May, 2004, was made public information that Jean-René Fourtou benefited hefty from a torrent of options: 1,000,000 thrust on him by the board at a price of €12.10 which represented a snowfall of €8,890,000 in paper profits, over and above the €2,256,000 – his annual salary.[2]

This snowfall of executive options was given to him in October 2002, a few months after he became Vivendi's CEO, and it has been a repetition of the policy followed by the ousted Jean-Marie Messier to award, through a rubber stamp board, a torrent of options to himself and his cronies. It should be recalled that Fourtou was appointed as Vivendi's CEO to clean up the mess – not to repeat the exploits of his predecessor.

Theoretically, there is nothing wrong with executive options. Practically, when they become a torrent they are a rip-off of the shareholders.[3] As if this very rich self-rewarding was not enough, another 500,000 options came as a second handout on 23 January, 2003, at an exercise price of €15.90 which represented a potential fallout of € 2,540,000 in early May 2004.

Moreover, French regulators have been investigating a Vivendi Universal bond issue of which the same Jean-René Fourtou made a large undisclosed purchase. This investigation is most embarrassing because, as already mentioned, Vivendi's new CEO was brought into the firm in July 2002 to clean up the company after corporate governance scandals, under his predecessor Jean-Marie Messier, had brought it to its knees.

In November 2002, the Janelly and Jean-René Fourtou Foundation, an entity set up in June 2002 while Fourtou was negotiating his conditions for joining the company, purchased €14.5 million worth of Vivendi convertible bonds, out of €115 million sold to retail investors in a refinancing that also raised €885 million from institutions. Most curious is the fact that Fourtou's children purchased a further €5 million tranche.[4]

In other terms, between the Fourtou Foundation and the offspring, the family's acquisition of 17 per cent of the retail tranche ended in very hefty profits, always at shareholders' expense. *If* this is not executive favouritism and self-gratification, *then* what is it? The difference between genius and stupidity is that genius has limits, as Winston Churchill once suggested.

## Notes

1. *Total Telecom Magazine*, April 2004.
2. Le Canard Enchaîné, 5 May, 2004.
3. D. N. Chorafas *Management Risk. The Bottleneck is at the Top of the Bottle*, Palgrave Macmillan, London, 2004.
4. *Financial Times*, 15/16 May, 2004.

# Index